THE DANUBE BASIN
AND THE
GERMAN ECONOMIC SPHERE

By ANTONÍN BASCH

COLUMBIA UNIVERSITY PRESS

NEW YORK : MORNINGSIDE HEIGHTS

COPYRIGHT, 1943

COLUMBIA UNIVERSITY PRESS, NEW YORK

First printing 1943
Second printing 1944

MANUFACTURED IN THE UNITED STATES OF AMERICA

TO MY WIFE

FOREWORD

IN THE SUMMER of 1941, Professor J. B. Condliffe invited me to undertake a study on the German trade drive in Southeastern Europe as a part of studies of the "Trade Regulation Project" directed by him and sponsored by the Rockefeller Foundation.

Such a study has to be set into the proper framework of an analysis of the economic and political situation in Central and Southeastern Europe prior to and at the time of the German economic offensive. It seemed particularly essential to deal with the causes and the very grave effects of the world economic crisis upon this part of Europe.

It was beyond the scope of this study to present either an economic history or to describe in detail the national economies of the countries concerned; chiefly those factors were discussed which relate directly or indirectly to the German economic penetration.

From the findings of this study I have tried to draw some conclusions bearing upon the rebuilding of Central and Southeastern Europe with special regard to the necessity of its economic integration with the rest of Europe. Balanced economic development might be a very important factor in protecting the backward part of this area against another economic aggression. It was not my aim, however, to offer here a detailed blueprint for a postwar reconstruction.

I am under special obligation to Professor J. B. Condliffe who devoted much of his time to my work, read the whole manuscript chapter by chapter. I owe him many valuable and stimulating suggestions.

Mr. Winton Pettibone, as my research assistant, was very helpful in preparing the documentation, as was my former assistant at Brown University, Mr. Allen Ferguson, in editing the manuscript. My sincere thanks are due to Miss Matilda Berg of the Columbia University Press for her extremely efficient assistance in the final presentation of the study.

ANTONÍN BASCH

Columbia University
July, 1943

INTRODUCTION: EAST OF THE RHINE

THE RIVALRIES and contradictions of economic policy in Europe have long been a source of international confusion and intrigue. It is not easy for those who live in a great country like the United States, where people of different races, creeds, and national origins live and work together under one government and in one economic system, to understand or sympathize with the national conflicts of a divided Europe. Western Europe is sufficiently near to the political and economic organization of the new world. But there is another Europe of small States whose undeveloped structure and economic weakness offer constant temptation to their powerful neighbors. Between the Germanic and Latin nations in the west and the Slavs in the east these frontier regions of the Roman Empire have never found a lasting solution for their political, economic and social conflicts.

Within the last few decades independent nations have been created by the breaking up of two old empires—the Austro-Hungarian and the Ottoman. These empires had begun to fall to pieces before the war of 1914–18. The shot which was the prelude to that war was fired at Sarajevo. It was merely the echo of struggling nationalisms and rivalries growing out of the new economic enterprise reaching through central Europe to the Near East. War speeded up the process of regrouping. At its close the map of central and eastern Europe was redrawn. Self-determination was the governing principle of the new order, but it was not completely realized, and indeed could not be, in such a tangle of mixed nationalities. The small States that were set up were not always united and some of them lacked any long tradition of national unity. They began to pursue their old enmities by policies that ignored economic realities and needs. Unfortunately the policies of restrictive nationalism that followed in the wake of monetary inflation were aimed primarily at the neighborhood trade between areas that had formerly been closely linked but had now become independent.

Rivalries among the great Powers complicated the situation and rendered futile all efforts to reach regional agreements for economic coöperation. Progressive impoverishment of a vast region that had

in any case lagged far behind the industrial progress of western Europe
was accentuated by the banking up of population increase that followed in the wake of migration restrictions. For a time this impoverishment was masked by a steady flow of international loans; but that flow
dried up at its source when the credit inflation collapsed in October,
1929. Banking intervention staved off the inevitable reckoning for a
few months more; but in May, 1931 the greatest bank in Austria was
forced to disclose its weakness. This bank, the Credit-Anstalt, had for
generations been the outpost of financial capitalism in central and
eastern Europe. Through it had flowed much of the capital for the
development not of Austria only, but of the whole area. Its difficulties
therefore revealed the essential bankruptcy of central and eastern
Europe.

So much of the government and business of this region had been
a doubtful risk that foreign investments were mostly on a short-term
basis, but at high interest. There was little local capital, and foreign
investors fought shy of local enterprises. When they lent, they did so
to banks which in turn made investments in local industry. The banks,
in familiar words, borrowed short and lent long. When the foreign
investors, through the "crack" of the Credit-Anstalt, caught a glimpse
of the flimsy financial structure on which eastern Europe rested, they
hastily withdrew what they could of their loans. Local capitalists and
speculators also tried to get out what they could before the national
currencies fell into depreciation and perhaps inflation. There was a
run on the banks and they could not call in their industrial loans. The
run became a panic and the panic spread like a prairie fire. The Credit-
Anstalt's troubles became known in Vienna in May, 1931. By the end
of June the big German banks were in serious trouble. By the middle
of September England was forced off the gold standard. In April, 1933
the United States followed suit.

Uncontrollable monetary inflation had been so recent in many
of these European countries that nervous owners of capital withdrew
their liquid funds at the first hint of any banking trouble. Capital
flight and speculation against the currencies grew to unprecedented
proportions. Governments, therefore, had no option but to clamp
down restrictions on the movement of funds. Thus sprang up within
a very brief time the confused and confusing mass of exchange restrictions that were gradually consolidated into powerful instruments
of economic nationalism. A new technical jargon emerged—clearing,

compensation and payments agreements, export subsidies, import premiums, mutiple exchange rates. Officials began to specialize on the incessant negotiations which were a product of the new regulations. Conferences met in rapid succession and the same faces appeared at all of them. Europe was caught in a tangle of administrative controls over trade and finance.

It was this tangle which gave the totalitarians their opportunity. They climbed into power on the backs of the unemployed. Once in power they found the regimented and centralized trade controls a most effective instrument of power policy. The second world war began on this economic front and within a very few years Germany dominated not only the trade but the internal economic policies of most central and eastern European countries. It took only five years to prepare the occupation of Austria, and once that was accomplished the way was clear for pressure upon the Czechs, for Berchtesgaden, Godesberg, Munich, the occupation of Prague and finally the second world war. In the years between 1933 and 1939, Germany had softened up her prospective victims and occupied strategic positions from which to launch further attack. This she accomplished mainly under cover of economic negotiations.

These are the events that Professor Basch essays to analyze and place in historical perspective. He himself was a prominent actor in the great drama. He was called in 1923 from a diplomatic post at Berlin to the double duty of economic teaching in the University of Prague and economic research in the National Bank of Czechoslovakia. In his official capacity he took part in practically all the meetings and conferences—at Geneva, Basle, Stresa, London, and many other centers —with which the record of these years is strewn. He knew and negotiated with the statesmen and experts who went from conference to conference. In 1934 he was called to be the head of the Czech chemical industry and in that capacity he participated in the equally frequent and important conferences of the numerous chemical cartels. When the Little Entente was constituted he was one of the Czech members of its Economic Board. There is no one better qualified, by economic training and practical experience, to analyze the economic background and present difficulties of Europe east of the Rhine.

The study which Dr. Basch has made rests soundly upon thorough and exhaustive analysis, supplemented by statistical measurements, of the economic facts. He is well aware of the political forces that were at work and of the underlying historical attitudes that must be taken into account. But he has tried to find a solid factual basis for his economic argument, so that his work is not a political tract.

The main conclusion to which he comes is not new; but it has gained new importance as a result of the present war. The backward economic development of eastern Europe, he concludes, is a constant source of political weakness and therefore a constant temptation to aggressive industrial powers. It follows that the industrial development of this great region is one of the keys to a solution of Europe's perpetual feuds.

This much is now generally agreed. Successive pronouncements of the United Nations clearly look forward to a program of economic development aimed at higher living standards. But such a program demands coöperative international action and for such action firm political control and clear authority are needed. Who is to create and operate the mechanisms that will be necessary if through railroads are to be built, industries promoted and banking systems reorganized? What governments will be recognized in Europe? Upon what conditions? And in which areas?

Dr. Basch does not lay down any dogmatic answers to these questions, and for very good reasons. At this stage of the war it is impossible to foresee what will be the ultimate answer to certain prior political questions. Much will depend upon the policy pursued by the U.S.S.R. in its relations with Poland and other central European states. Much will depend also upon the decisions reached with regard to a beaten Germany. And much will depend upon the attitude taken by Great Britain and the United States towards the little countries of Europe and international organization in general. Until these unknowns are determined little is to be gained by attempting to draw blueprints of economic development in central Europe.

There are those who dream of a United States of Europe in which all conflicting national interests, including those of a regenerated Germany, will be reconciled in a great federation. Within this federation communications by road, rail, river and air will be as free from local restrictions as they are in the United States. Free trade and migration will prevail over the whole area and economic activity will be re-grouped by economic forces without regard to political considerations.

At the other extreme are those who foresee a reconstitution of national units very much upon the prewar basis, with different boundaries, but on the old pattern.

Between these extremes lie varieties of regionalism sometimes envisaging blocs of smaller countries in the north, in the southwest, or in the east, to balance an undivided Germany. The notion of breaking up the German Empire—reverting from Bismarck to Metternich —has never been wholly forgotten. Another notion is that of forming a great buffer federation from Poland to Greece between Germany and Russia. Less ambitious are suggestions for local regional groupings in this area.

In all this confusion, which is now worse than in 1918, no one can really envisage a workable solution because no one can yet gauge the political forces that will be dominant at the war's end. But recent experience abundantly proves one basic economic fact. Europe, in whole or in part, cannot be organized on a basis of expanding welfare except as part of a world system. The autarkic unity which Germany has forced upon the continent is a unity of impoverishment. Only in a world trading system can the European peoples breathe freely. It is this fact, more than any other, which renders suspect plans for European federation. The German influence in such a federation would necessarily be dominant. Ingenious constitutions cannot outweigh the force of rich raw materials, integrated industry and massed population. One may well fear that a United States of Europe would quickly prove to be not a step towards a peacefully organized world, but the greatest bar to realizing that much desired goal.

Whatever pattern future events and policies may trace across the map of Europe, the distribution of economic resources is not likely after this war to count for as little as in 1919. When the time comes to reorganize the shattered continent, the facts and figures assembled and analyzed in this book will be invaluable. Beyond the facts and the figures, however, lie the policies and ideas that men have tried to put into effect. If there is any moral to the story which Professor Basch tells in the pages that follow it is that any solution of the problems of central and eastern Europe must be found in a setting wider than Europe. In the twentieth century men cannot safely allow themselves to be governed by feuds or dreams that draw their inspiration from the breakup of the Holy Roman Empire. Life runs most vigorously now in the world outside Europe. If the peoples east, and west, of the Rhine are to fit into modern society they must become part of a democratic world trading system. Twice in a generation both they and the peoples of the new world with them have paid a bitter price for their atavism. It is time that they were faced towards the future instead of the past.

J. B. CONDLIFFE
Professor of Economics

University of California
Berkeley, Calif.
May, 1943

CONTENTS

CONTENTS

TABLES

1

CENTRAL AND SOUTHEASTERN EUROPEAN ECONOMY BEFORE AND AFTER WORLD WAR I

AFTER World War I, the principles of self-determination and liberation of national groups wrought great political changes in Central and Southeastern Europe. Revolutionary forces caused the breakdown of the Austro-Hungarian Monarchy and freed the nations of the Danubian valley. Even before the Peace Conference started its real work, the dissolution of the Monarchy—which had long been in political difficulties—was an accomplished fact.

Out of the Monarchy arose Czechoslovakia, Austria, Hungary, and Poland (which also received parts of Russia and Germany). Rumania was substantially enlarged by acquisitions from Hungary, Austria, and Russia (Bessarabia). Serbia and Montenegro, together with sizable areas of the Monarchy—parts of Hungary, Austria, and Bosnia-Herzegovina—formed the new state of Yugoslavia.

Obviously the new political system entailed a new economic organization. Each of the liberated nations harbored great hopes for a strong and prosperous economic development. The peace treaties failed to attach proper importance to this particular problem, perhaps relying upon a restoration of the prewar system of world economy and international trade. As a matter of fact, problems of minor importance were dealt with much more adequately than were the economic problems.

Twenty years after the granting of independence to the smaller nations of this area, Central and Southeastern Europe was rapidly becoming a part of the German economic empire—Germany's dream had neared fulfillment. Step by step she had achieved economic penetration, and with the annexation of Austria and the occupation of Czechoslovakia she became master of the entire area. All this within twenty years—from freedom to a German domination surpassing in ruthlessness and thoroughness the German and Austro-Hungarian rule before 1914.

As we shall try to explain, it became clear that the so-called German solution to the problems in Central and Southeastern Europe cannot meet the basic needs of this region. Yet, even in the last few years, some writers and economists in the West [1] have considered that "the Germans are the only people capable of carrying through" [2] a suitable program here. According to this view—and it is not limited to a few experts—Germany has the necessary industrial resources and organizing ability,[3] and—most important—she is the natural export market. Nature, it was said, gave her a key position in Europe.

Such an opinion is based upon an inadequate analysis of the whole problem; its background is one of political expediency. Arguments of the kind go to prove how well German propaganda has succeeded in bringing to her side even experts who should know better. The fact that one country is an important natural market for the products of other countries does not automatically entail sole responsibility for organizing their economies. In the last years before the war, Great Britain took more than half of the Danish exports, nearly half of Finland's and about a quarter of those of Norway. Yet nobody drew the conclusion that she should therefore organize and control the national economy of these countries; on the contrary, she traded with them on the usual competitive and multilateral basis.

But because of Germany's continuous drive for expansion and her claim for larger living space, and deceived by the apparent success of German trade with Central and Southeastern Europe after 1933 (when, in fact, her previous policy had been one of the causes of the crisis here), many regarded Germany's right to rule as obvious at first glance, and the backward nature of the area only strengthened their belief. Let us therefore see how far Germany actually did succeed, before the outbreak of the present war, in solving the difficult basic problems of the area by her totalitarian commercial policy, with all its devices of clearing agreements, barter, subsidies, and the overvalued rate of the reichsmark—all based on the bilateral trade system. Here the political consequences of the German solution for the freedom of these nations are certainly not to be overlooked.

The argument in favor of the German plan always starts, of course,

---

[1] See C. W. Guillebaud, "Hitler's New Economic Order in Europe," *Economic Journal*, London, Sept., 1940, pp. 449–60; G. D. H. Cole, *Europe, Russia, and the Future*, New York, 1942, pp. 83–84; and a rebuke of this and similar attitudes in Paul Einzig, *Hitler's New Order in Europe*, London, 1941, p. 105.

[2] Guillebaud, *op. cit.*, p. 459.   [3] Cole, *op. cit.*, p. 69.

with Germany's providing a steady market at stable prices for all the agricultural and raw-material surpluses of the region, as was the case in the few years prior to the outbreak of the present war. Combined with this is the idea of a complementary *Grossraumwirtschaft* (economy within a large unit) without which such a secure market is supposed to be impossible. However, the countries concerned did not gain the advantages that they would have derived from a real customs or economic union with Germany, enabling them to buy and sell freely. Under the German scheme, no import or export was possible without licenses, nor was there any free movement of capital. Furthermore, Germany was not able to provide the agricultural countries with the needed long-term capital or to supply them with various necessary overseas commodities. Germany's economy was not adjusted to that of the partner—quasi-satellite—states; theirs had to be adjusted to hers,[4] under compulsion to produce what she thought was needed by her armed economy. The whole area was organized with the aim of attaining the greatest possible self-sufficiency for the German economic empire, with no concern for the welfare of the peoples involved.

The German policy was in direct conscious conflict with the concept of international division of production; its effect was therefore inevitably detrimental to the Danubian countries in the long run. By inflating prices, Germany divorced the price level of these agricultural countries from the world-market system, and, finally, reached the position of being able to dictate foreign-exchange rates favorable to herself.

Furthermore, it must not be forgotten that the whole trade policy was closely connected with German preparations for war. No proof was ever offered that Germany would be either willing or able to carry on such a policy once a peacetime economy was reëstablished. The stable market and the guaranteed high prices belong in the same sphere as other German economic "miracles," such as keeping the mark "stable" at the old parity or guaranteeing full permanent employment in a war economy. Now that all belligerent industrial countries have organized war economies, full employment and even labor shortages are no longer miracles or achievements of German genius. Their cause is clear. And clear, too, have become the ingenious

[4] G. D. H. Cole apparently did not realize this fact, remarking (*op. cit.,* p. 83) that in the purely economic sense "unification under the Nazis might be better than no unification at all."

scheme of a guaranteed market and prices, and the fictitious gold parity of the German mark.

There are still other aspects of the problems of Southeastern Europe. Germany, in her attempt to achieve the greatest possible self-sufficiency, made great efforts to foster the growth of products which are better suited to production overseas, and at the same time she checked the growth of demand for high quality foodstuffs.[5] This cannot be a desirable solution to the agricultural problem. Germany had no constructive program for mitigating population pressure in the agricultural area. She even contemplated settling German farmers there, regarding the region as her own living space.

One of the main possibilities for reducing the pressure on the land —industrialization—was definitely discouraged. The countries were to choose only industries and products complementary to German production and not in competition with it. If some economists point out that all this would have been changed once peace was established, it is only correct to answer that all the "advantages" with regard to purchases and prices were also the result of the same armed economy, and not therefore to be considered on the credit side.

Let us hope that after the defeat of Germany there will not be any serious suggestion of a German solution to the problems of Central and Southeastern Europe. For the years have fully demonstrated that there can be no durable peace in Europe unless the Central and Southeastern states are consolidated, developed, and built up as strong national economies within a framework of a proper political organization. It follows that if a good practicable system is to be worked out, Austria, like the other nations, must regain her freedom and the old historic borders of Czechoslovakia must be restored.

The German economic conquest raises certain fundamental questions. Was not the old organization sounder, safer, at least economically, for these nations? Did it not work more satisfactorily? Was the German conquest the inevitable result of the political situation, the economic structure, and local events in the area, or was it more closely related to the postwar European and world political and economic trends? Why did Germany succeed so easily, even before the present war started? A brief survey of prewar economic conditions in the Danubian valley will help in answering these questions.

[5] Doreen Warriner, *Eastern Europe after Hitler*, London, 1940, p. 25.

Very frequently we find the old Austro-Hungarian Monarchy regarded as the ideal economic unit. Such writers lay emphasis upon its large, protected domestic market. True, the Monarchy possessed the prerequisites for economic progress, but it lacked a definite and consistent program aimed at the general development of all its parts. People forget that it embraced one of the very backward regions of Europe. Bohemia, Moravia, Silesia, and substantial parts of Austria resembled the Central and Western European countries in their stage of economic development; we may characterize them as having a capitalistic economic system. But the eastern and southeastern parts of the Monarchy were only in the first stages of such development, with very primitive economic structures.[6]

The chief occupation of Austria-Hungary was agriculture, but its steadily increasing population (estimated in 1914 at about 52 million) created a real need for industrial development. In 1910, 56.8 per cent of the working population was engaged in agriculture (in Hungary, 68.6 per cent, in Bohemia, 40 per cent, as against 24.4 per cent in industry and 8.8 per cent in commerce and banking. In the last decade before the war, industrialization was in fact expanding rather rapidly: between 1903 and 1913 the number of factories increased by 40.6 per cent, and the number of industrial workers by 45 per cent.[7]

But economic and social progress was rather slow and the national income and the standard of living remained far below those of Germany or the countries of Western Europe. The prewar national income of Austria was estimated at Kr. 14.5 billion, that of Hungary at Kr. 7.5 billion at the maximum. This may be compared with Rm. 50.1 billion for Germany in 1913 (population, 68 million), and Fr. 36–38.5 billion for France in 1911 (population, 39 million).

Colin Clark's figures give us the basis for another comparison.[8] In 1913 the national income produced per head of working population (on the basis of a 48-hour week) was, in international units:

6 C. A. Macartney, *Problems of the Danube Basin*, London, 1942, p. 71.

7 Friedrich Hertz, *Die Produktionsgrundlagen der oester. Industrie vor und nach dem Krieg imbesondere im Vergleich mit Deutschland*, Vienna, 1917, pp. 5–10; Leo Pasvolsky, *Economic Nationalism of the Danubian States*, New York, 1925, pp. 21, 35.

8 Colin Clark, *The Conditions of Economic Progress*, London, 1940, pp. 92, 104, 135, 136, 148 (table).

An international unit is defined as the amount of goods and services which one dollar would purchase in the United States, taking the average of the period from 1925 to 1934.

Great Britain	966
Germany	764
Switzerland	655
France	629
Austria-Hungary	352
Austria, 452	
Hungary, 220	
Italy	328
Russia	306

The lower level income of this region was reflected in smaller purchases of various consumer goods, as compared with the more highly developed countries of Europe. It is estimated that before 1914 per capita consumption of meat, sugar, and tobacco was only three fifths that of Germany; cotton, one half; beer, two fifths; coffee, one third; and coal, less than one quarter.[9]

The system of public taxation was regressive. By far the greater part of the governmental income was derived from excise and indirect taxes, state monopolies, and customs duties, rather than from direct taxes. (This also explains the low consumption of various goods imported from overseas.) The standard of living varied widely in different parts of the Monarchy, the highest being in the industrialized areas of Bohemia, Moravia, Silesia, Vienna, and in some sections of Austria. In Galicia, a great part of Hungary, Bosnia, and Herzegovina the standard was very low.

One clear symptom of an unsettled economic status is constant emigration on a large scale, when the increase in the rural population cannot be absorbed. In the single decade 1900 and 1910 over 2,100,000 persons emigrated from Austria-Hungary to the United States (more than 200,000 yearly). Great numbers also went to other overseas territories and to other European countries (especially Germany and France). Moreover, there was a large-scale seasonal movement of labor. These emigrants sent back to Austria-Hungary large amounts of money as remittances, thus strengthening the balance of payments.

Austria-Hungary offered to industry and agriculture a large, protected—but as yet insufficiently developed—domestic market. The protection tended to favor agriculture; this placed Hungarian agriculture in a much better position than that of the Balkan countries, which depended upon foreign markets for the sale of their relatively small export surpluses. But in its foreign trade also, Austria-Hungary

[9] Macartney, *op. cit.*, pp. 74–75. See also League of Nations, *Report on Nutrition*, 1937.

lagged behind the Western countries. The value of foreign trade per head was only £3 (at the old parity), while in France it was £12, in Germany £13, and the United States £22.[10] It has often been said that agriculture and industry were unusually well balanced in Austria-Hungary and that consequently there was an extremely high degree of self-sufficiency. But a more appropriate explanation of the small volume of foreign trade might be the low level of living, coupled with the undeveloped mass demand for consumer goods. The balance of foreign trade showed an import surplus after 1908. The figures in million Kr. for the last years before the war are: [11]

	Imports	Exports
1910	2,929.7	2,587.6
1911	3,275.2	2,582.6
1912	3,669.9	2,926.7
1913	3,509.0	2,988.0

Pasvolsky[12] believes the primary cause of the steadily increasing imports was the rapid growth of population. Another reason might be the expansion of armaments and of investment in new industries and public works. If we take the year 1912 as typical of the period, the foreign trade may be broken down into the following categories (in percentages of the total):

	Imports	Exports
Raw materials	54.4	32.8
Semimanufactures	16.9	18.1
Finished manufactures	27.7	49.1

Germany was by far the most important source of Austro-Hungarian imports, sending over four times the value sent by any other single country. Next came the United States, followed closely by Great Britain, Russia, and British India. (In the period 1910–12 there were no significant changes in the proportion of Austro-Hungarian imports originating in the various foreign countries, nor in the relative importance of the various countries to whom Austria-Hungary exported). For 1912 the import figures (in percentages of total imports) are as follows:

10 Macartney, op. cit., p. 76.
11 Figures from Statistik des auswärtigen Handels, official annual publication of the Austrian Ministry of Commerce, for the years 1910–13. A krone equals $0.2026 (gold).
12 Pasvolsky, op. cit., p. 14.

Germany	39.3
United States	9.5
Great Britain	7.0
Russia	6.2
British India	6.1
Italy	4.5
France	3.4
Switzerland	3.3
Rumania	2.8
Bulgaria	0.4
Serbia	1.1
Greece	0.6
Turkey	1.2

Germany was likewise the most important market for Austro-Hungarian exports, taking more than four times as much as any other country. The figures (in percentages of total exports) are as follows:

Germany	39.0
Great Britain	9.1
Italy	8.5
Switzerland	6.0
European Turkey	3.6
Russia	3.4
Free Port of Hamburg	3.4
France	3.0
United States	2.3
Greece	0.9
Bulgaria	1.8
Serbia	1.6

Austria-Hungary's largest import balance in the period from 1910 to 1912 was with Germany, averaging Kr. 260 million per year; with the United States it was over Kr. 220 million. Exports to the Balkans were larger than imports from them, which may perhaps indicate some export of capital to those countries.

Germany therefore played the decisive role in Austria-Hungary's foreign trade, not only providing the Monarchy with German (manufactured) goods, but also delivering large amounts of raw materials from overseas—wool, cotton, crude metals, furs. On the other hand, various commodities exported to Germany were in turn reëxported via Berlin and Hamburg. Exports to Germany consisted largely of agricultural and forestry products; items exceeding Kr. 15 million in value (they included eggs, timber, barley and malt, hops, clover and other seeds, oxen, and bed feathers) alone comprised 37 per cent of the Monarchy's export to Germany. Industrial products accounted for one third of the total export.

Germany absorbed almost 40 per cent of the trade of Austria-Hungary, but the Monarchy held no such commanding position with regard to German trade; it received only 11.6 per cent of Germany's exports and provided only 7.8 per cent of Germany's imports. In world trade also the Monarchy's position was relatively weak; neighboring states absorbed from 68 to 70 per cent of her total trade in the period 1909–13. Of her total exports, 86.3 per cent went to Europe, from which she received 74.5 per cent of her total imports.[13]

The various parts of the Monarchy participated in its foreign trade to a different degree. This fact was later to have a very definite effect upon the postwar status of the countries arising out of the Monarchy. Whereas the territory of Czechoslovakia supplied by far the greater part of the Monarchy's total export, and had a large share also in the total import, Hungary sent 72 per cent of her exports to, and received 71.5 per cent of her imports from, other parts of the Monarchy.[14]

Because of the large import surplus, the problem of balancing payments became increasingly difficult. The biggest item on the credit side was emigrant remittances which amounted to Kr. 1,500 million in 1909–13, and to about Kr. 400 million in 1913. The tourist trade of Bohemia, Austria, and the Alps was an important credit item, as were the banking and other services available in Vienna. But on the debit side, besides the large import balance stood the ever-increasing item of interest and dividends on foreign debts. At the end of 1913, the Monarchy's total foreign indebtedness amounted to about Kr. 9,760 million.[15] Foreign investments were estimated at about one billion kronen; interest and dividends due on foreign debt amounted to Kr. 1,750 million in 1909–13, but returns from foreign investments yielded only Kr. 200 million.

In order to settle the balance of payments, it was necessary to contract new foreign debts. New capital was likewise required for economic expansion. In December, 1913, England had investments of

13 H. Liepmann, *Tariff Levels and the Economic Unity of Europe*, New York, 1938, p. 412.
14 Pasvolsky, *op. cit.*, p. 19. *South-eastern Europe* (published 1939 by the Royal Institute of International Affairs, Oxford University Press), estimates the trade of Hungary with other districts of the Monarchy at 75 per cent of her total trade.
15 *Ibid.*, pp. 5–6, 13.

£8 million in Austria-Hungary,[16] France, Fr. 2,200 million, Germany, Rm. 3,000 million. In other words, Germany's share in Austria-Hungarian investment was greater than that of France and Great Britain combined. Moreover, Germany was participating directly to an increasing extent in the Monarchy's industry, banking, and trade. Thus Germany's influence in the Monarchy derived from her political position, her major share in Austria-Hungary's foreign trade, and her growing role as a creditor.

On the whole the economic development of the Monarchy was retarded as compared with that of Germany or the Western parts of Europe, despite the fact that she possessed potential resources for improvement.

The necessary comprehensive, economic program could not be carried out without an adequate political program. A prerequisite for general economic progress was the coöperation of all the national groups contained in the Monarchy. Instead of this, two major struggles were maintained. Austria and Hungary were perpetually in conflict: different economic systems and policies had been established in each part of the Monarchy, and Hungary was ever trying to establish a more independent Hungarian economy. And superimposed upon this struggle was another between the ruling groups (the Germans in Austria and the Magyars in Hungary) and the ruled, but distinctive, racial groups. No far-sighted economic program, and therefore no significant progress, was possible without the full coöperation of all sections of the people. Moreover, such progress could have occurred only under an integrated national and foreign policy that would check Germany's steadily growing influence in Austro-Hungarian affairs.[17] Many of these problems, it is obvious, were to reappear after 1918. Apparently of recent origin, they had in fact existed before the war.

The three Danubian-Balkan states—Rumania, Serbia, and Bulgaria—were, of course, even more backward in their economic development than was the Austro-Hungarian Monarchy. Only recently established as independent political units, their political, social and economic

16 The Royal Institute of International Affairs, *The Problem of International Investments,* London, 1937, pp. 121, 125, 127.
17 The increasing German influence in the Austro-Hungarian economy was confirmed by the negotiations for a customs union in 1917–18. See Gustav Gratz and R. Schüller, *Die äussere Wirtschaftspolitik Oesterreich-Ungarns,* Vienna, 1925.

organization presented difficult problems. Like that of Greece—
which had a longer independent history but was also economically
backward—their economy was mainly agricultural, occupying nearly
80 per cent of the working population (even in Greece this proportion
was about 60 per cent). Agricultural production was carried on on the
basis of a small number of staple products, extensive rather than intensive methods being used. In some areas, a primitive patriarchal
system still remained.

In these countries, the level of living was very low and the population was steadily increasing,[18] although emigration offered a measure of
relief.[19] The volume and composition of foreign trade were adequate
to the economic and social structure; agricultural staples were the
principal exports and manufactured consumer goods the chief imports. Rumania held the strongest position in foreign trade, as the
following figures show (in millions of lei).[20]

	Imports	Exports	Export Surplus
1910	409.6	616.5	206.9
1911	569.6	691.7	122.1
1912	637.7	642.1	4.4
1913	590.0	671.0	81.0

The principal exports were wheat, corn, barley, flour—two thirds
of the total; benzine, and refined petroleum. With production of oil
mounting to two million tons shortly before 1914, there was a
government-encouraged tendency to promote industrialization, of
which the increasing import of machinery was symptomatic. Germany
was the most important source of imports (40 per cent of the total in
1913), followed by Austria-Hungary (23 per cent), and Great Britain
(9 per cent). Rumanian exports were more scattered; Belgium was
the chief buyer of cereals (27 per cent of the total export of 1913);
Austria-Hungary was second (14 per cent); next came Italy (10.6 per
cent), then France (9 per cent).

[18] The population of Rumania in 1918 was estimated at 7,897,000, of Serbia at 4,130,000
(Montenegro 200,000), of Bulgaria at 4,847,000 and of Greece at 5,017,000.
[19] In the period 1901–10, there were 53,002 emigrants from Rumania to the United
States; in 1910–14, 10,520. Corresponding figures for Greece are 167,519 and 61,504.
Bulgarian farmers and gardeners settled in Central and Western Europe. Royal Institute,
The Balkan States, p. 134.
[20] The Rumanian leu, Serbian dinar, Bulgarian leve, and Greek drachma were all equal
in value: one gold franc = $0.1929, gold.

Serbia's foreign trade was, of course, much smaller. (Figures in millions of dinars.)

	Imports	Exports	Balance
1910	84.7	98.4	+13.7
1911	115.4	116.9	+ 1.5
1912	106.1	84.2	—21.9

In 1912 the principal articles of export were cereals and fresh and salted meat (all together constituting two thirds of the total) and copper. Austria-Hungary and Germany were the principal participants in Serbian trade, taking the greater part of her exports (in 1912 Austria-Hungary took 42.8 per cent and Germany 21.7 per cent). They likewise provided 75 per cent of Serbian imports (Austria-Hungary 47 per cent in 1911, 44.9 per cent in 1912; Germany 29.33 per cent in 1912). Imports from Great Britain made up about 8 per cent of the total in 1912. Exports to Turkey in 1912 made up 8.54 per cent of the total.

Thus the foreign trade of Serbia—a country without an outlet to the sea—was really dependent on the Central Powers more than that of any other Balkan country. This dependence persisted, despite serious attempts to find other markets. A decline in the Monarchy's share in Serbia's trade after the commercial war of 1906–11 was compensated by an increased German participation.

Bulgaria's foreign trade was likewise that of a typical agricultural country producing a very limited number of commodities. The following figures are in millions of leva.

	Imports	Exports	Balance
1910	177.2	129.0	—48.2
1911	198.8	184.6	—14.2
1912	212.8	156.4	—56.4

In 1912 the principal articles of export were wheat and maize, eggs, and attar of rose (two thirds of the total). Half of the total imports came from the Central Powers, Austria-Hungary providing 29 per cent in 1913, Germany 19.6 per cent, Great Britain 8.9 per cent. In order of importance in the export market were Belgium (16.27 per cent of the total in 1913), Germany (18 per cent), Austria-Hungary (15.44 per cent) and Great Britain (8.5 per cent).

For Greece the Central European market was less important, because of her geographical position as well as the nature of her exports.

The foreign-trade figures for 1910–12 are as follows (in million drachma):

	Imports	Exports	Balance
1910	166.5	144.6	—15.9
1911	173.5	140.9	—32.6
1912	157.6	146.1	—11.5

Two thirds of the exports from Greece in 1912 were dried currants, tobacco, olive oil, and wine.

Great Britain was the chief single source of Greek imports in 1913 (23.4 per cent); next in order were Russia (19.9 per cent, mostly cereals), Austria-Hungary (16.4 per cent) and Germany (7.5 per cent). Great Britain was also the principal export market for Greek goods (23.9 per cent), with France (11.4 per cent), Austria-Hungary (10.7 per cent), and Germany (10.2 per cent), following. The two Central Powers together accounted for only one fourth to one fifth of the total Greek foreign trade.

The value of the imports and exports of each of these countries, translated into millions of gold dollars, was as follows:

	Imports	Exports
Germany (the 1911–13 yearly average)	2,668	2,330
Austria-Hungary (the 1911–13 yearly average)	702	578
Rumania (the 1911–15 yearly average)	101.7	116.8
Greece (the 1911–15 yearly average)	42.9	30.9
Bulgaria (the 1911–15 yearly average)	34.2	26.8
Serbia (the 1911–12 yearly average)	21.4	19.4

The commodities imported and exported by each country indicate clearly its economic structure as well as its stage of industrialization and of general economic development. Germany was plainly on a much higher level of industrialization than Austria-Hungary, which in turn was more advanced than the Balkan countries.

In summary, within this group of countries the Balkan states were chiefly exporters of foodstuffs, Germany of finished goods; Austria-Hungary exported manufactures to the Balkans and raw materials, foodstuffs, and certain specialized industrial products to Germany in substantial quantities. Whereas Austria-Hungary and Germany dominated the supply of goods sent to the Balkans (Greece, as stated, was an exception), the principal markets for Balkan exports were more widely dispersed and the proportion going to each country varied widely from year to year. From 1910 to 1912 Germany had an import balance in her trade with each of the Balkans, except Bulgaria. Austria-Hungary had an export balance with each of these countries and a large import surplus with Germany.[21]

The agricultural nature, together with the low standard of living of the Balkan countries, is sufficient explanation for their limited trade outside of Europe. Bulgaria sent 93.1 per cent of her exports to Europe in the period from 1909 to 1913 and received 98.6 per cent of her imports from there. Comparable figures for Serbia are 95.9 per cent and 99.7 per cent, for Rumania 96.2 per cent and 96 per cent, for Greece 83 per cent and 95.3 per cent.[22] In so far as overseas goods were consumed, they were largely in the form of manufactured goods, usually imported from Austria-Hungary and Germany, or, less frequently, through some other continental state. Thus the Central Powers provided the Balkan countries with goods in manufactured or unchanged form that they would otherwise have had to buy overseas. It was a common form of multilateral exchange of commodities.

The process of industrialization was slow, depending on the general economic development, and closely connected with the problems of capital and foreign credit. Credit to the Balkan countries was often used by the major powers as an instrument of power politics. Its chief feature was the struggle between the two big European blocs, the Central Powers and the Triple Entente. Loans were needed to build railways and other public equipment, and a very large proportion of foreign credit was used for armament purposes. It was but shortly before the First World War that foreign capital became directly interested in private ventures (oil, mines, factories and especially in banks). German capital predominated in Rumania,[23] while, in Bul-

[21] Although Germany could absorb the greater part of the grain surpluses of the Danubian States, she bought wheat from Russia, Argentina, the United States, and Rumania, in that order. (Germany purchased 2,721,000 quintals of wheat from Rumania in 1912.) Russia was also Germany's most important source of barley (supplying 21.7 million quintals in 1912), followed by Austria-Hungary (1.6 million q.) and Rumania. It was to Western Europe that the Danubian products were chiefly sent. The leading market for Rumanian and Bulgarian wheat was Belgium; Italy, the Netherlands, and France were also important markets. Rumanian maize went to Austria-Hungary, Italy, Belgium and Great Britain. Economic reasons (i.e., cost of transportation, transport by sea against rail, etc.), rather than political ones accounted for the destination of these commodities, in a time of multilateral trade before the ideas of complementary markets, of coördinated economies, were rampant.

[22] Liepmann, op. cit., p. 412.

[23] Herbert Feis, Europe, the World's Banker, 1870–1914, New Haven, 1930, p. 269; Royal Institute, The Problem of International Investments, pp. 121, 125, 127.

garia and Turkey, France exerted the greater influence. In Greece,
France and Great Britain held a traditionally firm position. By December, 1913, British holdings in publicly issued securities in the
Balkans totaled £17 million and in Turkey £24 million. French investment rose from Fr. 700 million in 1900 to Fr. 2,500 million in
1913; while German investment in the area in 1914 was Rm. 1,700
million and in Turkey, Rm. 1,800 million. Austrian investment may
be estimated at Kr. 500 million.

Only Rumania had an export surplus. Emigrant remittances (and,
in the case of Greece, revenue from shipping) were the main current
credit items in the balance of payments, and thus it became extremely
difficult for the majority of these countries to pay the interest on
foreign debt. But since domestic capital could not meet the need for
further public investment, for industrialization, and for armaments,
further foreign capital was essential; it was also needed to maintain
payments on the already existing foreign debts and, even more, to
accelerate economic development. The situation was very similar to
that in 1931 with one difference—there was no special problem of
transfer abroad. With the government as the principal debtor, the
difficulties of transfer became identical with the difficulties of payment.[24]

In our analysis of the main economic problems contributory to
the political unrest in this part of Europe before World War I, we
have arrived at the following conclusions: the standard of living in
this area was much lower than that of Germany and Western Europe,
with Austria-Hungary serving as a point of transition from West to
East; the western industrialized parts of the Monarchy exhibited
an economic development and level of living similar to that of neighboring Germany, while Galicia, a great part of Hungary, Bukovina,
and Bosnia were similar in their economic development and low
standard to the Balkans and to Russia.

In the greater part of the area there existed growing population

[24] It is interesting to compare the amount of foreign indebtedness existing before 1914
in this area (including Austria-Hungary) with that of the period 1931–32. The foreign
debt of the six Danubian countries, Greece and Poland in 1931–32 was estimated at
Fr. 24.35 billion, Fr. 6.1 billion being private debt. (Without Poland, the total figure was
Fr. 19.90 billion.) For 1914 we have the figures of long-term British, French, and German
investment in Austria-Hungary, the Balkans, and Turkey. The British figures are £49 million; the French, Fr. 4.7 billion; the German, Rm. 6.5 billion—a total of about 14 billion
Fr. If we take into account private investments and investments of other countries besides
these three, the volume of foreign debts and investments in 1932 does not appear very
different from that in 1914 (especially if we do not include Poland).

pressure; this was especially true in the agricultural countries where methods of production were prevailingly of an extensive type. A necessary outlet for this pressure was through large-scale emigration. There was a growing demand for industrialization especially in Hungary, Rumania, and Bulgaria.

Foreign indebtedness was increasing, with Germany taking an ever greater share in public as well as in private lending. German industrial and banking investments were expanding throughout the area, with more than 30 per cent of total German investments in long-term foreign loans centered here. The Austrian investment in the Balkans strengthened Germany's position politically. Germany's domination was further sustained by her decisive position in the Monarchy's foreign trade. The participation of both the Central Powers in the foreign trade of the Balkans was much greater than the share of other large countries. Nevertheless, the main agricultural products of the Balkans were sold abroad on the markets most satisfactory to the exporting countries with regard to price and quality conditions. The balance of the relatively small foreign trade of the whole area (including Austria-Hungary) showed an import surplus.

The situation could be remedied only by a general increase in economic activity and an advance in economic development. It is clear that this task had become even more urgent after World War I. The problem required a European solution with international support. It was beyond the capacity of these countries to solve it by themselves, for it involved not only increasing their foreign trade, developing their domestic market, and acquiring foreign capital, but it also involved the integration of the European economy.

2

THE PERIOD OF CONSOLIDATION AND
RECONSTRUCTION

THE PROBLEM of postwar reconstruction in Central and Southeastern
Europe was inevitably more difficult and of broader scope than that
of Western Europe. Similar factors of postwar reconstruction were
complete lack of food and raw materials; disorganized monetary
systems; large areas destroyed by actual warfare; inadequate transportation systems; and a substantial danger of social unrest. To the
ubiquitous problem of adjustment to various profound changes in the
world economy, there was added here an economic and social adjustment entailed by new political set-ups.

The independence achieved by the Danubian nations was not
confined to the political sphere; it permeated the economic life as
well, for once political emancipation was achieved it was inevitable
that a demand for economic strength should follow. The peace treaties
did not outline a common economic organization for these countries,
nor was the importance of a genuine economic consolidation of the
Danubian area clearly recognized and evaluated. Had this been the
case, and had the agreement of the Big Powers to such a plan been
assured, then perhaps a collective economic and financial reconstruction program would have been achieved. Nothing of that sort took
place, and while the League of Nations rendered valuable assistance
to several countries in their national monetary and financial consolidation, no real measures were contemplated to prevent the political
nationalism from acquiring a form of exaggerated economic nationalism. There is little doubt that if, in the peace treaties or immediately
thereafter, a desirable economic organization of these countries had
been created, their future development could have been directed in
such a way as to satisfy their reasonable demands. Simultaneously,
many mistakes which increased their difficulties later could have been
avoided.

When speaking of desirable economic organization, I am not of
the opinion that it was possible in the new political situation simply
to maintain unchanged the old customs unit of Austria-Hungary,

even if it were extended to other countries, or that it was feasible to retain the existing set-up of economic administration and the entire status quo in regard to power. A program of coöperation could succeed only if it took into consideration not only the purely economic points of view but also the unalterable fact that the new states were determined to develop their national economies and to achieve and maintain a position in the economic life of Europe. This implied a demand for the relative reduction of the predominant role of the German, Austrian, and Hungarian nations in the whole economic life of Central and Southeastern Europe. A tendency in this direction had long been apparent. A wise statesmanship, built upon facts and mutual understanding, was needed to evolve a program which would be advantageous to all nations concerned. But this was too much to expect, at the close of a war that had divided these nations into opposing groups of victors and vanquished.

Another aspect must be considered, namely the relation between the newly attained potentially democratic freedom and economic and social life. Newly attained political freedom creates a powerful economic incentive. Combined with a new democratic system, especially in the case of a young nation, it strengthens the determination to raise the standard of living, and to attain within a short time those things which have been hitherto neglected or denied. It is only too clear that these two forces, if uncoördinated in a comprehensive and farsighted policy and unsupported by a corresponding international movement, may encourage economic nationalism in international relations, and may also lead to difficulties in the national financial, social, and industrial policy.

Not all the Danubian states realized in time the responsibilities involved in their new independence. Political freedom did not bring them economic independence. I do not refer to their dependence on foreign capital, but to the fact that small states obviously must depend to a greater degree on international economic relations than do larger economic units. This sort of dependence is much greater in agricultural countries with limited numbers of staple products than in industrialized countries. The fact was underestimated at a time when protectionist policies were dominant. The new countries were soon faced with the difficult task of adjusting their national economies to the situation abroad and of integrating them with the

European and world economy. This task was made more difficult by the fact that some of their important former domestic markets became foreign markets.

We may summarize here briefly the main problems peculiar to each of these states.

Czechoslovakia's [1] important problem was the economic amalgamation of a highly developed western section (Bohemia, Moravia, Silesia) with a predominantly agricultural and retarded eastern region, formerly a part of Hungary (Slovakia, Carpatho-Russia). Another not easy task was the necessity to export a great part of her industrial production, competing with foreign countries on equal terms in what had formerly been her domestic market. Within a very short time she had to face the high protection of new industry in the Danubian area. At the outset she was somewhat financially dependent as a debtor nation upon Vienna and, to a less degree, upon Budapest. An energetic, anti-inflationary monetary and financial policy together with a steady increase of savings contributed greatly to a rapid consolidation of this country, based on an efficient industry and a progressive agriculture.

Austria's [2] development was, for various reasons, more difficult. For many years she had no clear political policy. Austrian patriotism and will to continue as an independent political unit conflicted with the demand of a part of her population for union with Germany. Her industrial situation was similar to that of Czechoslovakia, but her agriculture did not, of course, provide a like balance. Most important, the structure of the balance of payments was subjected to important changes. Invisible items in the balance of payments, resulting from the many financial and other services rendered by Vienna and by her position as capital of the old Monarchy, had been extremely important. The question arose as to which items and incomes could be retained and which must be lost. Needless to say, only those income items corresponding to various economic and financial services that Austria might usefully fulfill for Central and Southeastern Europe under the new order could remain in the long run. Conceivably

[1] Area: 54,244 square miles; population: 14.73 million (December, 1930 census), 15.26 million (1937 estimate). These, and the similar figures for other countries, are taken from the U.S. Department of Commerce, *Foreign Commerce Yearbook*, 1938.
[2] Area: 32,377 square miles; population: 6.53 million (1923 census), 6.76 million (1934 census).

Austria might render for this area services in reëxport, banking, insurance, and transport, similar to those rendered by England in world trade. On the other hand, many items, such as payments to Vienna as the headquarters of numerous corporations, her financing of purely national business, and the like would of necessity decline.

Austria began her new career as a large creditor nation, holding extensive investments in each of the Danubian countries and in Poland. In order to maintain her economic position it was necessary to achieve a new balance of payments by increasing production, and, if possible, by added strength in other sources of revenue. Considerable progress was in fact made in tourist traffic. But paramount was the necessity for adjustment to the changed situation—an adjustment which could have been instrumental in achieving a better balance between outgo and income in the Austrian economy. Of course the political (and psychological) issues were deeply involved in any question of economic policy.[3]

The problems of Hungary [4] were simpler in some respects. A country with an ample agricultural foundation, a surplus in food, and an industry employing a relatively small proportion of the population should have found no grave difficulty in balancing her foreign trade. The economic importance of Budapest to Hungary was never as dominant as that of Vienna to Austria. The new territorial status, however, necessitated many difficult economic adjustments. Before 1914 Hungary sold 70 to 75 per cent of her exports (which were predominantly agricultural) within the protected area of Austria-Hungary. This proved to be a serious obstacle when these products —less readily diverted to a new market than are industrial exports— had to compete with those of other agricultural countries. This should have been a powerful factor in promoting closer economic coöperation with Hungary's importing neighbors.

Hungary's policy of industrialization, begun long before 1914, was stimulated by the problem of the still-growing agricultural population and even more by the trend toward economic nationalism. But in contradiction to all other nations within the Danubian area, where a profound land reform was effected to divide large land-holdings among the peasants, Hungary maintained her semifeudal agricultural

[3] For further reference see: Antonín Basch and J. Dvořáček, *Austria and Its Economic Existence*, Prague, 1925.

[4] Area: 35,936 square miles; population: 8.69 million (1930 census), 9.03 million (1937 estimate).

system of large estates. It formed a vital part of her political system.[5]

The problems of reconstruction in Rumania and Yugoslavia [6] had much in common. Both countries were faced with the immediate necessity to repair the vast damage done by actual warfare (in prewar Rumania and Serbia). Both countries were primarily agricultural, 75 to 80 per cent of their populations being engaged in farming. Both obtained, in their newly acquired territories, important industries and moderately well-developed agriculture, thereby substantially increasing their natural resources. The organization of these greatly enlarged territories was a tremendous undertaking. It involved the amalgamation of three or four different systems into one economic and political unit, and the building up of a financial and credit system especially appropriate to the needs of agriculture and fitted to serve an enlarged territory. It included the modernization of primitive methods in agriculture, and the improvement of educational facilities in the general and in the technical field.

Clearly, it was a tremendous task to develop these backward economies, endowed with ample natural resources but almost completely lacking in capital, and possessing at the time inadequate organizing capacity. In both countries the problem of agricultural overpopulation became steadily more pressing; industrialization seemed to offer one possibility for its alleviation.

No such fundamental changes took place in Bulgaria and Greece,[7] though the impact of the World War following so closely on the heels of the two Balkan wars wrought grave difficulties. A special problem was created in Greece by the resettlement of more than a million refugees from Turkey; the resettlement of about 200,000 refugees from Greece in Bulgaria presented a similar problem there, though on a much smaller scale.

[5] "1232 large estates (over 1400 acres) representing 0.1 per cent of the total number of separate agricultural holdings cover 30 per cent of all the land. The 1,142,294 small properties (under 7 acres) represented 71.5 per cent of all agricultural holdings cover an area of 2,468,836 acres, i.e., 11 per cent of all the land. A small proprietor has an average holding of 2.13 acres. Forty per cent of the agricultural population has no landed property at all. Almost 80 per cent of the total agrarian population live on the outer fringe of proletarian existence." Oscar Jaszi, "Feudal Agrarianism in Hungary," *Foreign Affairs*, XVI (July, 1938), 714–16.

[6] *Rumania*—area: 113,887 square miles; population: 19.44 million (1936 estimate). *Yugoslavia*—area: 95,576 square miles; population: 13.93 million (1931 census); 15.40 million (Dec. 31, 1937, estimate).

[7] *Bulgaria*—area: 39,825 square miles; population: 6.017 million (1934 census), 6.28 million (1938 German census). *Greece*—area: 50,270 square miles; population: 6.20 million (1928 census), 7.00 million (1937 estimate).

Bulgaria and Greece were faced by the need to adapt their post-war economies to the new postwar conditions in general and in this area in particular. Bulgaria, a peasant farming country, was forced for various reasons to change the structure of her agricultural production. At the same time she made a serious attempt, though on a limited scale, to continue her prewar policy of industrialization. In Greece the increase of population called for expansion in national production both in agriculture and in industry. But on the whole the Greek economy belonged to the Mediterranean rather than the Danubian sphere.

While our survey cannot be even approximately exhaustive, we have attempted to indicate the principal postwar problems of the Danubian area: some were present before 1914; others had their source in the general consequences of the war; still others resulted from the new political regimes. Together they illustrate convincingly the scale of the task involved, not only in rebuilding areas destroyed by actual warfare, but also in laying down a firm basis for the future development of the region, for its economic recovery, for an improvement in its standard of living, and for relief of population pressure in the overcrowded areas. Obviously time was needed for even partial fulfillment of these objectives. It is equally true that economic success rested not only upon a predominantly coöperative spirit in the world economy, but still more upon the interest of the ruling economic powers.

In discussing the steps taken our first consideration will be monetary stabilization. In some nations of Central and Southeastern Europe the monetary situation was extremely difficult; it was aggravated by the German inflation, which had a marked influence directly and indirectly through its effect on foreign trade. Monetary and financial consolidation in these countries, exhausted by a long war and strained financially by postwar problems, required assistance from abroad. Czechoslovakia alone was able to carry out its monetary reform without contracting large foreign credits.[8]

Monetary and financial reform in the Danubian countries became an important part of the work of the League of Nations, which arranged for foreign loans and worked out schemes for Austria, Hun-

[8] A loan of £3.3 million and $14 million was contracted in 1922 to support the unnecessary deflation brought about by a sudden rise in the Kc. exchange rate. *De facto* stabilization was achieved in 1923; legal stabilization in 1926. (The law was passed in 1925.)

gary, Greece, and Bulgaria [9] (Rumania and Yugoslavia secured foreign aid without the assistance of the League). These schemes followed the traditional rules of monetary and budgetary policy, as restated by the Financial Conference at Brussels and later repeatedly emphasized. Doubtless, it was extremely important to introduce them in the Danubian area at a time when the solution of political and social problems threatened to overrule the equally important economic questions. On the other hand, the League should have supplemented its work by including various measures of a nonmonetary and nonfinancial character essential to an efficient national economy. For example, a direct approach to foreign-trade policy was certainly desirable. Greater coördination between the financial and economic measures would have been extremely useful.

As a matter of fact, at the time of the World Economic Conference at Geneva in 1927, the currencies of all the Danubian countries were stabilized, legally or *de facto,* and the monetary problem was thereupon regarded as settled and as offering a solid basis for international trade.[10] At that time, of course, there existed the general, optimistic belief that one of the most important steps had been achieved when the majority of currencies were brought into a firm relationship with gold.

As monetary stabilization advanced, attempts were made to restore more normal conditions in foreign trade. Various direct restrictions and quotas were abolished both before and after the Geneva con-

---

[9] League of Nations, Loans Committee, London, *Third Annual Report, June, 1935,* pp. 60–61.

Foreign Loans in Million £	(*£ at the Old Parity*)
Austrian Government Guaranteed Loan, 1923	£33.6
State Loan of the Kingdom of Hungary, 1924	£14.2
Greek Government Refugee Loan, 1924	£12.2
Kingdom of Bulgaria Settlement Loan, 1926	£ 3.4
Greek Government Stabilization and Refugee Loan, 1928	£ 7.5
Kingdom of Bulgaria Stabilization Loan, 1928	£ 5.4
Total	£76.3

[10] Throughout this work, unless otherwise stated, dollar means the gold dollar of pre-1933 parity—i.e., before the devaluation in April, 1933. For each country the date and rate of stabilization (in terms of the dollar) were as follows:

Austria (July, 1923): 1 s. = $0.1407; the schilling was introduced in March, 1925. *Hungary* (July, 1924): 1 pö. = $0.1749; the pengö was introduced in March, 1925. *Greece* (legal stabilization, 1928): 1 dr. = $0.1297; exchange-rate fluctuations were slight. *Bulgaria* (legal stabilization, November, 1928): *de facto* in 1924): 1 leva = $0.0072. *Rumania* (legal stabilization, February, 1929): 1 leu = $0.00598; there were few changes in the exchange rate after 1927. *Yugoslavia* (legal stabilization, June, 1931; *de facto* in 1928): 1 dinar = $0.01761. *Czechoslovakia* (February, 1926): 1 koruna = $0.0296.

ference. The objective was a policy leading toward free international trade and to a leveling of prices in various countries. But the postwar dislocations had not yet been overcome, and a new wave of protectionism increased the disparities in prices. It would be incorrect to assume that the introduction of the gold standard in its postwar form brought about the price-leveling process that existed before 1914. There had not been sufficient time, and economic reconstruction was not yet far enough advanced. As we shall discuss more fully later, in some of these countries the consideration of the prices of the leading export products is of greater significance than the comparison of the various price indices, as these were not always established by the methods used in economically developed countries.

The need for foreign credits was not, of course, limited to monetary and general reconstruction purposes. As we have seen, this entire area had been importing capital before 1914; now the need for it was, logically, increased. Foreign capital showed an interest in public and private investment in Central and Southeastern Europe, and the flow of foreign credits there increased during the general international credit expansion after 1925.

Czechoslovakia's position was quite different. Because of her favorable balance of payments and formation of national capital she was not eager to accept the foreign loans frequently offered her, especially for large-scale public investments.[11]

The new countries were considered good opportunities for investment in the expectation that development would be moderately rapid. In addition to loans to governments and credits for various public works—railways, construction of roads, water-power installations, gas works, telephone, and electricity—foreign capital concentrated more heavily in mining, lumbering, and various types of industrial production than before 1914.[12] It was interested in direct investment in the banking and insurance business, in mining, sugar, the metallurgical and chemical industry and, in almost all these countries, in the textile industry. The commercial banks of Vienna and Budapest obtained large amounts of foreign short-term credits which

[11] On April 1, 1928, possibly overestimating her financial strength, Czechoslovakia even repaid the American loan of 1925, the balance at that time amounting to $22,443,750. See *Ten Years of the National Bank of Czechoslovakia*, Prague, 1937, p. 165.

[12] For reference, see a very instructive article by Mirko Lamer, "Die Wandlungen der ausländischen Kapitalanlagen auf dem Balkan," *Weltwirtschaftliches Archiv*, 1938, pp. 470–524.

were used in many instances for middle-term and even long-term investments, not only in Austria and in Hungary, but also in the Balkan countries.

Foreign credits and investments were not limited to the big creditor countries—Great Britain, the United States, and France. Italy, Switzerland, Holland, Belgium, and Czechoslovakia also took part in this large-scale money lending in Central and Southeastern Europe which, together with Germany and Poland, was the center of international borrowing in Europe at the time. Germany was, of course, unable to participate substantially in these investments, since she herself was then the largest foreign borrower. The total foreign indebtedness of the countries concerned increased rapidly.

The flow of foreign capital, led by the profit motive, obviously followed the line of private interests on the private economy basis. The governments of the creditor nations exercised in general no direct control over the amount of the loans, nor did they investigate the purposes of the investments. There was no general program of economic development and reconstruction which could be taken as a guide for international credits. Financial circles gave little thought at that time to the question of how soon the debtor countries could repay the credits, or of their ability to maintain payments. The obvious relation between the balance of trade and the balance of payments was not taken too seriously. The prewar experience of the free movement of goods and capital was too recent. More imagination and thoroughness were needed to put these opportunities to best use, especially in making it clearly understood that capital should be accepted and invested only where the creditors were prepared for a long-term productive investment.

Industrialization in the agricultural states was greatly stimulated by the influx of capital. A substantial part of the new industrial enterprises and nearly all the new mining undertakings were created directly by it, with foreign technical assistance. In the first decade after the war greater attention was given to industry than to agriculture, despite the fact that the importance of agricultural production and export, especially in the prevailingly agricultural countries, should have been recognized before the crisis of 1930–31.

During the first years, national industry was supported by foreign trade and foreign-exchange restrictions (quota and licensing system), and in general by a well-developed policy of administrative protectionism for domestic industrial production. Later, the introduction of high protective tariffs in many instances counteracted the effect of the abandoned or reduced quota systems. Some countries actually increased their customs tariff protection shortly before the World Economic Conference of 1927 the better to prepare their economic arsenal for the eventuality that the Conference would result—as was the intention—in a general abandonment of the quota system and, perhaps, also in a reduction of customs barriers. Very high tariffs were introduced by Hungary in 1924, Bulgaria and Rumania in 1926; [13] a moderate protection of industrial production was instituted by Yugoslavia in 1925 and by Austria, which after 1927 also entered the ranks of industrial protectionist countries in Europe. Even Czechoslovakia [14] favored a policy of protectionism, which was not fully in accord with her strong industrial position and the great importance of foreign markets to her industry.

The volume of industrial production was rising; new products were introduced, with a greater increase in consumer goods than in capital goods, and with a particularly large expansion in the textile industry. Figures on the number of workers employed in industry, particularly in factories, imports of raw materials and machinery, and consumption of fuel confirm the rise in production. According to one estimate [15] the total output of Hungary, Rumania, Yugoslavia, Bulgaria, and Greece increased from 95.5 in 1927 to 104 in 1929 (1928 = 100), nearly 9 per cent. The record for the rest of Europe is similar: from 97 to 105.6. However, in 1929–32 the decline was more rapid in Western Europe (31.5 per cent) than in this area (16.7 per cent), where some industries actually continued to expand up to 1931.

Despite this rate of increase in the postwar years, the level of production attained should not be overestimated. According to rough

[13] Liepmann, *op. cit.*, notes that Rumania's textile duties were the highest in Europe (p. 160); Hungary's postwar economic policy was a strong protection of industry (p. 162); and Bulgaria's tariff levels on manufactured and semimanufactured goods were higher than in the rest of Europe in 1927 and 1931 (p. 170).

"The tariff position was most critical in Central and Eastern Europe. The nationalist policies formed in this region—especially in the new states—had on several occasions been criticised by international bodies." League of Nations, *Commercial Policy in the Interwar Period*, Geneva, 1942.

[14] "For the last five years protection in the form of customs duties upon industrial products has been the accepted policy of the country [Czechoslovakia]." *The Economist*, July 5, 1924, p. 21.

[15] German Institute for Business Research, *Weekly Report*, No. 17–18, May 4, 1938, pp. 34–36.

estimates in 1928 these five agricultural nations accounted for only 2 per cent of the value of European industrial output. In view of this relatively small production and the various types of industry involved, the question may well be raised as to whether the policy of high customs protection was justified by existing conditions or in proper relation to correctly estimated future possibilities. How much better and more efficiently could a program for a useful and necessary industrialization have been carried out had it been supported by an international program and coöperation! Needless to say, a preferential system or any sort of closer economic coöperation in the Danubian valley might also have served as a brake to uneconomic industrialization. In most instances the high tariffs (unless they were actually prohibitive) did not prevent the importation of industrial goods, but they were a definite factor in creating the tendency toward rising prices.

The rise in price of industrial goods, mostly to a much higher level than prevailed in the industrialized sections of Europe, necessarily affected the agricultural situation. The demand for agricultural products in the first postwar years and the disappearance of Russia as a competitor in the European markets may have caused the lack of attention to the problem of future agricultural export and production, particularly in reference to the stronger competition which was to be expected from overseas.

The agricultural exporting countries actually introduced export duties—in many instances they were very high—on agricultural staples. Since the income thus derived formed a substantial part of state revenue, the governments were very reluctant to abolish these duties even at a time when the entire price situation in the world market called for an immediate adjustment. Furthermore, little was done to improve the quality of agricultural production, to standardize it or change its structure, or to organize agricultural credit and coöperatives. Therefore, the price rise in various industrial goods, resulting from the protectionist policy, was felt as an actual burden upon and an injustice to agriculture. On the whole, the agricultural countries did not, at this time, develop any far-sighted program which would have helped them to overcome the approaching crisis and to adjust agriculture to the changed conditions. And no progress was made toward a leveling of prices in Europe or toward economic integration of the continent. On the contrary, the price levels of industrial goods in the agricultural countries were the highest in Europe as a result of the policy of protecting new (or future) industries, whose output was still very small. And, at the end of this period, Austria and Czechoslovakia, by protecting their agriculture, approached the high-cost European agricultural areas.

Development of foreign trade was similar to that of other countries; it increased in 1925–30. In some of the Danubian countries the increase was, perhaps, largely the result of large foreign borrowings. In general, the volume of trade reached its highest postwar level (in value) during 1929 or 1930.

The question has been raised frequently as to how greatly the new political regime changed the territorial distribution of the foreign trade of the Danubian countries, and especially how much it contributed to the relative or absolute reduction of the proportion of inter-Danubian trade in their total foreign trade. Obviously the territorial distribution of foreign trade was due to various changes in the direction of increased trade with other European countries and with overseas territories. There were several reasons for this. The tendency toward the achievement of a higher standard of living led to a greater import of various consumer goods, some from overseas. Industrialization obviously increased the import of raw materials and machinery from non-Danubian countries.

We have also to consider the fact that both industry and agriculture were forced to compete on the same terms with foreign production in their former domestic markets. Finally, the new policy of economic nationalism, in industry as well as in agriculture, was a contributing factor in the reduction of inter-Danubian trade. It is, of course, very difficult to say which of these factors was the more important. With the largely increased volume of trade a reduced percentage was not, of course, identical with a reduced absolute volume.

Figures for the three years, 1928–30 in Table 1,[16] show that the inter-Danubian trade was still a very important item for all countries concerned.

During 1928–30 the trade which these five states carried on with each other accounted for 31.2 per cent of total imports (an annual average of $1,462.1 million) and 35 per cent of total exports (annual average, $1,339.2 million). About two thirds of the total foreign trade was carried on by Czechoslovakia and Austria.

[16] League of Nations, *Chiffres essentiels du commerce exterieur des pays danubiens*, 1932, II.B.3.

TABLE 1

FOREIGN TRADE WITH THE DANUBIAN COUNTRIES IN PERCENTAGE OF TOTAL
IMPORTS AND EXPORTS (AVERAGE OF 1928, 1929, 1930)

Country	Imports	Exports
Czechoslovakia	17.9 (18.98) [a]	30.9 (39.25)
Yugoslavia	43.9 (44.94)	37.9 (46.8)
Austria	36.6 (41.4)	33.2 (36.8)
Rumania	31.7	30.9 (39.9)
Hungary	48.9 (60.21)	58.2 (68.4)

[a] Figures in parentheses are for 1924 and are from *The Economist*, May 14, 1924, p. 1062.

Figures for Bulgarian trade with these five countries in 1929–30 were: imports, 29.6% of her total imports; exports, 20% of her total exports.

The share of the intertrade declined in 1931 to 28.4 per cent in imports (the total import was $923.8 million) and to 28.5 per cent in exports (total $960.2 million). The Czechoslovak–Hungarian commercial war accounted, certainly, for a great part of the reduction of the inter-Danubian trade.

Germany's position in the foreign trade of the Danubian area during this period was a very important one, although her participation was considerably less than in the prewar era. In 1913 Germany absorbed 40.4 per cent of the total export of the Danubian countries and supplied 42.7 per cent of the total import. During the years 1929–30 her share was only 22.2 per cent of the exports and 17.2 per cent of the imports. This percentage rose in 1931 to 24.7 per cent and 17.4 per cent respectively. It must be kept in mind that the large transit trade increased the figures of the trade with Germany.

This trade with the Danubian area brought Germany a large export surplus—even during the time of her largest total import surpluses.

Italy was the second great power to make a great effort toward expanding her economic position in the Danubian area. In 1926–30, she bought 18–20 per cent of the total exports of the Balkan countries and sent them 10–13 per cent of their total imports. Comparable figures for the trade with Great Britain were 7.5–8 per cent of the exports and 10–11 per cent of the imports; France, 6–7.5 per cent of the exports, 7.5–9 per cent of the imports; the United States, 4.6–7.2 per cent of the exports, 5.4–7 per cent of the imports.[17]

An obvious effect of the period of heavy foreign borrowing was the marked increase in imports. In 1927–30 the balance of trade in

[17] Vladimir Pertot, "Einige Entwicklungstendenzen im Aussenhandel der Balkanländer," *Weltwirtschaftliches Archiv*, XLIX (1939), 369.

each of these countries, except Czechoslovakia and **Rumania**,[18] showed a large import surplus: the combined import surplus of Austria ($564.3 million), Hungary ($140.0 million), Yugoslavia ($37.4 million), Greece ($306.3 million), and Bulgaria ($4.7 million) was $1,052.7 million; the Czechoslovakian export surplus was $181.3 million, and the Rumanian was $25.6 million. Thus the net import surplus of the countries for the period was $845.8 million.[19] To complete the picture we must add that the great Czechoslovakian export surplus was chiefly the result of her trade with the other countries in the area, where she successfully competed with Germany. In this four-year period it amounted to more than $260 million.[20]

As we have noted, Czechoslovakia had not participated in the heavy foreign borrowing, but had used her foreign-trade surplus to reduce her foreign indebtedness. Nevertheless, the influx of foreign credits to Central and Southeastern Europe substantially increased her foreign trade and improved her balance of payment.

Germany's balance of trade also was greatly improved by the expanding economic activity of the area. For the years 1927–30 her import surplus with Bulgaria (Rm. 75 million), Greece (Rm. 72 million), and Rumania (Rm. 254 million) totaled Rm. 401 million; her total trade balance with the area represented an export surplus of Rm. 1,292 million (nearly $310 million). This was largely due to surpluses with Austria (Rm. 766 million) and Czechoslovakia (Rm. 410 million). She achieved a total surplus of Rm. 237 million with Hungary and Rm. 282 million with Yugoslavia. Thus, during the same four years in which Germany's import balance was Rm. 3,843 million, she achieved a substantial export balance in her trade with the Danubian countries. Germany's economy was thus strengthened directly by vast foreign credits and investments and indirectly by increased trade possibilities with the second largest borrowing area in Europe.

A study of the balance of payments throws light on the sudden and substantial increase in the total foreign indebtedness of Central and Southeastern Europe in the years 1924–30. Czechoslovakia was the

18 But even Rumania, with an established record of steady export surplus, ended the year 1928 with an import surplus of 4,611 million lei—the largest in Rumanian history—and of 668 million lei in 1929.
19 U.S. Dept. of Commerce, *The Foreign Commerce Yearbook*, 1938.
20 The total export surplus of Czechoslovakia for 1927–30 amounted to Kc. 6,481 million. Her surplus with Austria, Hungary, Yugoslavia, Rumania, and Bulgaria for the same period was Kc. 8,837 million—i.e., more than the total balance. Her foreign trade with the rest of the world showed a deficit of Kc. 2,587 million. Her balance with Austria was approximately Kc. 6,250 million.

only nation to improve the balance by using her large foreign-trade surplus to pay off foreign debts and for the repatriation of Czechoslovak holdings from abroad (particularly in Austria). Rumania was the single other member of the Danubian group to posssess a small export surplus. It was inevitable, therefore, that in the majority of these countries, the question should soon arise of maintaining the foreign-debt service without new borrowing. Austria, alone, had various substantial income items in her balance of payment, derived chiefly from the other Danubian countries. In Yugoslavia and Greece emigrant remittances were a relatively important income item; Greece had, in addition, a substantial income from shipping.

Thus at the end of the twenties the economic situation in this region at first glance gave reason to believe that a fair degree of consolidation had been achieved, that the work of reconstruction and development was proceeding successfully. Definite progress and increased momentum of activity could be observed in most places. The greatest postwar obstacles to an orderly economic life could be considered overcome. Monetary stabilization had been accomplished, and the budgetary position improved. Expanding national production had stimulated the trend toward a higher standard of living. The danger of sudden social changes seemed to have passed, and there were signs of improvement in political relations. There were important public as well as private investments, and the creation of national capital was proceeding more satisfactorily. Foreign trade showed a tendency to increase, and commercial relations were growing—also with countries outside this area. Foreign-trade restrictions in their most prohibitive and roughest form had been abolished, together with foreign-exchange restrictions.

On the other hand, there had been repeated complaints about the growing protectionism, paired with an apprehension of its effects on foreign trade. For the same reason it was felt that the growing foreign debts should no longer remain unnoticed. But the basic optimistic attitude, strengthened by the resolutions of the World Economic Conference in 1927 and other international meetings (including that of the International Chamber of Commerce in Amsterdam, 1929) was the belief that these difficulties were of a transitory nature, and that finally the world would return to a policy of a freely expanding international trade, which would automatically alleviate the growing difficulties in the Danubian countries.

Because of this optimistic attitude, it was not deemed necessary, or even urgent, to work out a special organization for them. The problems of Germany, reparations, and inter-allied debts were considered to be more crucial and of greater basic importance.

Thus, during this entire period of postwar prosperity, no program for closer economic coöperation was developed by the Danubian countries, nor had the Great Powers any concerted policy toward the achievement of consolidation and development of this area.

The treaties of St. Germain (Art. 222) and of Trianon (Art. 205) contained provisions for preferential tariff arrangements between Czechoslovakia, Austria, and Hungary, which were limited to five years after they came into force. It is clear today that these provisions should have been made compulsory, and should have extended to all succession states. They were never invoked in relation to Hungary, chiefly because of her basic political attitude. An attempt was made to use this preferential clause between Czechoslovakia and Austria shortly before the end of the five-year period specified in the Treaty of St. Germain. It was timed to coincide with a special examination by the League of Nations of the Austrian financial and economic situation in the summer of 1925. The League report [21] also was in favor of preferential treaties to support the Austrian export of industrial goods. But the attempt to arrange a special preferential regime based on the Peace Treaty failed, as did the Geneva negotiations for an even broader preferential basis.

During the Geneva Conference of 1927 certain of the Central European countries made a fresh attempt to obtain international recognition of the need for a regional preferential clause as a starting point for an economic rapprochement. After a long discussion which convincingly illustrated the scant enthusiasm of the big countries, the following very limited resolution was accepted as the result of a compromise: "For this purpose it is highly desirable that the widest and most unconditional interpretation should be given to the most fa-

[21] Layton and Rist, *The Economic Situation of Austria*, Geneva, 1925, p. 40. Pasvolsky, *op. cit.*, pp. 89, 90, 284, mentions Italy's demand to be party to the arrangement. The negotiations involved the establishment of a preferential tariff regime between Czechoslovakia and Austria, and Austria and Italy. Pasvolsky holds that Czechoslovakia was responsible for the failure of these negotiations because the scheme failed to fulfill reciprocal application of the most-favored nation principle among the countries entering the arrangement. But during these negotiations Germany's fundamentally hostile attitude became known (this fact has not been made public). She threatened Austria and Czechoslovakia with trade reprisals. Great Britain, too, was not in favor of any preferential regime following the classic most-favored nation clause. See also Basch and Dvořáček *op. cit.*, p. 93.

vored nation clause. This is not inconsistent with the insertion in any particular treaty of special provisions to meet local needs so long as such provisions are clearly expressed and do not injure the interest of other states." [22] This clause was not, of course, invoked. So long as economic prosperity persisted, the problem of an economic organization of Central and Southeastern Europe continued, more or less, to be merely the subject for discussion of various meetings, and for study by professional economists.

The big European countries did not follow an identical policy in this area.[23] Italy had exerted considerable effort, with some success, to expand her economic relations there. She was politically jealous of France, and was afraid that the old Monarchy would be replaced by a larger economic unit. Germany's interest was similar, but much more intensive and effective. Great Britain was fully maintaining her prewar trade position, whereas France was more active in the political and financial fields than in the development of exchange of commodities. Not only was there no common agreement among the big powers, but Germany and Italy had made it abundantly clear that they would not sanction any preferential Danubian regime to which they were not a party, thus making, a priori, any such plan impossible. Nor was there an agreement or common economic policy on the part of the states concerned, without which there could be no realization of any such rapprochement.

In his illuminating summary of the attitude toward an economic rapprochement or Danubian federation Pasvolsky states that Austria and Czechoslovakia would have welcomed freer trade relations among the Danubian countries, Austria in wholesale form, Czechoslovakia in the form of a preferential customs regime. To the primarily agricultural countries the disadvantages appeared to outweigh the advantages.[24] The primarily industrial countries could not substantially increase their import of agricultural products; therefore Danubian federation could bring only slight benefit to the agricultural countries

---

[22] Geneva Conference, 1927, *Documents*, p. 638a, under the heading "Commercial Treaties."

[23] J. B. Condliffe, *The Reconstruction of World Trade,* New York, 1941, pp. 300 ff.

[24] Pasvolsky, *op. cit.,* p. 563. He continues: "No serious discussions have ever gone beyond the scope of some sort of trade arrangement with a customs union as the ultimate limit." And throughout the entire period the following statement proved to be correct: "Not much has been heard recently about schemes for a Danubian Confederation. The real argument against such a project lies indeed in the fact, to which Dr. Beneš himself recently referred, that nobody wants it." *The Economist,* Dec. 16, 1925, p. 953.

from the point of view of an expansion of production. Hungary would have preferred an economic union with Rumania, Yugoslavia, and Bulgaria,[25] as a powerful agricultural bloc in which she hoped, in view of her industry, to obtain economic leadership. There was, of course, no possibility of realizing this solution. But Hungary would not have opposed an Austro-German union, which would have provided a potentially almost unlimited market for her agricultural goods.

Rumania felt that her interests were amply served by her favorable commercial treaties; from her point of view there was no reason for the creation of a Danubian economic union. Yugoslavia, also, did not consider that her interests would be better served by such a union; her favorable treaty arrangements with her Danubian partners were regarded as amply sufficient.

Thus the Danubian countries failed to arrive at any broader economic coöperation during these years, except in the enlargement and improvement of their trade agreements; they did not consider it either useful or necessary. The big powers shared no common program or policy in this direction, since their interests were divided. The Western Powers had attached no great significance to their trade relations with this vitally important area. The general attitude toward the economic situation was much too optimistic. The coming crisis was to show how fragile, unstable and unbalanced was the economic consolidation in Central and Southeastern Europe. It reflected, of course, the general stage of world economy.

25 Pasvolsky, *op. cit.*, pp. 379, 463, 536.

3

THE IMPACT OF THE WORLD ECONOMIC CRISIS

THE SHORT-LIVED period of "borrowed prosperity" was soon ended. The economic consolidation of Central and Southeastern Europe, scarcely in its beginning, and not yet based on a balanced situation in general, was profoundly shaken by the world economic and financial crisis of 1930–31. Its impact here was much heavier than in most other parts of the world, and its effects were not long limited to the economic and social field. In 1931, it became evident that the world crisis had reopened the entire problem of the Danubian order, in the economic as well as in the political sphere. Although the crisis did not initiate social unrest or a complete economic and financial breakdown, as was feared by many people, it called for an immediate, comprehensive international program and action, and, simultaneously, for a settlement of the various differences between the Danubian countries. But, as we shall see, nothing actually fundamental was achieved, nor even seriously attempted.

There were manifold reasons why the crisis should be felt so heavily. The complete structure and equilibrium of the economies of these nations were affected: the balance of payments was disrupted, the value and volume of exports declined rapidly, and the total national incomes dropped substantially. Great monetary and financial difficulties ensued to disturb the recently achieved monetary stabilization and consolidation of government budgets. The problem of public as well as private debts—especially those of agriculture—became extremely formidable.

We have already mentioned the particularly difficult problems of postwar reconstruction and consolidation in the Danubian basin. Obviously most of these problems were still unsolved when the world crisis broke out. The time had been too short for a fundamental economic readjustment to the changed conditions of world economy and to the new political organization. The general political atmosphere of Europe had not been sufficiently favorable for a far-reaching consolidation. The absence of Russia in the European sphere was a detrimental influence, politically and economically, particularly in the

Danubian valley, in view of the growing jealousies and conflicting interests of the big powers in this area. The unsettled situation in Germany had, in general, various troublesome effects; her policy of deflation and of reducing imports acted very unfavorably on the foreign trade of these countries, where she held an important role in the exchange of commodities. These problems, needless to say, were aggravated by her extreme protectionist policy in agriculture.

Finally, there was the question of population in the agricultural countries. The increasing difficulties of overseas immigration after 1924 closed a very significant outlet for the permanent population surplus. The impact of the world crisis fell first with the greatest intensity upon the agricultural countries, but it also directly affected Czechoslovakia and Austria. Their export of industrial goods to the Danubian countries declined rapidly, and at the same time they were subjected directly and indirectly in their foreign trade to the repercussion of the German deflationary policy.

The situation of the Danubian agricultural countries has often been compared to that of the overseas agricultural states, particularly of South America. Both groups shared in common the effects of the sudden marked fall in prices of their chief export goods. This change worked to the great disadvantage of their trade terms, for the prices of imported industrial goods declined more slowly and to a smaller extent. The price scissors operated definitely against those countries whose principal exports were agricultural produce and raw materials. It should be recalled that a similar relation had existed in the agrarian Danubian countries before the crisis, with an adverse effect upon agriculture. In general, prices for industrial goods were higher than in South America, largely because of the high duties on these products. Both groups were debtor nations; compared with South America, the foreign debt of the Danubian countries would seem to be rather light.[1]

But there were important differences in the situation of the two groups. The South American countries had no problem of war damages, reparation, or postwar reconstruction. Their capital was not exhausted during the war, nor were they faced with readjustment to a new political order. They had enjoyed a fair number of very

[1] League of Nations, *Economic and Financial*, II, B 7, 1935, "Considerations on the Present Evolution of Agricultural Protectionism," gives, on p. 32, the following figures.

Amount of issues of foreign securities in the United States, Great Britain, Switzerland, and Holland in 1924–28 (in millions of dollars): Issues for Non-European agricultural countries, 5,007; for European agricultural countries, 816; for Germany alone, 1,624.

prosperous years both during and after the war, whereas the prosperity of the Danubian valley was very short-lived. They were able to develop agricultural production, taking advantage of the new techniques, and were not faced, in a politically difficult period, with the problem of changing the methods and structure of their production. And, finally, in this thinly settled area, there was no difficult question of heavy population pressure in agriculture. Therefore, we are led to believe that the crisis penetrated much less deeply into the entire economic and social life of the South American countries than in the Danubian area. But if even in South America, which enjoyed relatively favorable conditions, it led to very serious disturbances in foreign trade, monetary stability, public finance, and the rest, with how much greater force must the blow have fallen upon the Danubian area! As far as I am aware, no suggestion was made that the basis of the crisis be solved by the creation of a South American customs union, whereas many persons thought that such a union would be the principal means of assisting agriculture in the Danubian area.

Agricultural products (including tobacco and timber) represented the major export item in the foreign trade of each of the five agricultural states concerned. The importing, industrial countries of Europe increased their protection of agriculture, particularly after the fall in agricultural prices, with the result that the Danubian nations suffered more than did the overseas states. They were affected not only by the general fall of prices, but also by the growing import difficulties in their old markets, where their competitive position was better than in the more remote consuming centers.

The leading agricultural exports (see Table 2) were cereals (and flour) for Rumania, Hungary, Bulgaria and Yugoslavia; livestock, meat and animal products for Yugoslavia, Hungary, and Rumania; fruits for Greece, Bulgaria, Yugoslavia, and Hungary; eggs and poultry for Bulgaria, Yugoslavia and Hungary; tobacco for Bulgaria and Greece. Timber was a substantial item in the export of Yugoslavia, Rumania, Austria, and Czechoslovakia, and sugar in that of Czechoslovakia.

It could be reasonably expected that Czechoslovakia and Austria would continue to buy their agricultural imports in the main from the Danubian countries for historical and geographical reasons. Although they were still important customers, they never possessed the capacity for absorbing the entire agricultural surplus of the valley.

TABLE 2

EXPORTS OF AGRICULTURAL PRODUCTS, INCLUDING TOBACCO AND TIMBER, IN PERCENTAGES OF THE TOTAL IN VALUE

	1927	1931
Rumania	73	61
cereals	48.9	35
timber	12.1	10.7
livestock	6.7	5.6
fruit, vegetables, and seeds	5.2	4.6
	1928	
Bulgaria	78.6	90.4
tobacco	36.0	43.5
cereals	12.6	20.1
livestock and animal products	11.4	14.3
vegetables and fruit	9.5	7.1
eggs	9.1	5.4
Yugoslavia	68.2	68.7
forest products	25.5	18.3
livestock	13.7	15.4
cereals	7.0	14.4
eggs and dairy products	7.3	8.3
fruit and vegetables	5.2	4.8
industrial and medicinal plants	5.9	3.2
meat	3.6	4.3
Hungary	64.8	62.1
cereals	17.9	9.3
flour	11.0	5.6
livestock	10.5	15.8
vegetables	5.4	5.4
animal produce	5.3	7.5
vegetable raw materials	5.1	6.3
poultry	4.9	7.9
other animal products	4.7	4.3
Greece	90.0	86
currants, olive oil, wine, figs	36.0	31.2
tobacco	54.0	53.5
Czechoslovakia	16.3	11.6
sugar	8.1	4.1
timber	4.2	2.3
cereals, vegetables, and fruit	4.0	3.2
Austria (timber only)	11.2	7.6

As a matter of fact, Czechoslovakia took 62.8 per cent of her cereal imports from the Danubian countries while Austria took about 75 per cent. During the 1928–30 period the wheat export surplus of Hungary, Rumania, and Yugoslavia was 816,900 tons; the corn surplus 938,600 tons. Czechoslovakia and Austria, taken together, absorbed more than one third of the Danubian cereal export. They formed its most important market for wheat and flour. The foreign trade between Czechoslovakia and Hungary was profoundly altered by the commercial war, begun December 18, 1930. Czechoslovakia's trade with Hungary was reduced to a small fraction.[2] The volume of trade between these countries never again reached its former level. The effect on Hungary became graver in the long run, since it was more difficult for her to find new markets for her agricultural produce than for Czechoslovakia to export industrial goods.

Germany, in this period, took 22.8 per cent to 24 per cent of the Danubian cereal export. Except for a small quantity of wheat, the chief product was fodder grain—corn and barley. Italy absorbed about 11 per cent. Thus, certainly more than two thirds (in some years three quarters) of the cereal export was sold in the neighboring states and Switzerland. This proportion was increased by exports to Turkey and Greece. Only Rumania succeeded—as she did before 1914—in selling a substantial portion of her export surplus to Western Europe, where Holland received 11 per cent of her cereal export, Great Britain 9 per cent, Belgium 5 per cent, France 4 per cent, and Gibraltar 8 per cent. In contrast, Hungary was able to place only 1 per cent in Great Britain, 1 per cent in Holland, and 4 per cent in Switzerland.[3]

This analysis clearly demonstrates the extreme importance (it was almost vital) of the old nearby markets to the export of the cereal surplus of the Danubian valley.

Turning to the livestock and animal products we find that Czechoslovakia and Austria, in 1929, absorbed 78.3 per cent of the pigs, 56.7 per cent of the meat, 55.3 per cent of the cattle, 25 per cent of the eggs, and 4.1 per cent of the mutton exports of Rumania, Yugoslavia, and Hungary.

There were other significant markets. For instance, in 1929 Germany received 47.2 per cent of the Hungarian egg export, 26.5 per

---

2 Czechoslovak export to Hungary declined from 1,005 million Kc. in 1930 to 289 million Kc. in 1931; her import, at the same time, declined from 922 million Kc. to 134 million Kc.
3 These figures are from League of Nations, *Chiffres essentiels du commerce extérieur des pays danubiens.*

cent of the Yugoslavian, about 30 per cent of the Rumanian, and 22.8 per cent of the Bulgarian (1931); Switzerland bought 19.3 per cent of the Yugoslavian and Great Britain about 30 per cent of the Rumanian. Italy purchased 40 per cent of the Yugoslav meat export and 7.1 per cent of her pig export. (Greece took 4.9 per cent). As for cattle import, Italy, together with Austria and Czechoslovakia, was the chief market. She procured 37.9 per cent of the Hungarian and 59.3 per cent of the Yugoslavian export. (The total export of cattle from these three countries in 1929 was 304,000 head, and of meat, only 31,900 tons.) Greece was the most important customer for sheep. She imported 725,000 head out of a total of 811,000 from Yugoslavia. The relatively small export of animal products was also dependent, in the main, on the nearby markets. The exporting countries had only slight success in finding other customers for these products, particularly in Western Europe.

On the whole, the nearby states were the principal buyers of the bulk of the agricultural products and timber exported from the Danubian area—even more so than in the prewar era when a larger proportion of the Balkan products were exported to Western Europe. But, measured in terms of European import of these commodities, the total agricultural export represented only a very small fraction in world or European trade. It is the more surprising, therefore, that there was such great difficulty in finding markets for so small a quantity of goods.

According to a statistical analysis published by *The Economist* [4] the Danubian countries (including Czechoslovakia) exported, in 1929, cereals totaling in value $123.1 million, whereas Europe imported cereals to the amount of $1,303.5 million, of which $1,099.8 million was from extra-European territory. The Danubian export represented, therefore, 9.5 per cent. Their share in Europe's meat import was much smaller; it amounted to $9.6 million, or only 1.7 per cent of a total European import of $575.8 million ($354 million from overseas). Her dairy products represented an almost negligible amount—$3.2 million or 0.6 per cent of a total import of $529.9 million ($160.4 million from overseas). These figures should, equally well, indicate future possibilities in shifting the structure of production.

Compared with the pre-1914 position, the Danubian share in world wheat export declined relatively and absolutely. Whereas their

[4] Dec. 29, 1930, p. 995.

export amounted, in the annual average 1909–13, to 1,905,600 tons or 11.2 per cent of the total world export, the annual average in 1926–30 was only 572,000 tons, or 3 per cent of world export, in spite of the fact that Russian participation during the same time was reduced from 24.1 per cent to 4.3 per cent.[5]

As already pointed out, Danubian agriculture, as well as that of all Europe, was forced to operate under strong overseas competition from countries with much more favorable conditions of production. In general, this competition affected the agricultural export countries far more than the import countries—even those with highly developed agriculture, which they were in a position to protect. The Danubian countries were compelled to face not only this powerful overseas competition but, at the same time, a vigorous policy of protectionism that spread throughout the industrial European nations, and in some countries, pointed toward a program for self-sufficiency in the staple agricultural products. There can be, therefore, no doubt that this policy aggravated the crisis, and that its effects could have been only slightly mitigated, even by the granting of import quotas, for import difficulties accelerated the fall in prices of these commodities.

The importing countries were not satisfied with merely increasing customs tariffs in realizing their protectionist aims. They took various other measures and instituted new devices. A whole arsenal of such weapons was used. Agricultural protection was already underway before the crisis occurred, possibly as a reaction against the neglect of agriculture in preference to industry during the first postwar period. It received great encouragement by the fall in agricultural prices. Germany led in this field, and as the second greatest European food importer, strongly influenced the exporting as well as the importing countries. Her average annual import of food and agricultural products was more than $1 billion.

She set out, after 1925, with a moderate customs protection, especially of bread cereals. By 1933 and 1934 complete protection was achieved through prohibitive customs duties and various other measures. The field was wholly organized—output was regulated and prices were fixed without regard to the world market.

[5] *Annuaire international du statistique agricole, 1930–31*, Rome, p. 96.

Warriner, *Economics of Peasant Farming*, p. 52, gives 4% as the 1925–29 percentage for Danubian wheat export in the world wheat trade. But in the prewar era, European producers supplied 34 million quarters of wheat out of a total European import of 47 million quarters. (*The Economist*, Aug. 1, 1925, p. 180.)

After 1929 the German tariff policy became protectionist in the extreme, particularly in the case of wheat; in October, 1930, a duty of Rm. 250 per ton ($1.62 per bushel) was inaugurated, greatly in excess of the world price. New restrictive and price-lifting devices were launched. Chief among them were the following: [6] the milling regulation of July, 1929 (maximum limitations of foreign grain to be mixed with domestic grain); a corn monopoly (March, 1930) designed for the protection of fodder cereals by limiting the import of corn, providing at the same time, an excellent instrument for a preferential treatment of foreign countries; government price-supporting and stabilization operation: (a buyer of the so-called eosin-rye destined for feeding purposes was permitted to import fodder barley at the reduced customs rate of Rm. 40 or 60 per ton, rather than at the regular rate of Rm. 120.)

Protection of bread cereals led to the protection of fodder grains, which was initiated in December, 1929. Duties on cattle and pigs followed, which were increased substantially between 1929 and 1931. Obviously the duties on meat had to be raised correspondingly. And next in succession were duties on dairy products—eggs and fats—which were raised in 1930 and again in 1932; and on bacon and lard in 1933, when a fat and oil monopoly was introduced to protect domestic fat production from margarine.

But high protection was not the only measure used against the importer.[7] The import quota system was extended permanently.

Import quotas were initiated in 1932, to include butter, bacon, lard, animals for slaughter, vegetables, fruits, tomatoes, and hewn softwood (a quota on sawn wood had been established earlier). Quotas for cereals were unnecessary; they were amply protected by prohibitive duties.

---

[6] U.S. Bureau of Agricultural Economics, *World Trade Barriers in Relation to American Agriculture* (73d Cong., 1st Sess. Senate Document, No. 70, Washington, 1933), p. 107.

[7] German grain duties of January, 1933, in gold francs per 100 Kg. as compared with those of 1913:

	1913	January, 1933
Wheat	6.79	30.93
Rye	6.17	24.64
Barley (for malt)	4.94	24.64
Oats	6.17	19.71
Corn	6.17	Monopoly
Wheat flour	12.59	53.17
Rye flour	12.59	56.87

From the International Institute of Agriculture, *Documentation for the Monetary and Economic Conference*, 1933, p. 27.

Domestic price fixing, originally restricted to wheat and rye, was extended to cover nearly all the important foodstuffs.

After cereal production was "freed from the tyranny of the free market," a comprehensive protection was rapidly introduced to embrace the entire field of agriculture, fully detaching its prices from those of the foreign markets.[8] Finally, in the early part of 1934, the "Nährstand" (Nourishment Corporation) was established for the purpose of regulating output, prices, sales, and profit margin in the trade of *all* agricultural products. The "protection" of agriculture was complete. Thus, the German agricultural policy, starting out long before the Nazi regime with a definite protection of bread cereals, favoring especially the northeastern estates with their poor soil, and obliged, step by step, to extend similar protection to other branches of agricultural production, ended in a system of completely planned, managed agriculture, detached from the world market, and, with the help of government intervention, divorced from the traditional price and cost rules. It should be emphasized once more that this policy which was put in operation in respect to foreign relations, was begun during the parliamentary regime of the Weimar Republic and was pursued very energetically, though not in conformity with the policy of deflation, under the emergency regime of Dr. Brüning and his successors. The East Elbe districts very cleverly gave the tone to Germany's foreign and trade policy.[9]

Totalitarian economy was first introduced in Germany in the agricultural sphere, with all the consequences noted above. Unfortunately, as so often happened, the world did not foresee in time the far-reaching effects of such a program. At the same time the agricultural interests in the import nations attempted to secure support for their products by means similar to those used by Germany, whereas the export states made a determined effort to obtain import possibilities in the German market.

It is hardly necessary to mention that the prices of agricultural goods were higher in Germany than in most countries of the world,

[8] For further reference see, for example, U.S. Bureau of Agricultural Economics, *World Trade Barriers in Relation to American Agriculture;* Carl Brandt, "The Crisis in German Agriculture," *Foreign Affairs,* X (1931–32), pp. 632–76; and, by the same author, "German Agricultural Policy," *Journal of Farm Economics,* XIX (1937), No. 1; also John Bradshaw Holt, *German Agricultural Policy, 1918–1934,* Chapel Hill, N.C., 1936.
[9] For further aspects of this question see J. B. Condliffe, *Agenda for a Postwar World,* 1942, New York, pp. 117 ff.

and that agricultural production increased [10] as imports declined rapidly. Self-sufficiency in grain (for bread) was nearly realized as early as 1931, and in all cereals in 1933, for the first time in two generations.[11] The need for meat imports almost totally disappeared, and the demand for foreign butter, eggs, fruit, and vegetables declined. Imports were maintained only in such products as important oil fruits and oilseeds, fodder, and lastly, tropical products such as oranges, bananas, etc., amounting approximately to double the quantity imported in 1913.

The record of German food imports during this period offers a graphic illustration of the development of this policy. The import of food and drinks declined steadily. The figures in million reichsmarks are as follows: 4,350 (1927), 4,188 (1928), 3,823 (1929), 2,969 (1930), 1,972 (1931), 1,082 (1933).

The reduction in food imports was more than Rm. 3 billion, or nearly $750 million. When we deduct Rm. 350 million in 1933 and 750 million in 1927 for those goods which Germany cannot produce (coffee and tropical products), we find the remaining figures to be Rm. 732 million in 1933, as against 3,600 million in 1927, representing a fall to only 20 per cent (approximately) of 1927 or 1928 imports. The import of cereals declined from Rm. 1,057.2 million in 1928 to 105.3 million in 1934, and to 55.5 million in 1935,[12] that is from 18.4 per cent of total import to only 6.8 per cent and 3.9 per cent.

The reduction of the German agricultural imports, chiefly as a result of her protectionist policy, and the changed structure of her production and foreign trade must have profoundly and substantially affected the world trade in agricultural goods and therefore world trade in general. Table 3 shows the German participation in world trade in certain products. It is evident from a study of these figures how difficult or nearly impossible it was to replace the reduced imports to Germany, and how great must have been the disturbance caused by her protectionist policy.

[10] Germany's wheat production increased from 2,597,200 tons in 1925 to 3,853,600 in 1928, 4,233,300 in 1931, and 4,532,600 tons in 1934. The average production in 1927–1931 was 3.7 million tons; in 1933–37 it rose to 5.1 million tons; imports, during these periods, declined from 1.6 million to 0.3 million tons. League of Nations, *Europe's Trade*, p. 62.
[11] C. V. Dietz, "Measures for Combating the Agricultural Crisis in Germany," *Proceedings of the Third International Conference of Agricultural Economists*, Oxford, 1935, p. 60.
[12] For further details see Reinhold Stisser, "Die Deutsche Getreidemarktordnung," *Weltwirtschaftliches Archiv*, XLVII (1938), pp. 322–72.

TABLE 3

WORLD TRADE IN SOME AGRICULTURAL PRODUCTS IN 1927–1933

Wheat Import (Thousands of Quintals) [a]

	1927–28	1929–30	1931–32	1932–33
All European importing countries (excluding United Kingdom)	117,979	82,499	99,448	57,581
Germany	24,099	13,039	6,311	1,366
Italy	23,895	11,524	9,052	3,019
France	12,819	2,982	20,977	8,667
Austria	4,331	5,171	3,670	3,605
Czechoslovakia	5,646	3,594	6,694	3,250

Import Balances of Beef and Veal (Thousands of Tons)

	1927	1929	1931	1933
Principal European importing countries other than United Kingdom	333.7	220.5	189.5	103.1
Germany	150.9	81.5	2.6	0.6
Italy	50.6	60.7	43.8	38.3
France	52.9	11.8	64.1	23.0
Austria	37.7	30.7	25.1	6.9
Czechoslovakia	1.6	0.9	0.7	0.1

Import Balances of Cattle (Thousands of Head)

	1927	1929	1931	1933
Principal European importing countries other than United Kingdom	602	806	308	203
Germany	331	317	54	40
Italy	84	265	98	117
Austria	125	98	54	19
Switzerland	8	7	22	Export
Czechoslovakia	19	93	20	0

Import Balances of Butter (Thousands of Quintals)

	1927	1929	1931	1932
Europe, excluding United Kingdom	1,219	1,478	1,476	1,057
Germany	1,082	1,354	1,001	591
Belgium	Export	30	176	121
France	Export	Export	135	61
Switzerland	84	75	106	5
Czechoslovakia	6	1	16	6

[a] League of Nations, *Considerations in the Present Evolution of Agricultural Protectionism* (Sir Frederick Leith Ross, "Agrarian Protection in Europe in the Post-War Period"), pp. 28–31.

After 1933 the German policy clearly pursued the course of self-sufficiency in foodstuffs at whatever cost. Naturally such a policy is not a one-way instrument; it strikes back as exporting countries retaliate or their purchasing power declines. Doubtless the policy of autarky was costly to Germany, but it was also costly to the whole world trade, and in particular to European trade. A foreign-trade multiplier does not operate only in the direction of expansion; its effects are similar in the direction of contraction.

German trade policy fell heavily upon the Danubian agricultural exporters. They lost, almost entirely, one of the most important markets for their grain exports. Their other exports, including animal foodstuffs, also dropped between 1931 and 1933, as a consequence of further restrictive measures of German agrarian protection. There remained scarcely any regular trade (in its previous form) in agricultural products with Germany, but the totalitarian organization was an apt instrument for granting preferential treatment—a method which later served as a basis of a "new" import policy. Using military terms, we may say that Germany wanted, first, to soften the countries which she was about to attempt to "save" and dominate.

Another blow to Danubian wheat export was delivered by Italy. Her "battaglia di grano," undertaken to improve the balance of payment and employment, aimed chiefly at an increase in wheat by more intensive production rather than an extension of the area sown; the measure of her success is shown by the rise of average production from 4,927,300 tons (yield 10.4 quintals per ha.) in 1909–14 to 6,160,721 tons (yield 12.6 quintals per ha.) in 1926–31. Grain and flour duties [13] reached prohibitive levels between 1929 and 1931, supported by a milling regulation of 1931 admitting only a small percentage of foreign wheat.

Duties on livestock, meat and butter were raised to similar heights in 1932; that on unprepared meats about 400 per cent.

Agrarian imports declined from Lire 5,320 million in 1927 to Lire

---

[13] Rates of important duties on principal cereals (in gold francs per one quintal):

	ITALY		FRANCE	
	1913	*Jan. 1, 1933*	*1913*	*Jan. 1, 1933*
Wheat	7.50	19.87	7.0	16.32
Rye	4.50	9.67	3.0	8.08
Barley	4.0	4.0	3.0	8.08
Corn	1.15	7.95	3.0	8.08
Wheat flour	11.50	29.77	13.50	32.32

From *Documentation for the Monetary and Economic Conference,* London, 1933, p. 27.

3,000 million in 1931, due in the main to the reduced wheat import from Lire 3,000 million to 840 million. Hungary, Yugoslavia, and Bulgaria suffered further from this development.

France, another customer of these same Danubian countries, did not lag behind the others in protectionist policy. She increased her duties on wheat and other cereals in 1929–31; in 1933 she imposed license taxes on all meat imports, which since 1931 had been subject to a quota system.

Austria considered agriculture as a possible and desirable sphere for expansion of her economic activity: declining income from the various invisible items of her balance of payment and difficulties in increasing export of industrial goods and in improving employment made some such development necessary. Domestic production and income had to substitute the declining foreign revenue. Austria succeeded in substantially increasing her production of wheat and flour, sugar, cattle and animal products and dairy products. Her agrarian import, though reduced from S. 1,065 million in 1927 to S. 680 million in 1931, still represented about one third of her total import, and was of great importance to the Danubian area.[14] Further foreign-trade restrictions, therefore, aggravated the Hungarian and Yugo-slavian problem, and were felt even in Czechoslovakia in such products as sugar, barley and malt, dairy products and cattle.

After a rather moderate tariff in 1927, which went into force in 1928 when the new treaty with Hungary was concluded, first the sugar duty was raised substantially in 1931. Customs tariffs were radically increased, though the full protectionist policy was not put into operation until the summer of 1932, when a quota system was introduced for the principal agrarian products. Austria moderated her protection by various treaties. Chief among them were those with Hungary and Yugoslavia. She could offer them market possibilities by reducing further her overseas imports, particularly cereals. By extending her livestock production, she could increase her fodder cereals import, however reducing to some extent her need for imported hogs and cattle.

Czechoslovakia also was influenced by the protectionist policy in the second half of the twenties, but her tariffs, especially for grain, livestock and dairy products, were moderate. In this instance the

14 Austria's average import of 1924–29 was reduced (in quantity) to the following amounts in 1932: cattle, 1/6; meat, 1/4; hogs, 1/8; lard, 90%; and flour, 40%.

protectionist tendency was certainly a reaction against the neglect of agriculture in the preceding years. Further strong impetus was given by the increasing difficulties in Czechoslovakia's agricultural export. There can be no doubt that Germany's policy, which materially affected Czechoslovak export of barley, malt, hops, ham, vegetables, fruit, sawn timber, and many other products, strengthened this trend. An added, and very important factor was the effect of the steadily declining sugar export, which led to a curtailment of sugar production.[15] A substitute crop for the land formerly planted by sugar beet (about 100,000 ha.) had to be found. Wheat seemed the most promising alternative.

In the discussion of Czechoslovakia's agricultural policy, it must not be forgotten that her not unimportant agricultural export declined in general. It dropped from Kc. 2,920 million in 1927 and Kc. 2,963 million in 1928 to Kc. 1,136 million in 1931 and Kc. 456 million in 1933 (only 15 per cent of the pre-crisis level). This development served to support the demand for protection and reduction of agricultural imports.

The commercial war with Hungary, following upon the expiration of the commercial treaty on December 15, 1930, definitely encouraged the trend toward an expansion of agriculture in Czechoslovakia, and gave considerable support to the Hungarian industrialization policy. The importance of the break in the old commercial relations between these two countries was certainly not rightly evaluated at the time. Each country speculated on the necessity for the other to conclude a new agreement within a short time, but relations were never restored to conform with the former pattern.

Though the new agrarian duties in Czechoslovakia substantially increased the level of protection, they were soon followed by other measures. In the summer of 1932 the existing import license system for cereals was replaced by an Import Syndicate. Its function was to regulate the imports and to stabilize the prices of grain and flour. The great increase in wheat and rye production made the execution of this project extremely difficult. Intervention purchases on account

---

[15] Production declined from an average of about 1,100,000 tons of raw sugar in 1927–1931 to 819,370 tons in 1932 and 519,000 in 1934. The sugar export of Czechoslovakia dropped from 562,000 tons, average of 1927–1931, to only 206,000 tons, average of 1933–1937.

The price quotation for sugar in New York (in cents per pound) fell from 2.565¢ in 1925 to 1.993¢ in 1930 and 1.220¢ in 1932.

by the government were demanded, and finally a Grain Monopoly was introduced in the summer of 1934. The import of livestock and animal products, regulated from January, 1932, by the Foreign Exchange Commission, was placed in January, 1933, under the jurisdiction of a new syndicate for the regulation of cattle and animal-products import.

Imports of the chief agricultural products and cereals declined materially, partially because of the reduced purchasing power of the great number of unemployed. The peak levels of agricultural import of Kc. 4,476 million in 1927 and of Kc. 4,203 million in 1928 were reduced to Kc. 2,715 million in 1931 and to Kc. 1,707 million in 1932. The 1933–34 average was Kc. 1,250, or little more than 30 per cent of the pre-crisis level. The decline in imports was greatest in wheat, corn, hogs, butter, lard, and eggs. Imports of cattle and meat dropped to a negligible volume.

Hungary in particular suffered from this development, for Czechoslovakia was her second-best customer. The other Danubian countries were similarly affected, though less severely. In the long run, Czechoslovakia's position in this area was weakened. Let us quote the annual report of the Czechoslovak National Bank for 1932: [16] "The restriction of imports which improved market possibilities and profitability of the pertinent agricultural products in Czechoslovakia, on the other hand of course, resulted in difficulties for the commercial policy, principally because a large part of the imports of the products mentioned came from countries of Southeastern Europe and in their relation to us at present serve as practically the sole means of payment of our exports."

Agricultural protection was not limited to the countries discussed here, but was applied, in various forms, in nearly all the importing states. Great Britain remained as the only large importer of agricultural products. Holland, Belgium, and Switzerland offered further possibilities. Their protection was moderate.

It can be stated with certainty that the policy of agrarian protection, led by Germany, in the importing nations at a time of a marked fall in prices, aggravated the depression in the agricultural countries. In contrast to the agricultural depression of 1875–95, when the European countries attempted to preserve their agriculture and to prevent a sudden fall in prices by successfully changing, in some cases, the

[16] Prague, 1933, p. 80.

structure of their agrarian production, at this time the importing countries continued to expand their food production, and some of them actually managed to increase prices. Thus wheat production in the importing countries increased from 999 million bushels in 1927 to 1,223 million in 1930, 1,102 million in 1931, and 1,358 million in 1933, whereas the exporting countries produced 2,352 million bushels in 1933, as compared to 2,524 million in 1928 and 2,653 million in 1931.[17]

With the high-cost producing agricultural area in Europe expanding, no progress could be expected toward an economic integration. In August, 1934, the German Minister of Food proudly pointed to the success of the German policy in keeping prices up. He compared prices (in reichsmarks) at home and abroad as follows: rye (ton), 159 vs. 58 (in Rotterdam); wheat (ton), 199 vs. 69 (in Liverpool); hogs (100 kg.) 47 vs. 12 (in Chicago); butter (100 kg.) 184 vs. 107 (in Copenhagen); eggs (one) 3½ pf. vs. 8 pf. (in Copenhagen).[18]

Even if Danubian countries had been able to obtain import quotas in their former markets—and their bargaining power as small units, negotiating separately, was rather weak—their entire trade would have suffered under this system of uncertainty, sudden changes, and pressure. They were obliged to look to the remaining distant markets. There they were handicapped not only because of higher transport rates, but also because of unstandardized production, and lack of a developed commercial and credit organization. We must not forget the basic difference in the New World and Danubian agriculture. In the countries overseas agricultural products are, for the most part, strictly commercialized; in Europe, agriculture still tends to be regarded as a means for providing employment. To increase output at the expense of contraction in man power was thought to be contrary to national policy. Agricultural competition was not based on even terms, and was often beyond the capacity of the Danubian states. This grave depression was even more serious because it was coupled simultaneously with an extreme financial and monetary crisis.

---

17 *The Economist*, Dec. 16, 1933, p. 1165.
18 *Ibid.*, Sept. 22, 1939, p. 585. This contrasts with the price decline in the agricultural exporting countries as measured by export prices in Rumania, per ton in lei (*ibid.*, Aug. 5, 1933, p. 269).

	Wheat	Corn	Barley	Timber
1928	9,122	7,556	6,866	2,522
1930	4,361	3,291	2,783	1,869
1932	3,222	1,931	2,708	1,326

4

ATTEMPTS TOWARD ECONOMIC RAPPROCHEMENT
AND INTERNATIONAL SOLUTION OF
THE DANUBIAN QUESTION

THE PROBLEM OF FOREIGN DEBTS

EVEN before 1914 the Danubian area had imported capital. For its vast program of postwar reconstruction and development the Valley needed extensive additional foreign investment. For purposes of reconstruction, long-term capital, primarily, was required. But, as was the case in other countries, huge credits were placed there as medium- or short-term capital, though the creditors should have been aware that the actual destination, in the majority of cases, was not the technical short-term credit, but medium- or long-term investment, even when the loans were formally designated as short term. The fact that the bulk of these short-term credits went to Vienna and Budapest is explained by the long-established relations of Austrian and Hungarian banks with world financial centers. The Viennese banks were thus able to continue their role in financing industry and trade in the entire Danubian area. The Czechoslovakian authorities attempted, with a certain degree of success, to avoid this short-term credit influx. We must not forget that, on the whole, foreign capital in whatever form was in general lent with the purpose of making a good, high-rate investment, based on an optimistic belief in future favorable developments.

The Danubian agricultural countries, before their economies reached the stage of higher development, could continue to pay their foreign debts and investment service only if they were to receive additional foreign capital in the future. Their balance of payments in which the foreign-trade balance was the chief item of income, could not be altered sufficiently within a short time to supply from export surpluses the necessary foreign funds to pay this debt service. It was evident that a decline in prices of the principal export products or a reduction in exports would immediately diminish this source of payment. Although there is no doubt that some credits were not put to the best economic use, and although it appears that some countries overborrowed abroad in relation to their capacity to repay, I do not think the following opinion renders justice to the whole situation: Capital invested in Europe was very largely used for "unproductive" purposes; it served to raise the standard of living in the borrowing countries, but export capacity was not sufficiently increased thereby to meet in full the service payments on foreign debt.[1] This may, in particular, be true of Germany, the greatest borrower, and in respect to the amount borrowed, also true of Hungary. But as for the Danubian agricultural countries as a whole, it should have been evident that the purpose of the foreign credits was to assist in developing their retarded economies, to modernize production, to increase transportation facilities, and to create industries. Such development certainly requires a much longer time than elapsed between the receiving of the loans and the outbreak of the crisis.

The turning point for the majority of the agricultural debtors came as early as 1929, when the prices of their chief export products [2] fell rapidly, thereby increasing the real burden of the debt. The bankruptcy of the Wiener Credit-Anstalt in May, 1931, marked the beginning of the credit crisis in Central Europe. Banking difficulties in Germany soon followed. It was thought at first that the main problem was that of banking liquidity and short-term debts, which had reached dangerously high levels in Austria, Hungary, and of course, Germany.[3] Attempts were made to consolidate these debts, and new substantial short-term credits were provided for Austria, and also for Hungary. Within a short time special standstill agreements had to be arranged for Austria and Hungary, but only after a large amount of foreign capital had been withdrawn. About S. 1,000 million was withdrawn from Austria within one year. Czechoslovakia [4] did not take advantage of a similar standstill agreement, relying upon

[1] Royal Institute, *The Problems of International Investments,* p. 279.

[2] In 1929–34, average gold export prices declined as follows: wheat (U.S.A.), 71%; butter (Denmark), 73%; corn (Argentina), 65%; sugar (Czechoslovakia), 57%; bacon (Denmark), 52%. From League of Nations, *Review of World Trade,* 1935, pp. 14–15.

[3] H. S. Ellis, *Exchange Control in Central Europe,* Cambridge, Mass., 1941, p. 55. The amount of the Austrian short-term foreign debts in 1932 was S. 1,287.4 million of a total foreign debt of S. 4,251 million.

Ibid., pp. 74, 80: Hungary's total short-term indebtedness amounted to pö. 1,838 million of a total foreign debt of pö. 4,310 million.

[4] In April, 1932, Czechoslovakia obtained a new five-year credit of French Fr. 600 million in Paris, but the amount of French short-term credits, alone, withdrawn and repaid before that time was substantially higher than the total of this new loan.

the circumstance that her credits abroad were greater than her debts. But she also was obliged to repay within a few months about $100 million. She found it impossible to cash many of her credits, some of them being frozen as medium-term banking investments in Germany, others in the Danubian states. The sudden and massive withdrawal of short-term capital of course increased the existing tension and aggravated the already difficult situation.

The real nature of the credit crisis should have been clearly illustrated by Hungary, whose situation was made the subject of a special League of Nations investigation in October, 1931. The total amount of Hungary's indebtedness as related to the balance of trade brought the entire problem in close relation not with the banks or the debtor's solvency, but with the possibility of transfer of payment abroad in general. Although Hungary's foreign debt was relatively the highest of the Danubian countries, a similar problem existed in each of the agricultural states. The domestic situation took an equal turn for the worse. Sinking prices increased the burden of debt, placing the debtors in a difficult position and immediately affecting their creditors, the banks. Within a very short time the governments were called upon to render agriculture effective assistance, in particular in the form of debt relief.

A realistic, far-sighted international economic policy on behalf of the creditor nations—which should have taken some measures to check the crisis and to prevent the spread of distrust or even to restore lost confidence—would have required as part of a comprehensive program not only a consolidation of the greater part of these so-called "short term" debts, but also a rapid settlement of the whole foreign—debt problem, if only for a certain time. This would have meant a reduction of some high-interest rates, voluntarily negotiated moratoria for debt service, and finally, actual new supervised credits for overcoming the crisis and for productive purposes. It may be taken for granted that the creditors would have been competent to demand numerous measures and supervision, on the same basis as did the League of Nations Commissioner in Austria.

The total long-term indebtedness, though very great for the agricultural countries, was, in truth, relatively small for the three large creditors—France, Great Britain, and the United States—in comparison with their other overseas investments. The postwar French and British loans and credits to the governments of these countries amounted,[5] for Great Britain, to £65.93 million (at the old gold parity), for France to French Fr. 3,506 million. The American Dollar Bond issues of 1920–31 for this purpose were $150.5 million.[6] The total for the three countries was approximately $600 million. Public long-term debt represented the greatest part of these postwar long-term foreign debts in the Danubian states. With the necessary understanding, and with the aid of competent central banks and governments, there is no question that a plan could have been devised to prevent the full outbreak of the crisis. The losses resulting from the crisis were greater than would have been entailed in concessions granted under the necessary guarantees precisely at this time. But again the atmosphere was not yet prepared, nor sufficiently harmonious; the large creditor nations, having of course much greater and, to them, more important investments in other parts of the world, and faced with an increasingly serious development in Germany, were perhaps reluctant to show a far-sighted and wise policy toward this particular area. And, in some circles, the strictly orthodox point of view may have been held that there can be no "economic reasons for not making payments in full if only a sufficiently ruthless deflation is carried out." [7]

And thus, although Hungary's insolvency was evident during the League of Nations investigation, she continued to pay her full service in foreign debts to the end of 1931, when a moratorium, declared in December, 1931, was put in operation on January 1, 1932. The conclusions reached by the League of Nations in regard to her position were neither very new nor bold. They demanded a reduction of public expenditures, and a balanced budget, and advised a curtailment of imports to improve the balance of payments. These measures were, of course, to be supported by a pertinent central-bank policy. This was not sufficient to set in motion the energetic and rapid action needed. Within a short period, five additional countries declared partial moratoria (later, in many instances, changed to full moratoria) for foreign-debt transfer: Greece and Bulgaria early in the spring of 1932, Yugoslavia in November, 1932, Rumania on January 1, 1933, and Austria in June, 1933.[8] Czechoslovakia alone remained solvent.

---

[5] Hamilton Fish Armstrong, "Danubia: Relief or Ruin," *Foreign Affairs*, X (1931–32), 610.
[6] Madden, Nadler, and Sauvain, *America's Experience as a Creditor Nation*, New York, 1937, p. 76. The grand total of this type of United States investment was $3,898.5 million.
[7] *The Problem of International Investment*, p. 286.
[8] For further details see Madden, Nadler, and Sauvain, *op. cit.*, pp 115–19.

And, with gold and foreign-exchange reserves substantially reduced, foreign-exchange and trade restrictions steadily increased, and were made more severe in all these countries.

The League of Nations did not remain inactive. The report of the 55th meeting of the Financial Committee in March, 1932, was very eloquent. It dealt at some length with the basic problems [9] involved, and contained some exceedingly important statements. Referring especially to Austria, Hungary, Greece, and Bulgaria, which had all received League of Nations loans, the committee repeated its previous judgment that whatever errors in budget or loan policy may have been committed, the strain upon these countries was mainly due to world causes over which they had very little control. It pointed out that the wholesale prices of raw materials and foodstuffs (in gold) had fallen approximately 40 per cent since 1928 and that, as a result, the burden of fixed charges on producers had increased by some 70 per cent.[10] Turning to the creditor states, the report asked them to recognize the temporary necessity of the debtor countries and to accept the goods which alone constituted the major means of payment. If they refuse, the debtors cannot continue to meet their obligations. Because the fundamental causes of the crisis had not been dealt with, the Committee, believing that there was no present possibility of final solution, emphasized "that action must be taken with the least possible delay both to avert the grave consequences of a further financial collapse in many parts of Europe and to give a chance for remedial measures which require further time for their development. It [the Committee] has reached the conclusion that there is urgent need for immediate action in the form of loans to be raised on international markets under government guarantees." Moreover, the report supported the attempts toward a closer economic coöperation of the Danubian countries (the so-called Plan Tardieu), advising that Bulgaria be included in the group affected. Further action was expected from the Lausanne Reparation Conference of July, 1932. This Con-

[9] League of Nations, *Economic and Financial*, 1932, II, A 5, pp. 2–5. In this connection we might refer to a recent statement in a League of Nations publication (Commercial Policy in the Interwar Period, Geneva, 1942, p. 133), to the effect that the problem constituted by the multiplicity of small and poor economic units in Central and Eastern Europe, heavily indebted to the Western World, was extremely complex, and purely economic measures could only have made a partial contribution to its solution.

[10] Bulgaria's export is cited as an example. The weight of her export increased in 1930 by 80%; in value it dropped by 3%; in 1931 weight increased by 40%, value dropped by some 4%.

ference, which in large measure settled the German reparations, proposed an international loan of 300 million schillings to Austria. In addition it appointed a Special Committee with the duty of submitting proposals as to measures required for the restoration of Central and Southeastern Europe, and, in particular, "measures to overcome the present transfer difficulties of those countries and to make possible the progressive suppression—subject to necessary safeguards—of existing systems of foreign-exchange control. Further measures to revive the activity of trade both among these countries themselves and other countries and to overcome the difficulties caused to the agricultural countries in Central and Southeastern Europe by the low price of cereals—it being understood that the right of third countries remain reserved."

The duties assigned this Special Committee became the program of the Stresa Conference, which dealt exclusively with the economic and financial problems of Central and Southeastern Europe. The program was extremely comprehensive, and there were many who believed that Stresa would prepare the solution to the two main problems facing Central and Southeastern Europe: financial and transfer difficulties, and questions of export, especially of agricultural goods. The Conference from the outset of its work recognized the intimate relation between financial, monetary, and economic questions; it contributed very much to the general knowledge of the foreign-debt problem of the Danubian countries in all its complexity. So far as was possible, complete figures on foreign indebtedness were compiled and were related to the existing foreign-trade situation. These figures, which include the prewar debts, are given in Table 4.[11]

The total external debt of these seven countries (not including Poland)—of which a not negligible part represented prewar debts—was, therefore, Fr. 19,902 million, gold (about $3,900, gold), in 1931–32. Public debts formed the major part: Fr. 15,443 million, gold. Service of the external debt for 1931–32 was Fr. 1,069 million, gold, of which 783 million was for public debt. This amount was compared with the external trade figure, after deducting the trade of the countries concerned *inter se*. This gives an extremely interesting picture, showing that the foreign trade of these countries with the rest of the world had always an adverse balance during the preceding years. The adverse

[11] Since the Conference dealt also with Poland, figures for that country are included. League of Nations, *Political*, 1932, VII, pp. 7–8.

Table 4

Foreign Indebtedness of the Danubian Countries

	Total (in Million Gold Fr.)	Total per Head of Population (in Gold Fr.)	Total Service of the External Debt in 1931–32 (in Million Gold Fr.)	Total as a Per cent of Exports in 1931	Balance of Foreign Trade for 1931 (in Million Gold Fr.)
Austria	2,423 (731) [a]	361	214	22	−622
Bulgaria	715 (34)	118	35	16	+ 47
Czechoslovakia	2,037 (138)	138	105	5	+213
Greece	2,418 (71)	378	140	49	−259
Hungary	3,774 (1,408)	432	248	48	+ 16
Rumania	5,226	292	203	28	+192
Yugoslavia	3,269 [b]	235	124	29	− 15
Poland	4,457 (1,782)	139	268	24	+242

[a] Short-term debts are in parentheses. [b] Public debt only.

balance amounted in 1929 to gold Fr. 1,378 million, in 1930 to gold Fr. 305 million, in 1931 to gold Fr. 136 million, and in the first half of 1932 to gold Fr. 213 million.

The foreign-trade balance permitted no service payment from that source on debts incurred [12] outside the area. In 1932 it was not sufficient to cover import charges (or the payments for import), though imports had been substantially reduced. This gave clear proof that the problem of transfer of payment abroad was as great for the Danubian countries as for Germany, though the latter question was more widely discussed. But Germany's export, as an industrial country, possessed greater flexibility than is generally true of agricultural exports. Further, Germany's balance of payments contained various substantial items of invisible income. In contrast, the balance of payments of the Danubian agricultural nations was dependent in large measure upon their balance of trade, with little flexible export. Yet Germany asked for an active balance even with these countries, arguing that she needed foreign exchange to buy raw materials from overseas. Both questions were, in the ultimate, related to the problem of the European Continental balance of payments with the rest of the world.

Stresa did not encourage new loans. Rather, it advised the creditors to assist the debtors to return to normal conditions, suggesting that any measures taken at this time be of a temporary rather than a final nature. The Conference not only recommended direct contact between debtors and creditors, taking into account the real value of the credits and making the necessary adjustments, but also suggested the creation of a Currency Normalization Fund whose immediate object would be to assist Central Banks by increasing their reserves at the opportune moment, to facilitate the final abolition of exchange restrictions. The governments were to make the necessary sums available, and the leading powers, of course, were to contribute. But this fund, called by the Chairman of the Conference, a fund for European solidarity, was never established. The Commission for European Union, whose "most important task" was to prepare the formation of this "common fund," decided, merely, to request the

12 "For the service of their debts abroad the majority of the Central and Eastern European countries have essentially at their disposal only the surplus of their trade balances. There is a correlation between the means of payment available and the export capacity and secondly between that capacity and the price-level of exportable products." League of Nations, *Political*, 1932, VII, p. 10.

Council to arrange for a detailed and thorough examination of the draft of the fund and to discover whether and how it could be combined with the contemplated fund for the revalorization of cereals.

The Stresa Conference, though it contributed to the general knowledge of the importance of the foreign-debt problem and formulated certainly very useful recommendations, fell far short of preparing any bold or immediate measures, which alone could have halted the deepening crisis. In its monetary and financial report much, obviously, was expected from the general revival of trade from the abolishment of trade and foreign-exchange restrictions and revalorization of the prices of agricultural goods. But, as a matter of historical fact, no collective action was taken in the field of foreign debts and no visible progress was realized.

ATTEMPTS TOWARD INTERNATIONAL ACTION AND ECONOMIC RAPPROCHEMENT

International action in foreign trade was centered upon two questions: improvement of prices and export of agricultural products, and the possibility of closer economic coöperation among the Danubian nations. The first move in this direction was consideration of preferential customs duties which the European importing countries should grant to the Danubian Basin and Poland in respect to cereals, and, possibly later, to other agricultural products. Two tendencies became evident, interrelated to some extent, but with clearly different economic and political objectives. Whereas the French political system definitely leaned toward the establishment of a close economic coöperation of the Danubian countries, Germany, with her greater economic weight and steadily increasing power, preferred, unquestionably, the system of preferential treatment.

The system of preferential duties raised several important problems. Should it be of limited duration or permanent, pointing to a basic impossibility of competing with overseas production and perpetuating the existing maladjustments? Should it be negotiated in bilateral agreements or introduced by collective action? To which products and to which countries should it be limited? Would not a country with protective duties gain inordinately by granting preferential reduction as compared to a country possessing only moderate agricultural protection or none? These and other questions, particularly the repercussion of the entire most-favored-nation clause, were the subject of wide discussion, reminiscent of the discussion following a similar request for introducing preferential duties for European cereals against overseas competition in the 1880s.

An open claim for the granting of preferential customs treatment by the European importing countries for cereals and agricultural products of European origin was addressed to the League of Nations by the Warsaw Conference [13] of the Central and Eastern European Agrarian Bloc as early as August, 1930. This Agrarian Bloc, including the representatives of six governments—Bulgaria, Hungary, Poland, Yugoslavia, Rumania, and Czechoslovakia (first in the capacity of observer)—at the outset outlined a far-reaching program. The program included not only such topics as rationalization of agriculture, improved marketing, grain standardization, a plan for the reduction of crop areas and agricultural credit, but an attempt to elicit agreement to present a united front against overseas competition, coupled with the demand for preferential treatment in Europe. Throughout its activity, the Agrarian Bloc never attained the concerted action found in the international industrial cartel agreements—further evidence of the great dissimilarity, in this respect, of the agricultural and industrial situation, not to mention the widely divergent interests of the several countries involved.

Furthermore, there is no evidence of a single instance in which the Agrarian Bloc, as such, negotiated as a representative of the exporting countries with an importing country. Such negotiation, implying collective action, would have placed the exporting countries in a much more favorable bargaining position than could be attained in bilateral agreements. It was, at that time, difficult to secure an understanding with industrial Europe which would have provided an assured market for agricultural products at remunerative prices. Reliance upon the effects of preferential duties as a solution to the crisis was certainly too optimistic.

The League of Nations, which had followed this problem for some time, admitted the desirability of a preferential-customs regime for cereals from the agricultural states of Central and Eastern Europe.

13 This Warsaw Conference was attended by Bulgaria, Czechoslovakia, Estonia, Latvia, Poland, Yugoslavia and Rumania. Similar meetings of the Agrarian Bloc were held, during the next years, in Bucharest, Belgrade and elsewhere. For details concerning the Agrarian Bloc see M. Hodža, *Federation in Central Europe*, London, 1942, pp. 103 ff. Also Elemer Hantos, *Le Regionalisme èconomique en Europe*, Paris, 1939, pp. 19 ff.

The admission was made in November, 1930, at the meeting of a second Conference with a View to Concerted Economic Action, and again in May, 1931, by the Commission of Enquiry for European Union. The conference regarded preferential treatment as an emergency measure only—applied under abnormal circumstances in order to adapt the level of export prices of the principal agricultural products to their cost level price [14]—and emphasized that it was a conditional, exceptional, and limited derogation to the most-favored-nation clause, limited to cereals and their derivatives from the agricultural countries (Rumania, Bulgaria, Hungary, Yugoslavia, and Poland).

We may note that the conference pointed out that a Danubian preferential regime in cereals would not harm the interests of the overseas exporting countries; the latter would always be the main providers of Europe, and the cereal exports of Central and Eastern Europe were negligible in comparison with the aggregate imports of other European countries. Furthermore, transportation costs made Germany, Czechoslovakia, Austria, Italy, and Switzerland the natural and most important cereal customers of Central and Eastern Europe. Correspondingly the regime would not endanger the protection of the agrarian interests of the importing countries, whose total imports should not increase at the expense of domestic production.

According to this attitude the cereal export of the agricultural European states should not increase at the cost of either overseas import or domestic production of the importing countries. With no rapid increase of consumption in sight how could an increase of volume of export be expected? Improvement of the agricultural states should come through preferential reduction of duties, which would supply the needed margin for price adjustment. With the scope and aim of preferential agreements thus defined, no considerable help could be expected from such action particularly if the customs and other barriers were to continue to increase.

But the granting of preferential duties was obviously subject to an agreement with those countries enjoying the most-favored-nations clause. No preferential regime could be applied without their consent. Any granting of preferential duties should be unilateral; it was not expected that preferential treatment be conceded the industrial products of the partner.

With all the exceptions and reservations made by the Conference,

[14] League of Nations, *Economic and Financial*, 1932, II, p. 52.

the results were of limited success only. It should have been clear at the time that the system was more fitted to Germany's needs than to those of any other nation. She was still an important customer, and by introducing exceedingly high agricultural duties was in a better position to grant preferential duties, perhaps, in fact, at a higher level than were the normal ones before the recent increase.

The Agrarian Bloc again pressed the preferential problem in the Wheat-Sub-Subcommittee of the Briand Commission for European Union, where it was accepted for cereal export, with such countries as Holland and England abstaining.[15]

Germany, growing in power politically and economically, entered upon negotiations for preferential treaties with the Danubian states. She persisted in regarding this area as a special sphere of interest, hoping to regain there her prewar position and influence. It was obvious that the growing export difficulties of these countries, for whom Germany was an old and important market, would soon lead them to ask her for that kind of concession. And with her extremely high duties and corn monopoly she was well prepared to negotiate preferential agreements. After the failure of the attempt to establish a customs union with Austria during the summer of 1931, Germany devoted considerable attention to this question. In July, 1931, she granted Rumania, by commercial treaty, 60 per cent preferential reduction on corn and 50 per cent on fodder barley and other cereals for specified quotas of these commodities. She concluded similar agreements with Hungary and Bulgaria.[16] These preferential duties were unilateral; Germany did not demand that any preference be granted her export.

The whole situation was somehow paradoxical. The state which had initiated the extreme agricultural protection which had basically disturbed the foreign markets for agricultural products, was now diligently offering preferential treatment to some of the very nations to suffer most as a result of that policy. No wonder the agreements aroused no great enthusiasm among the other nations at that time!

[15] According to M. Hodža (*op. cit.*, p. 107), M. Briand offered to secure the purchase of 10% of Central European wheat surpluses. And Hodža remarks that, since France was practically self-sufficient in cereal production, it was little more than a symbolic gesture, sufficient to make a very favorable impression upon the governments of Central Europe for the time being.

[16] Bulgaria obtained in her 1932 treaty with Germany 60% preferential reduction of corn, 50% of barley, and 25% of wheat. Milka Deyanowa, "Die staatlichen Massnahmen zur Förderung der Ausfuhr der Agrarprodukte Bulgariens," *Weltwirtschaftliches Archiv*, LI (1940), p. 417.

They could not be put in operation because some of the most favored nations (among them Argentina, Czechoslovakia, and Turkey) refused their consent. Others (United States, Russia, and Denmark) reserved their decision. Later a number of other countries joined the opposition, even India being one of them.

As German activity in the Danubian area increased, discussion continued not only in respect to the market for agricultural products but to the general organization of the Danubian Valley. France, having the closest political associations and having won influence, prestige, and responsibility after the 1931 Schober-Curtius Anschluss incident, was called upon to take the initiative for an economic rapprochement here. And thus the so-called "Plan Tardieu" was proposed.

The chief proposals of the Plan were, in the main, as follows: Austria, Czechoslovakia, Hungary, Yugoslavia, and Rumania should be organized to form a special economic system without the participation or interference of the great powers. They were to grant each other a preferential tariff reduction of 10 per cent, which was not to be considered in disagreement with the most-favored-nations clause. They were to abolish all import and export prohibitions among them, cancel exchange restrictions, and, possibly, establish a common currency. A reconstruction loan was suggested, to which France would subscribe £10 million ($40 million).

In April, 1932, at London a short meeting of the four big powers, Great Britain, France, Germany, and Italy, ended in the failure of the Plan Tardieu over mere question of procedure—an incident managed by the German and Italian delegates. The big powers were not in agreement on the plan as a whole. France was in a position to offer the greatest financial aid, but in view of her economic structure and policy, offered little prospect of considerable purchases of goods. Italy was fearful that a realization of the plan would result in the restoration of something similar to Austria-Hungary under the influence of French diplomacy and finance.[17] To Germany it sounded the death knell of the Anschluss and of any "future revival of the Drang nach Osten." [18] It was pointed out that Czechoslovakian and Austrian in-

[17] For further details see: Hamilton Fish Armstrong, "Danubia: Relief or Ruin," *Foreign Affairs*, X (1932), pp. 600–616; also Josef Hanč, *Tornado across Eastern Europe*, New York, 1942, pp. 114 ff.

[18] Armstrong, *ibid.*, p. 605. A resolutely negative German attitude was also displayed at the special meeting of the International Chamber of Commerce in Innsbruck in April, 1932.

dustry would gain advantages which might harm the competing industries of Germany and Italy, who were prepared to grant unilateral agricultural preferences to the exporting countries. Great Britain's attitude to the whole plan was rather lukewarm. She was apprehensive of its effects on British exports, and was never actually in favor of a preferential system.

There is the possibility that, if the Danubian countries themselves had stood together and, as a united bloc, had pressed for coöperation, they could have changed the attitude of the big powers. Such unity on their part did not exist. Hungary, and also Rumania, did not consider the plan to be a satisfactory or permanent solution because it did not give them a large enough market for their agricultural surpluses. In the Hungarian opinion, German and Italian help was essential. Further, the Hungarian Government attempted, as it always did, to press revisionist demands, combining economic negotiations with political considerations. It refused to join any organization that would preclude a future revision of the Peace Treaty.[19]

Let us now examine the Tardieu Plan chiefly on its economic merits, its prospects, and the obstacles it met. In addition to the objection against the small amount of the reconstruction loan—which amount, of course, was only tentative—it was argued that the Plan did not provide a large enough market for agricultural surpluses, that inter-Danubian trade represents about one third only of the total foreign trade of these countries. Moreover it was calculated that even though the Danubian countries were to purchase all their agricultural and industrial goods within this area, united by a preferential system, total inter-Danubian trade could not be substantially increased, and the Valley would still be compelled to look to other markets for their agricultural and industrial surpluses.[20] There was further a suspicion or fear, especially in England, that such federations, while reducing customs duties among members, might raise them in trade with other countries.

[19] The Hungarian Foreign Minister Kánya wrote on Sept. 16, 1933, in *Europe Centrale*, Prague: "Once more let it be known that Hungary would join no kind of Central European Bloc or Danubian Federation unless and until a measure of treaty revision had either been granted or guaranteed. The first point in our program can be nothing else than the revision of treaties by pacific means."

[20] The total import of the five Danubian countries (excluding Bulgaria) was in million dollars: 1,578 (in 1928); 1,256 (1930); 924 (1931), of which inter-Danubian import amounted to 482, 402, and 262, respectively. Similar figures for export were 1,375 (1928), 1,232 (1930), 927 (1931), and 487, 419, and 262. From League of Nations, *Economic and Financial*, II, 1932.

On the other hand, 10 per cent of preferential reduction was not a satisfactory basis for solution of the problem. If the preferential system served only to replace import from other countries by Danubian import, that would have meant merely a shift but not an expansion of foreign trade, and would probably soon have been followed by the loss of foreign markets. The real question was whether the Danubian countries were determined to continue their efforts toward a marked reduction of customs duties and other obstacles in their mutual trade. Would they even go so far as to introduce a customs union? We need not speak of the general advantages of a greater economic unit, but we may point out that if, during the agricultural crisis, the agricultural export states had been able to present a united economic front, their bargaining power for trade negotiations with other countries would have been infinitely stronger. And it would have been vitally important in the near future in their relations with Germany.

Not only were there political difficulties, but there was also lack of economic support. Czechoslovakia and Austria were not ready for a customs union, or, for that matter, for substantial preferences on a free-trade basis without import quotas with regard to their agriculture. The other countries, in direct opposition, were perhaps even less ready for such a system in respect to their new industries. Cost of production and prices diverged steadily in the different succession states. The divergence in prices of industrial goods was still greater than that shown for agricultural products.[21]

Both political agreement and bold imagination on the part of the big powers and the Danubian states were needed to outline and carry out a sound economic program which could serve as a basis for an economic and also a political rapprochement. It was unfortunate that at that time it was more common to think in terms of economic contraction than to visualize the prospect of expansion, which alone could have solved the extremely difficult problems.

[21] As an example of price differences we quote Oscar Jaszi, "The Economic Crisis in the Danubian States," *Foreign Affairs*, II (1935), No. 1, 98–116: "The result [of agricultural protectionism in Austria and Czechoslovakia] has been that whereas in Budapest, Beograd, Bucharest a quintal of wheat costs about $1.50, in Vienna and Prague it costs from $3.50 to $4, (p. 103), and . . . it was calculated by the Hungarian Chamber of Agriculture that whereas in 1913 a plow cost 240 Kg. of wheat, in 1933 it cost 1330 Kg.; a ton of coal cost in 1913 45 Kg., in 1933—320 Kg. of wheat. The buying power of agricultural products has decreased by two thirds of the 1913 figure." (p. 104.) See also *The Economist*, May 21, 1932, p. 1122.

The Stresa Conference, called in 1932, gave fresh hope to Central and Southeastern Europe. Besides the problem of foreign debts the Conference was concerned in particular with the question of revalorization of cereals. The necessity for strengthening economic position by close coöperation among themselves was placed in the background.

We have already spoken of the general recommendations made in the field of foreign debts. The Conference emphasized a similar liberal doctrine in reference to foreign-trade policy. As a solution to the most crucial point, that of finding markets for the agricultural surpluses of Central and Southeastern Europe, Stresa proposed a new plan for revalorization of cereals. It suggested that a revalorization fund of gold Fr. 75 million yearly for a period of 5 years should be created to subsidize the export of cereals from Central and Eastern Europe (including Poland). The importing countries were to contribute to this fund according to a certain scheme, such as, for instance, the total value of their foreign trade. The fund should be a factor in raising the prices of the export surpluses, and it was hoped that, indirectly, the total level of domestic prices would thus be maintained without the need of direct intervention. A beautifully simple idea if the desired effect could be achieved by so modest a means!

The subsidy was to apply only to the average quantity of cereals exported in 1929, 1930, and 1931; gold Fr. 2 per quintal of wheat and gold Fr. 1.50 per quintal of barley and corn. The total amount was only 52.5 million quintals: 16 million q. of wheat, 15 of barley for fodder, 13.5 of corn; rye, barley for brewing, and oats made up the remainder. The total current value was between $120 and $150 million.[22] A revalorization fund of gold Fr. 75 million (less than $25 million) obviously would not be sufficient if these quantities could not be sold. It was a great pity that the governments, especially those of the Western Powers, were as yet unaware of the device of preëmptive purchases, a device often used later as a weapon of economic warfare. They were equally unaware that unusual steps and measures of governmental intervention were required to fight an economic crisis, not

[22] The tobacco-exporting Balkan countries pointed out that conditions for tobacco and cereals were the same—production suffered from New World competition. (This was especially true of the British market.) The total production of Bulgaria, Greece, and Turkey did not represent more than 3% of world production.

The Conference expressly mentioned the Austrian marketing difficulties (for industrial goods) and trade negotiations with a view to improving the general situation of that country. A preferential system was proposed, all the rights of third states, naturally, being reserved.

only in national economies, but also in international economic relations. The old conceptions were entirely inadequate in the situation.

It was decided at the Conference that states granting by bilateral treaties preferential treatment for cereals from the Central and Southern European countries would be released from contributing to the revalorization fund. The report stated expressly that Germany, for her part, was to acquit herself of her contribution through bilateral treaties concluded or to be concluded with the beneficiary states. Other importing countries intended to do the same.

The Stresa Conference cannot, certainly, be regarded as having brought the settlement of all these questions any nearer fulfillment. Some very useful and wise general principles [23] were emphasized, but nothing was contributed to the most urgent problem of foreign debts, and very little to the question of the agricultural export of the countries of Central and Eastern Europe; no consideration was given to the problem of a new economic regime in the Danubian Valley. The only tangible results were the subsidies envisaged for cereal export and the accepted system of preferential duties.

The Stresa program was approved in principle at the next meeting of the Commission for European Union in spite of opposition by certain Western countries. Those countries with duty-free import of cereals (or negligible duties), such as Great Britain, Holland, and others, were opposed to the idea of preferential duties and to the contribution to the revalorization fund. Russia's attitude was also far from encouraging.[24] Neither the revalorization fund for cereals nor the proposed currency normalization fund were ever created.

The high expectations and the few false hopes (for a rise in prices, for instance) of the Danubian countries were shattered. Great disappointment spread throughout the Valley nations; they lost confidence

[23] These principles were summarized by Mr. Eden at the meeting of the Commission for European Union on September 30, 1932. (League of Nations, *Political*, 1932, VII, p. 13.): "A strict budgetary and credit policy should be followed by the states which had been compelled to impose foreign exchange restrictions, that they should arrive at a position of equilibrium between their internal price level and the price level ruling elsewhere, whether by a policy of deflation or by a change of monetary policy and that all questions concerning their external debts should be negotiated directly between debtor and creditor."

[24] M. Litvinoff remarked at the meeting: "The proposals are more in the nature of pious hopes than of schemes capable of realization." And, "The impossibility of putting into practice these recommendations would emphasise the fact that conflicts of interests both between nations and within nations could not nowadays be overcome in the interest of international solidarity."

in international action, and learned that they must not expect a remedy in "Utopia," but must travel the hard road of negotiations and extreme internal efforts. The opinion was expressed that what was needed was not subsidies or preferential duties but free markets, which Stresa failed to provide, and, further, that the Stresa suggestion for removal of currency restrictions in the Danubian states, though sound in principle, was impracticable of application without, first, the settlement of the foreign-debts problem.

After three years of international meetings and conferences none of the most crucial problem of the Danubian countries was settled. The problem of foreign indebtedness remained open and thereby aggravated the monetary and foreign exchange position. The export situation was becoming worse as foreign-trade obstacles steadily increased, particularly as agrarian protectionism climbed to new heights. The major powers had arrived at no agreement which could serve as a workable basis for a comprehensive and constructive economic program for Central and Southeastern Europe. Weighty points of disagreement in world politics threw their shadow over the Danubian Basin; questions vital to its economic existence were linked with the political fight between the Great Powers.

Though the crisis shattered the roots of the economic stability of the Danubian countries and the social stability of some of them, it brought them no unity of action. They did not arrive at agreement among themselves, nor did they work out or even outline a constructive joint program which would have made it possible for them to present a united front in relations with the rest of the world. The cleavage between the industrial and the agricultural countries widened.

The only device used for the betterment of conditions which obtained a certain importance was a *preferential* treatment, thought of first in terms of unilateral preferential duties granted, in the main, to agricultural exports. But these countries were very soon to learn how, in a world of expanding barter and clearing payment system, this device was to be transformed into a bilateral preferential system, ushering in a system of bilateral trade. They were to learn also how difficult under this system was to become their position as smaller countries in negotiation with a major power on whose market they were dependent. By that time they became convinced, certainly, that a Danubian economic unit—even though based on the very imperfect

Plan Tardieu and unable to absorb a great part of the agricultural surpluses—would have provided them with a much firmer bargaining position than could be obtained within the most ideal preferential regime. And it may be said that, had such a unit been created, future events might have taken another turn, especially in relation to Germany.

Of course there was no hope of justifying the establishment of this unit so long as an exaggerated nationalism, both political and economic, prevailed, and so long as the main problems between the major powers remained unsettled and unsolved. And thus "as a result, the year 1933 found Southeastern Europe hopelessly divided against itself, disillusioned . . . and confronted with yet another problem in the shape of a resurgent National-Socialist Germany." [25] It was impossible to insulate the economic from the political sphere.

[25] The Royal Institute of International Affairs, *South-Eastern Europe; a Political and Economic Survey,* London, 1939, p. 25.

5

THE FIGHT OF THE DANUBIAN COUNTRIES
AGAINST THE CRISIS

ALL ATTEMPTS to bring about international action for the purpose of consolidating the desperate economic and financial situation of this area had failed. However, the financial crisis of 1931—which was mainly the result of developments abroad—forced the Danubian states into immediate action to protect their national economies and their currencies. They had no long-run policy in mind; measures were taken largely in reaction to immediate events or in the attempt to prevent undesirable developments. It was not until later that these measures were integrated into a sort of united economic policy, characterized almost everywhere by an expanding governmental interference and piecemeal planning.

Looking back upon this policy, one might be tempted to say that foreign-exchange control, transformed into a policy of a managed (manipulated) balance of payments was considered the most powerful instrument for preventing the deepening of the crisis and for stabilizing the economic situation. As a matter of fact, after 1931 the situation of Central and Southeastern Europe was characterized by a disintegrating international trade, by evergrowing foreign-trade barriers coupled with a most exaggerated protectionism, by government interference increasing to the point of very extensive indirect planning, and by an industrial boom in the agricultural countries and agricultural prosperity in the industrial nations. After 1933 the growing influence of Germany quickly became evident and those national economies entering into close coöperation with her moved, on the whole, in quite another direction than did the economies of the western European countries.

FOREIGN EXCHANGE CONTROL

After the outbreak of the financial crisis in 1931 the structure of the balance of payments in all of these nations underwent profound change. The majority (practically all five of the agricultural states) could achieve equilibrium in the balance of payments only by obtaining new foreign credits. This entire trend of receipts of foreign credits from abroad was reversed. Short- and medium-term loans were withdrawn, and there was scant possibility of obtaining new foreign credit.[1] These foreign credits were repaid by reducing, in the last instance, the gold and foreign-exchange reserves held by Central Banks, reserves which on the whole had never been very high. Obviously, it was also necessary to call upon the foreign-exchange balances of private banks and industry. In nearly all of these countries the urgent need of foreign exchange for repayment of withdrawn credits and for payment of the regular service of debts and investments was seriously augmented by an increasing flight of capital as a result of general lack of confidence. The devaluation of the pound in September, 1931, contributed, certainly, to this monetary uncertainty, which, of course, affected the financially weak countries more severely. This development was accompanied by an increasingly difficult situation in the export markets. Little hope remained for the possibility of achieving a substantial export surplus which would check the unfavorable trend in the balance of payments.

Each of these countries was confronted by the same problem: was it possible to maintain the balance of payments while keeping the foreign-exchange rate stable without depreciation and freely satisfying all demands for payments abroad? Or was it necessary to introduce foreign-exchange restrictions which would lead, very soon, to a policy of a managed balance of payments, this in turn necessitating control of the entire foreign trade and an expansion of governmental intervention in economic life? The decision was made in 1931–32 to establish foreign-exchange control in each of these countries, including Czechoslovakia which, because of her highly favorable balance of trade in the previous years had ceased to be a debtor country on a substantial scale. The Danube valley embarked upon a new era of economic organization.[2]

[1] Exceptions were the international short-term credits granted to the Austrian and Hungarian National bank, the new Austrian loan and the French loan to Czechoslovakia in 1932.

[2] Foreign exchange control was introduced, first, in Hungary on August 8, 1931; in Czechoslovakia on October 2, 1931; Yugoslavia, October 7, 1931; and Austria, October 9, 1931. Bulgaria renewed this control on October 15, 1931, and Greece introduced it on September 28, 1931. Rumania was the last of the group to follow the plan, on February 27, 1932. She had hoped that it would not be necessary to establish foreign-exchange control, owing to the relatively high monetary reserve of the Rumanian National Bank and a favorable development of her balance of trade.

The chief purpose of foreign-exchange control was to prevent devaluation of the external value of the national currency and to prevent destruction of monetary stability by too great and too sudden demands for payment abroad. In consideration of the fact that the original purpose, namely to avoid devaluation, was not realized in any of these countries, it is logical to ask whether the introduction of foreign-exchange control, which became one of the contributing factors in the disintegration of foreign trade, was actually necessary, or whether the same results could not have been achieved some other way. Theoretically, there were two possible methods of obtaining such general price adjustment—deflation or devaluation.

The policy of deflation proved to be quite unsuccessful in Czechoslovakia. In practice no country succeeded in sufficiently adjusting its level of prices by deflation, as the history of the gold-block countries clearly illustrates. It is scarcely necessary to add that the devaluation of the pound, the dollar and other currencies, and organized German dumping, increased the difficulties to be expected in carrying out a policy of deflation in modern industrial states.

In agricultural countries, such as the majority of the Danubian states, where these difficulties were present only to a minor degree, deflation could be achieved more easily. However, we must remember that, in these only partially developed economies, there were not present the instruments for an effective deflationary policy. The drop in agricultural prices was sufficient to threaten the entire weak economic structure.

The second method for obtaining general price adjustment, namely devaluation, was put into operation by the British in September, 1931. Many experts advocated its use in the Danubian area. But devaluation was equally difficult here, for psychological and political reasons even more than for economic ones. The war and particularly the postwar inflation was too recent a memory. People looked upon stable money as an absolute necessity. Any change in official parity would have increased the general nervousness and intensified the flight of capital. Devaluation was identified with inflation; the people made no distinction between them. Devaluation of the exchange rate of the national currency had been regarded in the past as the result of inflation, and therefore even political and financial circles could not believe that there might be devaluation without inflation.

It was, of course, even less possible to follow the British example of devaluation without an immediate new stabilization, i.e., pegging the new parity to gold.

Without international agreement and collective action there was no hope that, in the presence of repayment of debt and growing export of capital, the exchange rate could be adjusted to some level to restore the equilibrium of the balance of payments. It is, perhaps, useless to speculate upon what might have happened; nevertheless no country could thus plunge into complete uncertainty in the midst of growing economic unrest. The frequently repeated rule that the exchange rate would have found a level, and upon that basis a new equilibrium in the balance of payments could have been established hardly apply here. There was not sufficient reason to believe in an effective automatic adjustment, especially in the agricultural countries. We have discussed the problem of foreign debts, export possibilities and difficulties in these debtor countries. They give ample proof that there was very little hope of adjustment by free development of the rate of exchange in a world of paralyzed credit markets and increasing foreign-trade difficulties.

The introduction of foreign-exchange control was, certainly, not a step toward the solution of the crisis, but rather a measure of defense, regarded as a temporary instrument in a time of emergency. No country foresaw in 1931–32 that this measure would soon become one of the chief devices not only of the monetary and foreign trade policy but of national economic policies in general.

MANAGED (REGIMENTED) BALANCE OF PAYMENTS

The nature of the foreign exchange control introduced in 1931–32 in the countries of Central and Southeastern Europe was, in most cases, very different from that applied before the stabilization of their currencies after 1918.[3] Its definite objective was to maintain a stable exchange rate of the national currency, although an attempt was made in the initial stages to retain the exchange rate at the original parity.

Monetary stability was not particularly menaced by budgetary inflation. The main danger came from a sudden and very unfavorable

[3] See the author's "Probleme der Devisenkontrolle," *Mitteilungen des Verbandes oester Banken und Bankiers*, Vienna XIV, No. 9–10.

development of the balance of payments. Because of its basic objective, foreign-exchange control was no longer designed to defend the balance of payments against illegitimate or economically unjustified demand for foreign exchange as was mainly the case in the first years after the war, while observing the principle that such control must not interfere with the payment of justified claims. Moreover the idea was *to exclude from the foreign exchange market all demand, all claims, which would threaten the equilibrium of the balance of payments and therefore, the stability of the national currency.*

According to this concept the volume of obligations and payments abroad were to be related to the expected income from abroad (after using a great part of monetary reserves). Payments in excess of this amount were not allowed to be effected even if based on legitimate claims such as debts, payment of dividends, payment for imported goods, and so on. In practice a great variety of foreign-exchange control methods developed.

In general it may be said that the actual demand for foreign exchange was reduced to the point at which it could be satisfied without menacing the stability of the external value of the national currency. Therefore, the *debit* side of the balance of payments was cut down in order to avoid a fall in the exchange rate by too heavy demand for payment abroad. Obviously this reduction again was concentrated first on all unjustified demand, such as export of capital, flight of capital, and granting of credit abroad. But in the current situation resulting from the world crisis, this was not sufficient in most of the countries here under discussion. Therefore they attempted to exclude also from payment and transfer abroad justified claims, and various debts. In the majority of instances this was done by one-sided decisions, without consultation with the foreign creditor or his country.

Foreign-exchange control was thus transformed into a manipulated, managed balance of payments. Equilibrium of the balance of payments was to be achieved not by the effect of the exchange rate but by quantitative regimentation, particularly of the debit items. The greatest element of flexibility was therefore lost; it became increasingly rigid, no longer dependent upon the interplay of the market, but subject to the arbitrary decisions of the governments or central banks. As we have pointed out, Czechoslovakia alone maintained throughout this whole period the principle of satisfying all legitimate foreign claims, though she, too, exercised severe exchange control. She did not find it necessary to introduce any type of debt moratorium. Within a short period of three years Austria also was able to return to this important principle.

In other states where foreign debts were extremely heavy, various difficult questions arose: which legitimate foreign claims should be paid abroad and transferred; which could be paid on blocked accounts within the country; and, in this latter group, which payments should be postponed at all.

From the outset of this policy there was conflict between the payments for imported goods and payments of a financial character. Here again Czechoslovakia followed a different policy than did the other countries. She felt that it was better to control and reduce imports but to make full payment for them than to continue upon a free import basis without allowing payment abroad. This point was heavily stressed at the Devisen Conference of the Central Banks at Prague in November, 1931, called by the Bank for International Settlements. It was pointed out that, for the Danubian countries at least, it was most essential to maintain orderly payment for imported goods. By doing so they would avoid any further feeling of insecurity, which at this time, would affect not only the banking or financial sphere but also the normal functioning of foreign trade. Such feeling would certainly arise if bona fide exporters were to receive no payment because of foreign-exchange restrictions rather than insolvency of their debtors. Unfortunately Czechoslovakia was alone in her attitude at that time. Although it was evident that it would be difficult for several of the countries of the Danubian area to pay for freely imported goods, they felt that it was preferable to maintain imports without quantitative restrictions, even though in all probability there would be slight possibility of providing the necessary foreign exchange for their payment fully or on time. Frozen or blocked commercial debts for recent imports began to accumulate in Austria, Hungary, Yugoslavia, Greece, and Bulgaria, and later in Rumania. Germany introduced quotas for payment of imports often not sufficient for the payment of the purchased goods; it was not until July, 1935, that she also issued an order prohibiting import of goods for which Devisen allocation was not assured. This widespread establishment of blocked accounts created, in itself, an acute and difficult problem.

Within a short time many other blocked payments (accounts) were arranged for all types of the various financial claims, including services. It was the duty of the foreign-exchange control authority to decide which payment for what title in what time order was to be allowed for transfer abroad; other creditors were obliged to await payment, sometimes for an indefinite period.

This chaotic and arbitrary system led to grave consequences in the foreign trade and monetary sphere, which certainly were not foreseen by those countries who practiced it.

The policy of quantitative regimentation of the balance of payments endeavored to limit demand for foreign exchange by forbidding some payments entirely, or by permitting payment on some blocked account within the country. Legitimate foreign claims remained unsatisfied. The general method of execution was by arbitrary decision. No agreement was reached in advance with the creditors or their countries; standstill agreements for short-term debts were the exception. The most disturbing element in the whole situation was the fact that there was no regular allocation of foreign exchange for the payment of imported goods. It resulted in retaliation on the part of the creditor countries and in attempts by private creditors to obtain some payment, even though at a lower rate.

Because the majority of these countries were unable to effect the payments due for imported goods and because foreign creditor claims were frozen and blocked, private creditors applied to their governments and central banks for assistance. Assistance was given, in particular, in the financially weak countries and where the frozen claims were large. The usual method was to prohibit payment in free exchange for imports from those countries which, by their own decision, had discontinued totally or partially payments in free exchange. These imports were to be paid for either in the currency of the country from which imports came or in the blocked balances of the importing country. In this fashion bilateral exchange relations began to replace multilateral trade operations, and led very soon to bilateral clearing payments agreements. It was a further very decisive step toward the degeneration of international trade.

When various legitimate and justified payments abroad were not permitted, it was perhaps assumed that this demand would actually be earmarked or sterilized, that the debit side of the balance of payments would be shortened and the pressure eased. But to achieve this goal it was necessary to have either an agreement with the foreign creditors or a very efficient control preventing any transfer abroad that did not correspond with the intention of the foreign-exchange control. In both cases, time was needed to achieve these prerequisites, and in the meantime creditors, anxious to collect their claims and disturbed by the one-sided proceedings of some countries, attempted to sell their blocked balances or their claims. This transfer was not allowed; rates for this type of foreign exchange sank below the official parity. Varying rates developed in accordance with the purpose and the risk involved and in accordance with the objectives for which these accounts could be used. There were big loopholes in the initial foreign-exchange control of every country; a balance which was not allowed to be directly converted in foreign exchange could be used for other purposes without openly breaking the foreign-exchange rules.

Different exchange rates for one and the same currency developed from such transactions and were later often recognized by the exchange authorities. The practice of blocking legitimate and due foreign claims or prohibiting their transfer abroad without an agreement with the creditors had resulted in the differentiation of the foreign-exchange rate (multiple rates) and in the disintegration of foreign-exchange relations.

The original authority granted to the foreign-exchange control, the measures it introduced and the weapons it devised, proved to be entirely inadequate to carry out the policy of a managed balance of payments. The problem of foreign debts had not been satisfactorily settled; the adjustment of the price level was not generally sufficient to restore a new equilibrium in the balance of payments; the trend of the flight of capital from lack of political and economic confidence had not been stopped. These factors contributed to the continued pressure on the monetary reserves and the balance of payments. It was an unceasing, day to day battle to defend the stability of an exchange rate unsupported by an established equilibrium of the balance of payments. It might be compared to the fight against the effect of inflation upon the level of prices—a struggle with symptoms while the chief causes are not removed.

Following the pressure on the balance of payments, new steps were taken, or attempts were made to close some loopholes. In general, the official policy lagged behind the actual occurrence.

Private holdings in foreign exchange from current and former business transactions were called upon for surrender. In some states, including Czechoslovakia, the surrender not only of foreign exchange and gold was required, but also compulsory delivery and sale to the central banks of all types of foreign securities. The proceeds of these sales were used to strengthen the foreign-exchange reserve. This meant, of course, a reduction of the country's foreign assets as a whole and also a successive liquidation of international financial relations.

As for demand, everything was done to curtail, first, economically unjustified demand such as granting of credit, traveling expenses, and other unnecessary payments. But even the suspension or reduction of services of foreign debts proved an insufficient means of establishing the desired equilibrium in the balance of payments. Under the existing circumstances it was found that a necessary corollary was foreign-trade control and quantitative regulation of import. Thus foreign-exchange control became the initial phase of a kind of planned economy, in which the greatest emphasis was placed upon foreign-trade control.

PLANNED FOREIGN TRADE

The quantitative regimentation of import was introduced for monetary reasons to improve the balance of trade by reducing imports. The majority of the Central and Southeastern European countries adopted this system in varying forms during 1931 and 1932. In its rudest form the control operated indirectly. Imports were left free but foreign exchange was allocated for payment according to differing schemes. Priority was given to raw materials; so-called luxuries— a very flexible term—were excluded, and a differentiating payment plan was followed including varying treatment of export countries. This type of foreign-trade control was gradually abandoned and an import-permit system was generally accepted to prohibit import of goods for which an import license had not been granted in advance.[4]

We shall not describe the various direct and indirect quantitative regulations of import. The most important difference between them was whether payment for imported goods was assured or not. We repeat, the reason for the introduction of this quantitative control was the permanent pressure on the balance of payments. The purpose of

[4] The last country to introduce an import-permit system was Yugoslavia. Her growing balance on the German-Yugoslav clearing account made the step advisable in June, 1936. Before that time she too had made no guarantee of payment for imported goods.

the measure was to improve the balance of trade by reducing imports —therefore clearly a monetary and not a foreign-trade policy. But within a short time it was discovered that to carry out an import-license system simply from the foreign-exchange point of view became increasingly difficult, because the various pressure groups in all countries looked upon it as a welcome opportunity to protect their special interests. They, of course, tried to prove that their interests coincided with monetary necessity.

If the import-license system were introduced for monetary reasons one should have expected to encounter no difficulties in imports from debtor countries or in imports paid for by means of blocked balances owned by the country's nationals. But this was not the case. The following examples, which could easily be amplified, illustrate this fact. In the first Austrian licensing system list of May 1, 1932, three quarters (in value) of the restricted products were agricultural,[5] imported even from countries in which Austria held blocked accounts or maintained a surplus in the balance of payments. Certainly no demand for free foreign exchange was created by this import. An Exchange Commission was set up in the Ministry of Finance of Czechoslovakia in January, 1932, its leading purpose having been officially stated as protection of monetary stability. From the first months of the existence of this control, import (payments) licenses were refused, especially in the agricultural bracket, for goods from countries where Czechoslovakia possessed large blocked amounts which could be freed for such purposes.[6]

A similar development took place in each country where the introduction of a quantitative regulation of imports was regarded as a necessary measure. A step which had been contemplated as protection of monetary stability had become an instrument for the extreme protection of domestic production whether justified or not by monetary reasons. On the contrary, the effects of this regimentation of import and protection of domestic production on the level of prices made in some countries further adjustment of prices to the world market extremely difficult, and reflected very unfavorably upon the balance of trade.

The system of import licenses acted as a powerful incentive toward

[5] See H. Heuser, *Control of International Trade,* London, 1939, p. 134.
[6] "The control of imports exercised by the Foreign Exchange Commission proved to be the most effective measure for a large part of agricultural production." *Annual Report* of the National Bank of Czechoslovakia, 1932, p. 79.

further industrialization in the five agricultural countries. Not even the high customs tariff had been as powerful an instrument in preparing the ground for the development of new industry or for the expansion of existing production. Later, after 1934, a new element supported this tendency, namely the policy of producing armament and other goods important for national defense, so far as possible, at home. A decided industrial boom was produced. In general there was no great danger of foreign, cheaper competition. In the majority of cases the granting of an import license was refused where the same or similar goods could be purchased in the domestic market, regardless of price. It was an experience not completely new. Whenever an import-license system is established there is a tendency to regard as an exception the granting of licenses for goods which are also produced at home. The idea of competition disappears within the comprehensive quantitative import regimentation.

We have already mentioned the fact that in both Austria and Czechoslovakia the system of import control served to protect agricultural production, which increased during this period. It was also used to protect the industrial output. Imports of industrial goods were reduced. Since each of these countries was vitally dependent upon export of industrial goods to the large Western markets, they followed the necessary policy of refraining from inviting retaliation against their own industrial export by reducing imports of industrial goods from those countries which had little or no foreign-exchange or foreign-trade control. This consideration set, therefore, a definite limit to the tendency to use the license system as a new and extensive protection of industry.

The situation in this respect was different in the agricultural states. They believed that their export possibilities were limited in any case in view of quotas, high custom duties, and low prices paid abroad. And they saw large opportunities in expanding their industrial production. The following figures clearly illustrate this development.

Whereas before the crisis the increase in production had been more pronounced in the consumer goods industries, during the thirties capital goods also expanded substantially. Accompanying a further increase in the textile, leather, and food industries, there was a large increase in the capital goods, particularly in Hungary, Rumania, and Yugoslavia. This was partly due to the armament policy. New metallurgical plants, chemical factories, and machine factories

TABLE 5

INDUSTRIAL PRODUCTION [7]

1928 = 100

	Southeastern Europe (Bulgaria, Rumania, Yugoslavia, Hungary, Greece)	Rest of Europe
1929	104.0	105.6
1930	99.7	97.8
1932	86.6 (the lowest point)	72.3
1934	112.6	87.7
1935	120.4	95.2
1936	133.1	103.3
1937	137.3	112.6

were established, and the mining industry was intensified and enlarged. Hungarian industry enjoyed the greatest protection; industrial interests succeeded in obtaining a guarantee that future imports would not be allowed even when their factories were still unbuilt.

An obvious consequence of this industrialization policy of protection by a thorough import-control system was the further rise in prices of industrial goods, in spite of the fact that in some instances the refusal of foreign-import permits was linked with the administration of a definite price policy (no increase in prices, and sometimes even a price reduction).[8] This price development added to the existing difficulties of price adjustment in agricultural goods, necessary for export. The situation became worse, of course, when the new German purchasing policy developed fully.

From foreign-exchange control, contemplated as a temporary measure, and from import control, introduced as a device to support

[7] *Weekly Report* of the German Institute for Business Research, May 4, 1938, p. 34. The number of persons employed in industry although still relatively small, increased absolutely to a greater extent than before the crisis. Thus in 1938 there were engaged in industry of all kinds (including handicrafts), 702,000 persons in Hungary, 800,000 in Rumania, 700,000 in Yugoslavia, 430,000 in Greece and 230,000 in Bulgaria—probably not much more than three million in the whole area.

If industry is understood to exclude cottage industry this number is greatly reduced: in 1933 there were 264,300 factory workers in Hungary, about 350,000 in Rumania, perhaps 250,000 in Greece, 100,000 in Bulgaria, and about 300,000 in Yugoslavia, or 1.2 to 1.3 million in the entire area against 18 million engaged in agriculture. (Royal Institute for International Affairs, *South-Eastern Europe,* 1940, pp. 100–101.)

[8] The growing difficulties of providing the foreign exchange needed for raw materials placed a definite limit upon the steady increase of industrial production. This was especially true after the trade with Germany expanded.

monetary stability, the system was transformed into a kind of planned, managed foreign trade. New vested interests had been created, opposing any substantial change in the regime. There was no comprehensive, balanced, economic plan in general; the system operated with short-term dispositions and was increasingly influenced by growing pressure groups.

Foreign-trade transactions were subject to governmental decisions, long-term commercial treaties were replaced by three-, six-, and, if successful, by twelve-month agreements. The purpose was not to lay a general framework for a mutual exchange of commodities carried out by private trade but to fix quotas on various imported commodities for a short period.

There was, in general, no elaborate legal mechanism defining the procedure of making decisions on applications for import licenses; the matter was decided more or less arbitrarily by the authorities in question.

It is perhaps not too much to say that the entire import-control system became a proving ground upon which the test was made as to whether and how a parliamentary democracy could successfully make decisions in daily foreign-trade transactions, which could satisfy only a small minority, and where strong influence on the part of pressure groups was to be expected.

The experience gained during this period in all countries served to underline the difficulties inherent in the governmental planning of daily business transactions in a parliamentary democracy, though but one segment of activity had been touched upon.

The interrelation between foreign exchange and foreign-trade control, the growing tendency toward rigid bilateralism and what was thought to be a new element in foreign trade, namely clearing payment agreements, had served to increase the difficulties and complicate the whole economic situation.

CLEARING AGREEMENTS AND THE IDEA OF BILATERALISM

It would be incorrect to suppose that the policy of foreign-exchange control as carried out and the policy of clearing agreements were the outcome of a well preconceived, systematic plan. They were, more truly, the offspring of a difficult situation where palliative measures were taken with no fundamental principle in mind. The origin of the clearing-payments system lay in the bottleneck of international payments. Some nations had stopped the transfer of payment for various foreign debts, including those for imported goods, because foreign-exchange difficulties had arisen in spite of their solvency.[9] The retaliatory measures taken by the countries of the creditors involved actually threatened to bring foreign-trade relations to a standstill or to reduce them to primitive barter trade. Such a situation was developing when the 1931 Prague conference of the Central Banks convened. Its purpose was to try to discover means to alleviate the growing difficulties. It was Dr. Reisch, the President of the Austrian National Bank, who advocated the introduction of clearing agreements.

Dr. Reisch's proposal was to discontinue the usual direct method of payment between exporter and importer by means of foreign exchange and to establish cumulative accounts of the central bank of one country with the central bank of the other. The importer was to pay the amount due for his imported goods to the central bank of his own country in his national currency. The exporter was to receive payment from his central bank in his national currency. There would be no import difficulties or restrictions because of uncertain payment in the country of destination; foreign trade would not be burdened and subsequently reduced for reasons of foreign exchange. Dr. Reisch hoped that not only the existing volume of foreign trade would be maintained but that the system would be so flexible as actually to increase it.[10] Very little attention was paid to the question as to how and in what time periods the balances on the cumulative accounts were to be settled. Without a satisfactory solution of this point difficulties would inevitably follow within a very short time. It could equally well be foreseen that clearing agreements would develop into a system of balanced foreign trade between two given countries. Austria, which maintained an import surplus with most countries, thought, perhaps, that this would work to her advantage.

On the other hand, Czechoslovakia, which opposed the clearing system (as a country enjoying an export surplus with many countries she could hardly be in favor of it), pointed out that the real reason for

[9] League of Nations, *Enquiry into Clearing Agreements*, 1935, II. B. 6, p. 10.
[10] The National Bank of Hungary expressed a similar opinion in its *Annual Report*, 1932, p. xiv: "We did not oppose the introduction of this [clearing] system on the assumption that the increased freedom of international trade incidental to the clearing system will increase not only our imports but also our exports. But they [the clearings] have greatly increased undesirable imports without considerably promoting exports and thus tended to make our foreign trade balance adverse."

the bottleneck was that some nations had stopped payment for imported goods and had continued the plan of free import without a guaranteed allotment of foreign exchange. She felt that a better method than the clearing scheme was to follow her own practice, namely to maintain full payments for imported goods. According to this view, even a reduced import, by quotas, but fully paid for, is to be preferred. It preserves the old trade channels, the established foreign-trade relations and maintains the principle of multilateral trade. Furthermore, the quota system, with assured payment, may serve as a sound basis for the negotiation of an expanded volume of foreign trade.

Within a very short time the majority of the countries in question were convinced that clearing agreements offered the easiest and most flexible solution to the problem. The system of such agreements was introduced throughout Central and Southeastern Europe.

It was not long before the clearing plan proved to be one more step toward the further disintegration of international trade rather than an expansion of foreign trade.[11] The general problem of clearing payments has already been discussed in detail by others;[12] our attention will therefore be concentrated on some special features as related to the situation in Central and Southeastern Europe.

Clearing agreements as concluded in the first years contained clauses which fixed the ratio between the currencies of the two countries in question, usually at the legal parities. In those instances where there was depreciation of currencies *de facto* these parities became fictitious, but since they were clearing-agreement parities they often operated in the opposite direction from what had been expected and was desirable. These parities acted as an obstacle to export and a premium for import in the debtor countries, and therefore aggravated

---

[11] See H. S. Ellis, *Exchange Control in Central Europe,* p. 44. As a participant in this Prague conference I have reported some of the unpublished details because they are very informative as to the motives underlying the original introduction of clearings. Mr. Richard Schüller, who headed the economic and financial section of the Austrian Foreign Office during 1917–1938, writes in a recent article (published after this manuscript was completed) that under the existing circumstances he thought of introducing the clearing device. Austria, whose imports were always larger than her exports could offer to other countries the choice of buying more from her or selling less to her. But Mr. Schüller adds that he has no reason to be proud of his "invention." "Commercial Policy Between the Two Wars," *Social Research,* X (1943), No. 2, 159.

[12] In addition to the books by H. S. Ellis, by H. Heuser, by J. B. Condliffe (*Reconstruction of World Trade*), and by Margaret Gordon (*Barriers to World Trade*), see two memoranda of the League of Nations, *Enquiry into Clearing Agreements* (1935, II. B. 6), and *Report on Exchange Control* (1938, II. A. 10).

further the difficult problem of balances. Later the rates of exchange as stipulated in the clearing agreements were altered, and more flexible rates were adopted which should have corresponded to the so-called "real" external value of currency. It was thought that this measure might remove one of the major defects of the system, especially the tendency for the balance of trade to turn in favor of the free-exchange countries or countries with so-called strong currencies. Still later, when less rigid forms of bilateral payment were used, it was possible to settle the exchange rate by a kind of private payment agreement which lay, nevertheless, within the framework of the basically bilateral payment mechanism.

Although these steps pointing to a real rather than an artificial rate of exchange were very useful and important, they did not change the basic system of bilateral relations which attempted to balance the foreign trade between a given pair of countries. This basic feature of the entire system was the result of the fact that the proceeds of export were permitted to be used only within the buying country and only for certain purposes. Originally the scope of the agreements was confined to payment for import and export, but it was soon extended to include payment for practically every type of claim (financial, pensions, royalties). In other words all the claims, balances, and amounts belonging to the residents of one country were used solely for payment in connection with the relations between the two countries in question. The principle was followed that no payment could be affected in the currency of a third country or by exporting goods to a third country.

In this fashion a more or less complete bilateralism in payment between two countries had evolved. Whether it took the form of a clearing agreement or other payment agreement of a more flexible character was not material to the principle itself. Obviously, the system directly affected the evolution of the exchange rate. An exporter who knew that he would be unable to obtain the countervalue in free exchange or payment without delay took this fact into consideration as a type of greater risk and expressed it by means of higher prices. Higher prices for goods exported in countries lacking free payment became the rule. In actual fact, therefore, there was depreciation of currency in spite of an official rate based on the so-called "real" value.

Those countries possessing an import surplus thought that the clearing plan might serve as an effectual and efficient instrument for achieving a balanced foreign trade by forcing the exporting countries to use the total countervalue for purchasing their goods. For instance Mr. Yovanovitch [13] writes that the measure adopted by the Yugoslav National Bank in 1932 by which payment for imported goods was allowed only in "dinars blocked provisionally" was intended "to compel foreign countries to conclude clearing agreements with Jugoslavia." Possibly this was the general idea expressed in the League of Nations report on clearing agreements in the sentence, "To have a good clearing system you must have a bad balance of trade." [14]

Therefore it was rather surprising that some creditor countries, even those with an export surplus with a certain country, took the initiative in concluding clearing agreements. They thus attempted to obtain payments for goods previously delivered, to continue as far as possible and upon a reduced scale if necessary their exports to the country in question, and to secure at least partial payment of their financial claims. The conflict between the financial and trade interests often played a very significant role.

Agreements of this kind had various undesirable effects upon the Danubian countries, among them the necessity to import goods in accordance with the clearing accounts and not with their actual need. In some cases this meant importing luxury goods from the Western countries when agricultural equipment, ordinary consumer goods, raw materials, were needed.

The balancing of foreign trade, if it were reached, was usually attained through a smaller volume of trade. Dislocation of the old channels of foreign trade, limitation of buying abroad with unfavorable repercussions on prices and lack of the price competition accompanying multilateral trade were all felt rather soon. The first answer to these difficulties was not to liquidate the system of clearings but to attempt so far as possible to increase export into nonclearing countries, in general into countries not employing exchange control.

A new criterion was introduced in foreign trade: a distinction between the trade with free or with clearing countries or generally with foreign-exchange-control countries. Within a brief period different prices and conditions were applied to each of these groups; Europe was divided into countries with prevailing clearing or free-payment

[13] A. Yovanovitch, *Memoire sur le controle des changes en Jugoslavie,* 1939, Paris.
[14] League of Nations, *Inquiry into Clearing Agreements,* p. 35.

TABLE 6

RELATIVE SHIFT IN FOREIGN TRADE FROM 1929 TO 1934, IN PERCENTAGE OF
TOTAL EXPORTS [a]

	To European Countries (other than Germany) with Exchange Control		To Germany		To Other Countries	
	1929	*1934*	*1929*	*1934*	*1929*	*1934*
Austria	51.6	49.8	16.5	14.8	31.9	34.3
Bulgaria	49.9	25.5	29.9	42.8	20.1	31.7
Czechoslovakia	42.5	30.2	19.3	21.5	38.2	48.3
Greece	25.4	20.3	23.2	22.5	51.4	57.2
Hungary	69.0	48.4	11.7	22.2	19.3	29.4
Rumania	45.4	35.8	27.6	16.6	27.0	47.6
Yugoslavia	75.5	59.3	8.5	15.4	16.0	25.0

[a] League of Nations, *Report on Exchange Control*, 1938, p. 53.

trade systems. The agricultural countries of Central and Southeastern
Europe all belonged to the clearing payment group.

Another important point may be emphasized here. Whereas in
trade with the Western countries the majority of the Danubian
debtor nations attempted to maintain or to return later to the free-
payment system, they introduced the clearing-payment plan in dealing with each other practically without exception. Their trade with
Germany and Italy also was organized on a clearing basis.

The system of clearing agreements, which aimed to balance total
payments abroad for all purposes with each individual country,
brought about a fundamental change in the inter-Danubian trade—its
further reduction. The system operated in the identical fashion of a
new quantitative limitation of this trade. The most important item of
trade was the exchange of commodities between Czechoslovakia and
Austria on one side and the five agricultural countries on the other.
There was, further, very significant trade between Czechoslovakia and
Austria; intertrade between the agricultural nations was with some
exceptions of minor importance.

The introduction of the clearing system for all payments meant
that in practice in Czechoslovakia, for instance, the value of the export from Czechoslovakia to Yugoslavia was limited to the value of

export from Yugoslavia to Czechoslovakia, plus any amount invested or loaned by Czechoslovakia to Yugoslavia, and plus the expenditures made by Czechoslovak tourists in Yugoslavia. In the same way, Austria's import surplus was paid for by various other items of the balance of payments.

Returning to the example of Czechoslovakia and taking the balance of trade as by far the most important item in the balance of payments we reach the conclusion that the limit of her export to each one of the Danubian countries was set by the amount of her import from the respective country unless she was prepared to grant new credits. Consequently an increase in export was possible only if she increased her import from the country involved. With reference to the agricultural countries, this could be done either by shifting the import from some other country at the risk of losing export there, or by increasing domestic consumption (even importing for future use as was done in the case of tobacco) or finally by reducing domestic production.

This system of clearing agreements contributed even more to the abandonment of the old trade channels among the Danubian countries than the other factors. The agricultural countries had been accustomed to buy a great part of their industrial goods in Czechoslovakia and Austria, but these two nations had never been in a position, even before the wave of high protectionism, to absorb as much as half of the agricultural surpluses of these five states. This old established trade between neighboring states, operating on a multilateral basis, was replaced by trade with other countries founded on clearing agreements. The agricultural countries were forced to turn to other markets for the goods and commodities which they needed, sometimes receiving goods of inferior quality or nonessential materials.

The trade between the five Danubian states (Czechoslovakia, Austria, Hungary, Yugoslavia, Rumania) had fallen more than 70 per cent from 1929 to 1935, while their combined total trade had decreased only 65 per cent.[15] In percentage of total trade, the figures for inter-Danubian trade show the following development: 1928, 36.3; 1929, 32.3; 1930, 33.5; 1931, 29.1; 1932, 28.9; 1933, 28.9; 1934, 26.7; 1935, 27.5. This was a decline similar to that which resulted from the effects of the creation of the new political and economic order after

15 League of Nations, *Survey of World Trade, 1935–36*, p. 195.

1918. The system of clearing agreements and foreign-exchange control may be considered as an even more powerful obstacle than protectionist policy to the trade relations of the Danubian nations. Improvement in the situation could have been effected only by a return to multilateral trade, based, of course, upon a change of the basic trend in foreign-trade policy.

But during this period the exchange restrictions and the attending factors had become an integral part of the economic, social, and even political system in Central and Southeastern Europe, and as *The Economist* remarked, perhaps too sharply, "The trade in the Danubian valley is a chain of barter and political agreements; even a more liberal currency policy could not revive international commerce in the absence of a political truce." [16] Certainly government interference with foreign trade increased everywhere, and in this area transactions ceased to be a matter to be settled between businessmen. It became, rather, the subject of detailed, rapidly changing governmental directives, justified in the main for monetary reasons, but very often satisfying the demands of various pressure groups.

[16] *The Economist*, Dec. 22, 1934, p. 1196.

6

THE PROBLEM OF PRICE ADJUSTMENT: EXPORT SUBSIDIES

IT WAS extremely difficult to achieve the purposes for which control of foreign exchange and foreign trade had been set up. In many cases the policies controlling different branches of economic activity were in direct opposition to one another. This was clearly illustrated in the adjustment of domestic prices, where revision downward was needed to meet the declining prices in the world markets; yet the import restrictions and various measures introduced to support higher domestic prices had precisely the opposite effect.

During the crisis the value and volume of foreign trade dropped to low levels. The decline was of course felt much more severely in small countries, which depend upon foreign trade to a much greater degree than do large nations. In Czechoslovakia and Austria, industrial employment was directly related to export. In the agricultural countries export not only provided the only means for obtaining raw materials and industrial goods not available in the domestic market, but also affected domestic prices of the chief agricultural products and the purchasing power of agriculture.

The extremely unfavorable development in the foreign trade of each of the Danubian countries was, therefore, of even greater significance than the decline of foreign trade in those countries which possessed greater resources and more completely consolidated national economies. Table 7 illustrates the decline from 1929 to the lowest period in the crisis.

The decline in exports was greater in Czechoslovakia and Austria than in the agricultural countries with the single exception of Hungary, which had been unable thus far to find a substitute market for her exports to the old markets and in particular to Czechoslovakia.

For the correct evaluation of these figures it may be added that the distribution of the total foreign trade of the seven countries in 1929 was as follows: Austria and Czechoslovakia, 59.2 per cent (23.1 and 36.1, respectively), the five remaining countries, 40.8 per cent (Hun-

gary 11.1 per cent, Rumania 10.5, Yugoslavia 8.2, Greece 7.9, and
Bulgaria 3.1). Czechoslovakia's foreign trade and export alone was
greater than that of the three chief agricultural countries, Hungary,
Rumania and Yugoslavia; its marked decline, the sharpest in all of
these countries, together with the great reduction of Austrian trade,
indicate the severity of the effects of the crisis upon this area.[1]

With the exception of Czechoslovakia, who practically lost her export surplus, the balance of trade of the Danubian countries improved. Austria and Greece greatly reduced their import surplus and
the other four countries achieved an export surplus, which they maintained throughout the entire period. The new equilibrium, so far as
it is possible to call it so, was founded on a much lower level of
foreign trade, even taking into account the fall of prices. Each country aimed definitely to increase exports and to reduce, as far as possible, imports. Unfortunately this policy was applied also to the
exchange of commodities between Czechoslovakia and Austria on the
one hand and the agricultural countries of the Danubian valley on
the other, and also to the trade between Austria and Czechoslovakia,
although it should have been evident that the balance of trade could
not be improved by cutting down this intertrade. However, the practice dove-tailed with the high protectionist policy, and was supported
by many arguments. It is not necessary here to explain in detail how
few are the advantages to be gained within rather small economic
units by following a policy which attempts to cover the demands of
domestic production. There were many possibilities, theoretically at
least, of increased or new industrial production in the agricultural
countries; possibilities of increased agricultural production in
Czechoslovakia and Austria were obviously more limited. Greece,
especially, was in a position to increase both agricultural and industrial production substantially with the help of quantitative import

---

[1] The estimates of national income (in billions of national currency) may be used to
complete this picture:

	1929	1934	Percentage of 1929 income
Czechoslovakia	90	56.2	62.3
Austria	7.41	5.69	76.8
Bulgaria	56.2	34.5	61.4
Hungary	5.89	3.54	60.1
Rumania	201	99.3	49.4
Yugoslavia	69	32 (1932)	46.5
Greece	41	30 (1931)	73.1

From League of Nations, *World Economic Survey*, 1938–39, p. 84.

TABLE 7

VALUE OF FOREIGN TRADE (IN NATIONAL CURRENCIES) IN 1929 COMPARED
WITH THE LOWEST LEVELS REACHED IN THE CRISIS

Country		1929	Year of Lowest Level 1932	Lowest Level in Per Cent of 1929 Figure
Greece	Export	6,960	4,576	65.7
(figures in	Import	13,276	7,851	59.1
million dr.) a	Balance	− 6,316	− 3,275	
Hungary	Export	1,038.5	334.5	32.3
(figures in	Import	1,063.7	328.5	30.9
million pö.)	Balance	− 25.8	6.0	
Yugoslavia	Export	7,921.5	3,055.6	38.5
(figures in	Import	7,590.2	2,823.0	27.1
million din.)	Balance	331.3	232.6	
			1933	
Austria	Export	2,188.5	774.7	35.0
(figures in	Import	3,262.5	1,148.1	35.2
million s.)	Balance	− 1,074.0	− 373.4	
Czechoslovakia	Export	20,485	5,483	28.9
(figures in	Import	19,942	5,799	29.1
million kc.)	Balance	543	44	
Rumania	Export	28,960	14,166	48.9
(figures in	Import	29,626	11,739	39.2
million leu)	Balance	− 666	2,427	
			1934	
Bulgaria	Export	6,388.5	2,534.6	39.0
(figures in	Import	8,321.3	2,547.0	27.0
million leva.)	Balance	− 1,932.8	287.6	

a Greek currency was devalued already in 1932.

regimentation, since she was an importer of staple agricultural goods
and had little industrial development.

This policy was coupled, logically, with a tendency to export as
much as possible into the so-called free countries outside the clearing system, where there were no foreign-payment restrictions. As a
matter of fact such export was necessary in order to provide foreign
exchange for the import of vital overseas raw materials and various

other commodities. Clearly this was again of greatest significance to the industrial countries, Czechoslovakia and Austria. But, following the development of industry, the other countries of this area were likewise immediately obliged to consider the problem of providing industry with raw materials not available in the domestic market or in the clearing countries—an obvious effect of the disintegration of multilateral trade. This problem, more than any other, proved the need for price adjustment in a country which must maintain regular export trade with free countries. But the task and the burden imposed on the economic structure of these countries was too great and complex.

They attempted to maintain the original parity (of 1931) of the national currencies and to improve substantially the balance of trade, and endeavored to protect domestic production and to hold the prices of the chief agricultural products even in exporting countries at much higher levels than those in the world market. On the other hand it was necessary to adjust the prices of the outstanding export goods in order to maintain or increase exports on the free markets. There was no consistent policy embodying these principles. Rather, many nonrelated measures were taken, each of them enacted in the hope of solving some particular problem regardless of its effect upon the situation as a whole.

The forces working to maintain prices were definitely stronger than those operating in the direction of price reduction. When we compare price development and indices in some of these countries with similar indices in economically developed countries we are aware both of the imperfection of the indices and the comparison. Obviously the most important problem for countries exporting a limited number of staple articles was to adjust, in particular, the price of these staple commodities (for instance, cereals, timber, oil, tobacco, lard and hogs).[2]

The quantitative regimentation of imports by a system of quotas creates, of itself, a tendency toward increased prices, by limiting competition. In general, the prices of domestic and imported industrial goods were higher in the agricultural nations of the Danubian area than in the rest of Europe. The import restrictions introduced

[2] This question cannot be answered by a simple comparison of price indices, but it is necessary to examine the conditions under which price adjustment of these goods can be made and whether or not the adjustment can be made in time.

here had partially removed foreign competition, in many cases leaving the market completely to the protected national industry. When the quota system was established, providing for a quantitative limit of imports, all incentive for foreign competition was removed, and prices rose still further. Finally, the rapidly expanding clearing system, based upon the principle of bilateralism, deprived foreign trade of one of its most important functions, namely the maintenance of competitive standards. Within a very short time two systems of prices developed: one for export paid for by clearing, and one for export paid for in free exchanges.

There were no forces to counteract these price raising tendencies except, of course, the fall of prices of imported raw materials and other important commodities when purchased at an official exchange rate and sold without extreme profit. We have already mentioned the difficulties of deflation.[3] But in addition, how could it have been possible to bring about price adjustment when, in the majority of these countries, every effort was being made to prevent a fall in agricultural prices and to maintain or guarantee certain prices for the chief farm products, such as grain, in order to preserve the purchasing power of agriculture? Certainly price adjustment of these commodities presented no great difficulty in importing countries such as Greece and Austria (it was rather more difficult in Czechoslovakia), but how could the problem be solved in countries dependent upon their agricultural exports? How could they find a means to maintain their former monetary parity, and keep their domestic price level substantially higher than that of the world market and at the same time continue or increase their exports of these same commodities on the free market? The conviction grew that it is impossible to achieve a large-scale price adjustment. "The world market prices of the most important export commodities of the country had declined so heavily that the domestic price level could by no means, not even by a most drastic intervention, have succeeded in catching up the fall," was the comment in the Hungarian case.[4] Opinions of this sort were supported by arguments pointing out that the possibilities to export into the most important markets were already limited by quotas and other

---

[3] "Deflation was not possible because of the fixed costs of enterprises, costs which in their majority were established according to the level of prices existing before 1929." *Le Commerce extérieur de la Roumanie pendant la periode 1920–1938*, Paris, 1939, p. 13. A rather surprising statement for an agricultural country to make.

[4] *Hungarian Foreign Trade Policy*, Paris, 1939, p. 24.

restrictions and that a price reduction would not increase export. The entire policy moved in a vicious circle and brought about further disintegration in foreign trade.

TABLE 8

GENERAL LEVEL OF WHOLESALE PRICES IN TERMS OF GOLD (1929 = 100) [a]

	March, 1932	March, 1935 [b]		March, 1932	March, 1935
Hungary	81.8	70.2	United Kingdom	57.4	44.2
Germany	72.7	73.4	Sweden	57.7	44.6
Austria	69.6	65.6	Belgium	64.4	52.6
Bulgaria	64.9	54.9	France	70.8	53.4
Czechoslovakia	75.4	63.6	U.S.A.	69.3	49.2
Yugoslavia	67.4	48.0	Switzerland	69.9	61.2

[a] League of Nations, *Report on Exchange Control*, 1938, p. 51.
[b] Between 1932 and 1935 the currencies of Austria, Czechoslovakia and Yugoslavia were devalued.

The differences in the general level of prices, as given in the above table, indicate how much more difficult it was, in this respect, to bring about price adjustment in the Danubian countries than in the free-exchange nations. But an even more significant fact was the existence of higher domestic prices of the leading staple export goods. A bottleneck appeared which had to be cleared: what measures were to be taken to make it possible to export these products at the old monetary parity, and still later at the new stabilized rate? This problem was of major import in the foreign-trade policy of all of the Danubian countries, particularly during the first years of the crisis.

The need for aid for the export of agricultural products had arisen in 1930, before the financial crisis of 1931. It was regarded in the main as a temporary need, for which public subsidies or government export monopoly would soon be supplanted by better remedy.

This brings us to the question of how far an agricultural exporting nation may go in subsidizing the export of its chief agricultural products. Here several wrong conclusions were drawn from Germany's success. She had maintained a fictitious monetary parity, yet had been able to compete successfully in the foreign market. Without entering into a general analysis, we shall try to give some examples of the difficulties involved in export subsidies in agrarian and small, economically undeveloped states.

The Yugoslavian scheme for wheat export subsidies is an extremely instructive case in point. The law of April 15, 1930, provided for the establishment of a special-privileged corporation, known as Prisad (Privilegovano Izvozno Akcieonarske Družstvo), for the management of cereals export. Its purpose was to intervene in the domestic market of the principal agricultural export products in order to improve prices. The corporation received a governmental credit of 50 million dinars. The new organization was unable to prevent the decline of the price of wheat from 250 to 120 dinars per 100 kg. It was estimated, however, that the export subsidy granted under this system in 1930–31 was merely 1,000 dinars per 10 tons of wheat or corn (that is, 10 din. per 100 kg.), which certainly cannot be considered as being a sufficient amount to compete in the world market.[5]

In order to protect the domestic price of wheat (not corn or other agricultural products) a complete wheat monopoly was introduced in 1931; "Prisad" was entrusted with the administration and was obliged to maintain the domestic market price of wheat at 160 dinars per 100 kg. franco Danube. The Liverpool quotation for wheat at this time was approximately 60 dinars, taking the transportation cost into consideration. It was estimated that the Yugoslavian wheat export would be 5,000,000 quintals, a deficit of 500 million dinars under this subsidy system. This was too great a burden for the Treasury to carry. It was believed that the creation of a domestic monopoly would afford a solution. Accordingly "Prisad," as a sole buyer, was to purchase all wheat on the domestic market at 160 dinars per 100 kg., and sell it to the flour mills at 240 to 270 dinars. The profit thus realized was to cover the losses expected from the export subsidy.[6] Unfortunately the actual development differed very much from the theoretical assumptions.

During the first year of operation, 1931–32 (July 1, 1931–June 30, 1932), "Prisad" sold 599,550 tons of wheat (this included stocks from previous years), which represented only 20 per cent of the total amount of wheat in the country. Of this quantity "Prisad" exported 426,880 tons, or 71 per cent of its holdings. Approximately 80 per cent of the Yugoslavian wheat had been consumed, traded on the domestic market, or stored without the direct participation of

[5] Vladimir Pertot, "Die Weizenregulierung in Jugoslavien," *Weltwirtschaftliches Archiv,* XLV (1937), 631.
[6] S. D. Obradovič, *La Politique commerciale de la Jugoslavie,* Paris, 1939, p. 20.

"Prisad" or of any other authority.[7] The price margin on domestic wheat sales—bread, and flour—fell far short of financing the export subsidy scheme. The profit margin, though it amounted to 80–110 dinars per 100 kg. on 172,670 tons of wheat sold to the flour mills, did not, certainly, cover the loss on 426,880 tons exported.

This fact, among others, that only a small fraction of Yugoslavian wheat enters the market was overlooked. The better part is consumed directly by the local population who have their grain ground at the local flour mills for their own consumption. It is not traded on the open market and could not, therefore, contribute to the subsidy plan. This condition would apply to any country of a similar economic structure. In addition, the high price of wheat and wheat flour provided a strong incentive for backdoor markets, where control was very difficult. The minimum wheat price—100 per cent over the world market price—was high, certainly.[8] The failure of the monopoly came, in the main, from the fact that the quantity of wheat entering the domestic market through "Prisad" was too small. It did not provide the broad basis required for collecting the margin needed to cover export losses resulting from the difference between the world market price and the higher domestic price.

According to M. Pertot "Prisad's" losses from wheat export were 336.1 million dinars, of which only 136.9 million dinars were covered by the margin on wheat sold at home; the remainder (about 200 million dinars) was paid for directly by the Treasury. The domestic wheat monopoly was abolished by law on March 31, 1932. Thereafter Yugoslavia supported the domestic price of wheat by export subsidies given to "Prisad" directly by the government. The various preferential agreements in which Yugoslavia was a partner should have eased this financial burden.[9] However, when the government's financial situation did not improve and the basis of the preferential system proved to be very uncertain, the new German trade policy was wel-

[7] Pertot, op. cit., p. 644.
[8] On the average, 45 per cent of the export value was paid for by the domestic producers. The difference between the purchasing price and world price parity amounted to 52.5–57.6 per cent in August–October, 1931. Pertot, op. cit., p. 651.
[9] Austria granted a preferential duty of 3.60 gold crowns for 50,000 tons of Yugoslav wheat. Yugoslavia took advantage of only a portion of this amount in 1932 and 1933 because the Hungarian preference was higher. Czechoslovakia granted a restorno of custom duties of 18 Kc. for 100,000 tons of wheat. The restorno could be applied to a part only of this quantity. France's promise of a custom duty restorno of 30% of the duty on wheat for a quantity up to 10% of total imports remained on paper. Obradović, op. cit., p. 20.

comed as a solution to the problem. M. Obradovič writes, "The question was solved only in 1934 when Germany according to the new commercial agreement started bulk purchase of the Jugoslav wheat at remunerative prices." [10]

This Yugoslavian experience in price adjustment illustrates the difficulties involved in attempting to manipulate the price of just one product dependent upon foreign markets. The exporters of corn and various animal products demanded similar subsidies. But if Yugoslavia had attempted to arrange for export subsidies for these products by taxes imposed on domestic sales of these same products or by price margins through monopolies she would have encountered difficulties similar to those involved in the wheat subsidy scheme. To impose the entire burden upon the government budget would have created an extremely grave problem.

The exporters of animal products, hogs and cattle, urged the Yugoslavian Government to enter into agreement with those importing countries which guaranteed higher profits on a quota basis—quota profits. Again, there were similar attempts to obtain preferential duties. Finally, as in the case of wheat, massive German purchasing of cattle, hogs, horses, meat, lard, eggs and poultry, was the chief factor contributing to the success of the price policy in the animal products field.[11] In spite of the relatively short experience in the system, it can be assumed that it would scarcely have been possible to maintain high domestic prices for agricultural products in Yugoslavia by paying export subsidies from the government budget or by charging high prices in the domestic market. The domestic agricultural market, not identical with domestic consumption, was not large enough for this purpose; only a small part of the agricultural products consumed in the country entered that market. Price adjustment would have led to further increases in the prices of industrial goods or to an inflationary budget. In either case adjustment to the world market would have become more and more difficult.

The situation in the other grain exporting countries was similar. Hungary's policy was to maintain the domestic price of wheat at as high a level as possible. As early as 1930 she introduced the so-called Boletta (grain-ticket) System. Purchasers were required to buy this ticket with each quintal of wheat and rye. The system provided for a bonus to the wheat sellers in the domestic market and the full boletta

10 Obradovič, op. cit., p. 21.   11 Ibid., p. 22.

amount to exporters of wheat and wheat flour. "The development of agricultural prices was thereby isolated from the unfavorable world market price level and at the same time prices were raised." [12]

In the first year (1930–31) the entire proceeds of the 3 pö. per 100 kg. of wheat and rye, which was the price of the boletta went to the grain producers.[13] In the years following the boletta price was increased (to 10 pö. in 1931–32) and the producer received a part of this subsidy (6 pö. as the farmer's share of the boletta was highest during this year); the remainder was deposited in a government fund for agricultural (grain) export subsidy.[14]

During the four years of its existence, the boletta system proved to be a heavy burden on state finance. The income of the Boletta Fund was supplemented from extrabudgetary excises and sales taxes. The original excise duty placed on flour was not sufficient to cover the costs of the system. In order to make up the deficit an excise duty was levied on tea, coffee, and rice, a special tax was placed on textiles and coal, and all cartels were obliged to pay a small registration duty.

Here again we find that the duty imposed upon the domestic sales of grain (a price margin) did not provide sufficient funds for the export subsidy. The primary reason was that the quantity of grain entering the domestic market was not more than the amount usually exported.

The basis for collecting the subsidies needed to counteract the great discrepancies in price was too limited, though wider than in Yugoslavia. Hungary also attempted the use of preferential agreements, which in reality increase export prices. The so-called Brocchi system introduced in Austro-Hungarian relations in 1931 and applied also in 1932 to Italy provided for preferential treatment *de facto* for certain commodities, including wheat and flour. France promised a reduction of customs duties in 1932 on wheat and corn; Germany offered preferential treatment for corn in 1933.

The situation was definitely changed by the signing of the Rome Protocols on March 17, 1934 (see pp. 159 ff.). Italy and Austria, under this agreement, undertook the purchase of large quantities of Hungarian wheat (and flour) at remunerative prices. The Boletta Fund was abolished in 1934, since the price of wheat could be regulated by

[12] International Institute, *Hungarian External Economic Policy*, p. 62.
[13] Ellis, *op. cit.*, p. 111; *The Economist*, July 12, 1930, p. 73.
[14] For a description of the boletta system see U.S. Dept. of Agriculture, *World Trade Barriers in Relation to American Agriculture*, pp. 401–3.

the guaranteed Italian and Austrian purchases and by some other exports. Nevertheless the Hungarian government concluded contracts with several trade and coöperative organizations by which they agreed to maintain a fixed minimum price of wheat whenever the market showed any signs of weakness.[15]

Several other commodities required subsidy, if they were to be sold on the foreign markets. Hungary made a great effort to find new markets in the Western countries for her agricultural products. The "Agricultural Relief Fund," established in 1934, had as its chief purpose the subsidizing of agricultural exports. It was financed by indirect extrabudgetary taxes, and its expenses amounted on the average to 50 million pö. yearly. We could easily calculate what the expense would have been if Hungary had not increased—almost doubled—her exports to Germany in the following years. No subsidy was required for this export since high export prices to Germany were guaranteed.[16]

The Hungarian policy did not aim to adjust agricultural prices to the world market. On the contrary Hungary preferred to detach agricultural prices from the world market and keep them at a high artificial level. The cost of export subsidy was a large item of state expense and was, at the same time, a price-raising factor. The possibility of exporting at higher than world market price to Germany, with no need of subsidy, presented therefore a welcome opportunity to relieve the state budget.

Rumania also wished to prevent a fall in the domestic prices of agricultural goods. To this end she provided subsidies for cereal exports. An export subsidy of 10,000 lei per 10 tons of wheat was granted for the first time in 1931.[17] The system of export subsidies remained as a firmly established feature of Rumanian economy throughout the period; the rates were changed from time to time. In 1934 the government created a fund of 900 million lei for the purchase of high quality domestic wheat. By this means the price of the better grade wheat was maintained between 31,000 and 35,000 lei per 10 ton, and at the same time an export premium was granted on the finest grain sold abroad. In spite of her increased cereal exports to

15 Gordon, op. cit., p. 337.
16 *The Development of Hungary's Foreign Trade between 1930 and 1936,* International Institute, p. 42.
17 *Le Commerce exterieur de la Roumanie pendant la periode 1920–1938,* Paris, 1939, p. 10.

Germany,[18] Rumania made a great effort to place larger quantities on the free markets, which required, of course, government subsidies. These subsidies were continued even after the introduction of exchange premiums; they were administered by a "Commissariat for Valorization" which was replaced in 1936 by a "Central Office for Wheat Valorization." For 1935–36 a minimum wheat price of 34–35,000 lei per 10 ton was fixed, and a wheat export subsidy of 10,000 lei per 10 ton.[19] To meet the expected costs of these subsidies (500 million lei for an export of 500,000 tons) a special tax of 900 lei per ton of the wheat and rye flour was introduced to be collected from the commercial flour mills. The figures of the proceed of this tax are not available. But the government advanced in this year 360 million lei to the National Bank for the Office of Valorization and in all succeeding years this was increased to 400 million lei (or approximately equal to the amount needed for paying the subsidies). The rate of subsidies fluctuated during each year, being highest after the harvest; lower subsidies were paid if the prices on the world market went up.[20] The payment of these subsidies was a charge on the government budget. The government had not considered these sacrifices high and was content with the results thus obtained, especially with keeping prices of wheat at a remunerative level for the producers.

In 1930 Bulgaria established a special government institute—"Chranoiznos" (Institute for the Purchase and Export of Cereals)—delegated to maintain the prices of all cereals, especially of wheat. The method of operation of this institute was to purchase at fixed prices, higher than world market prices, all stocks of cereals offered on the domestic market. Its activities were soon limited to wheat and rye and it functioned as a monopoly for these two cereals, buying them during the great price fall at prices twice or even three times over the market price.[21]

This method of operation led to heavy deficits and the system was changed.[22] "Chranoiznos" had a buying monopoly with regard to the

[18] *Ibid.,* p. 43.
[19] *Bulletin d'information et de documentation,* National Bank of Roumania 1936, p. 193.
[20] *Bulletin d'information et de documentation,* National Bank of Roumania, June, 1938, p. 273.
[21] Constantin N. Bobtcheff, "Reglementation du commerce et politique commerciale en Bulgarie," Paris, 1939, p. 38. Milka Deyanowa, "Die Staatlichen Massnahmen zur Förderung der Ausfuhr der Agrarprodukte Bulgariens," p. 411.
[22] The deficit for the year 1930–31 was estimated to be 350 million leva. *The Economist,* August 22, 1931, p. 357.

producers and a selling monopoly with regard to the flour mills and exporters. It was financed by the consumers through the intermediary of the flour mills. The price paid by the flour mills showed the difference between the price paid to the domestic producers and the price paid by the exporters.[23] Bulgaria's situation in this respect was less difficult than that of the three other agricultural states because the absolute quantity of her cereal exports was not large; it amounted to merely 8–13 per cent of the total value of Bulgarian exports (less in proportion than the fruit exports and not higher than the egg exports).

Keeping prices of a few agricultural products at a higher level by means of subsidies and governmental intervention without question affected the prices of all agricultural goods. The whole idea of keeping the foreign value of the monetary unit unchanged and at the same time maintaining prices of the staple export products on the domestic market at higher than world market prices by means of subsidizing the export of these products at the direct expense of domestic consumption or the government proved, obviously, to be wrong.

The proper conditions for such a price policy were not present in the Danube valley. A comparison with the German system will further clarify this statement. The total German export in the period 1934–38 supplied only 6–8 per cent of the German national income; little more than three fifths of that export was subsidized. German economy was organized on a totalitarian basis and the yearly subsidy amount (750–1,000 million Rm.) was collected in the form of a small quasi sales (turnover) tax paid by all industrial enterprises. This meant that the subsidies were financed collectively on the basis of a developed market economy. The yearly amount of the subsidies did not exceed three per cent of the national income. Even under these circumstances Germany was able to maintain only a fictitious parity of the reichsmark, not its real international value.

The national economies of the agricultural countries of the Danubian area did not offer a similar basis for the financing of subsidies, especially in respect to the domestic markets. A very great proportion of the agricultural goods consumed did not enter the market.

[23] C. Bobtcheff, *op. cit.*, p. 39. Average prices for wheat and rye over a long period are represented in Institute transactions: wheat was bought for 2.70 leva and sold for 3.90; rye was bought for 1.46 leva and sold for 2.50. *The Economist*, March 17, 1937, p. 576.

It is not correct for this purpose to calculate the value of export as a part of total production. The necessary calculation is a comparison of the export to just those goods which actually enter the domestic market. Goods consumed which do not enter the market should be excluded. Both the Yugoslavian and Hungarian experience clearly demonstrated that the proportion of exports to the amount of goods entering the domestic market was too great to allow for the market of the same group of goods to support the export subsidies.[24]

Since the general financial and economic situation had made it very difficult for the various governments to grant large export subsidies, other means were sought to support and encourage export. Exporters were to obtain higher rates than the legal parity for the exchange derived from their exports, but a direct currency devaluation had to be avoided. The first attempt to secure a higher price for foreign exchange was by means of the so-called compensation premiums, "additional export" systems, and other similar devices.

Yet it soon became evident that the necessary price adjustment on the basis of the old monetary unit could not be achieved, in spite of the most severe foreign-trade and exchange control coupled with various export subsidy schemes. Since price adjustment was indispensable, the nations of Central and Southeastern Europe turned to monetary adjustment—devaluation—as the only other solution. Each of the Danubian nations accepted the evidence that devaluation was inevitable. The industrial countries, Austria and Czechoslovakia, felt the need for it more keenly; they were dependent upon the world market for a large part of their exports and were obliged to provide the foreign exchange necessary to pay for the raw materials imported. The agricultural countries, which had experienced greater difficulty in price adjustment of their chief exports, were expanding their foreign trade in the clearing area, particularly with Germany, where they received prices higher than world-market prices.

[24] The situation in Czechoslovakia was quite different. There the grain monopoly could bear the losses sustained by the export of cereals because the relation between the quantity of export to the quantity sold for domestic use was 1 to 10, or 1 to 8.

However Czechoslovakian sugar presented another picture. The quantity of sugar exported was equal to the amount consumed at home. Export was possible only by maintaining the domestic price at three times (or more) the world market price, by completely regulating production and prohibiting expansion of output. Even in this case when the world price of sugar continued to decline it was difficult to keep the proportion of export and domestic consumption at 50 to 50.

7

THE POSITION OF THE INDUSTRIAL COUNTRIES

CZECHOSLOVAKIA

THE NEED for foreign-exchange and foreign-trade control in Czechoslovakia may be questioned. A country with a relatively small foreign debt, extensive foreign trade and a large export surplus, a consolidated financial situation, strong capital formation, and a firm technical monetary position could, perhaps, have followed the example of Switzerland, Holland, and Sweden, and have avoided the use of foreign-exchange control? This much is certain, had Czechoslovakia joined the sterling bloc in the autumn of 1931, and devalued her currency at that time, her position would have been less difficult in the ensuing years. She would not have suffered so severe a decline in her foreign trade and she would have been in a position to withstand the effects of the crisis more easily and to recover from them more quickly. But it is doubtful that she could have avoided the use of foreign-exchange control by joining the sterling bloc. The impact of the crisis upon her economy was no less severe than upon Germany's, though the world was less aware of it. The figures below will illustrate the really serious character of the Czechoslovakian crisis.

The mass withdrawal of short-term credits was a feature common to all countries in the Danubian area. Czechoslovakia was the only member of the group to repay these credits without standstill agreements or moratoria. In the year 1931 alone, she lost approximately 2,000 million Kc. from the exchange funds of the National Bank and the commercial banks. She could not make up this loss by calling upon her assets abroad. Not only were her financial claims (short- and medium-term credit) frozen (mainly in Germany), but increasing exchange restrictions and moratoria prevented her from cashing her export claims. The total of these frozen claims at the close of 1931 was estimated to be between Kc. 1,500 million and 2,000 million Kc.[1] The monetary reserves of the country declined.

At the same time her balance of trade was, of necessity, profoundly changed. The export surplus of 1,354 million Kc. in 1931 did not

[1] *Ten Years of the National Bank of Czechoslovakia*, p. 173.

represent a cash income for the balance of payments, since her frozen claims were greater than the entire surplus. In 1932 Czechoslovakia's foreign trade ended, for the first time, with an import surplus of 144 million Kc.; in 1933 the export surplus was only 23 million Kc. These figures do not indicate the full effect of the change upon her balance of payments, for her deficit with the free countries was even greater.[2] However, her foreign-trade balance shows the gravity of the crisis much less than the really catastrophic decline of foreign trade and its structural changes. Total exports fell from Kc. 20,499 million in 1929 to merely Kc. 5,923 million in 1933—a drop of 71.5 per cent (or to 28.5 per cent). Total imports declined from Kc. 19,988 million in 1929 to Kc. 6,125 million in 1933—70.8 per cent (to 29.2 per cent), which was greater than the 65 per cent decline in world trade during this same period. (The volume of foreign trade showed a 29 per cent decrease.) Unemployment reached its highest level; the number of unplaced applicants for work was 738,300 in 1933 (annual average) compared with only 41,900 in 1929.[3] The national income dropped from Kc. 90 billion to 53.6 billion—or to 59.5 per cent of the 1929 figure.[4] The relation between export and employment was absolutely clear.

The decline in foreign trade was not evenly distributed. Imports from the foreign-exchange control European countries decreased by 72.5 per cent, exports to them receded by 78.7 per cent; imports to the stable-currency nations dropped by 64.3 per cent, exports by 55.1 per cent, and in trade with the free-market countries of depreciated currencies imports declined by 68.1 per cent, and exports by 71.2 per cent. The greatest loss in trade came from the exchange-control group, which included, of course, the Danubian countries and Germany. The total value of Czechoslovakia's exports to these nations decreased to only one fifth of the 1929 figure. The structural changes which took place are indicated in Table 9.

We find that export fell from Kc. 6,476.9 million in 1929 to only Kc. 1,351.3 million in 1933, or to merely 20.8 per cent of the 1929 level; imports dropped from Kc. 3,459.7 million to Kc. 920 million,

[2] Czechoslovakia, as the only nation in this area to continue full payments abroad, had become the dumping ground for imports from all countries since the beginning of the payment difficulties in the autumn of 1931.
[3] The index number of persons employed dropped 100 in 1929 to 75.4 in 1933 and to 75 in 1934. *Statistical Year Book* of the League of Nations, 1941, p. 45.
[4] *Bulletin* of the National Bank of Czechoslovakia, 1939–40, p. 34.

TABLE 9

FOREIGN TRADE OF CZECHOSLOVAKIA WITH THE DANUBIAN COUNTRIES

(IN MILLION KC.)

Danubian Countries	1933			1932			1929		
	Imports	Exports	Balance	Imports	Exports	Balance	Imports	Exports	Balance
Austria	298.5	721.8	+423.3	450.3	1,038.7	+588.4	1,565.3	3,074.0	+1,508.6
Hungary	166.9	190.5	+ 23.6	120.7	201.3	+ 80.6	967.0	1,305.7	+ 338.6
Yugoslavia	230.9	197.4	− 33.5	389.1	404.2	+ 15.1	340.1	1,154.6	+ 814.5
Rumania	176.6	222.1	+ 45.4	334.9	301.8	− 33.1	473.4	769.7	+ 296.2
Bulgaria	47.1	19.5	− 27.6	54.2	63.2	+ 9.01	113.9	172.9	+ 59.0
Total	920.0	1,351.3	+431.2	1,349.2	2,009.2	+660.01	3,459.7	6,476.9	+3,016.9
Greece	41.6	22.9	− 18.6	48.4	28.9	− 19.5	183.3	118.4	− 64.9

or to 26.6 per cent; and the export surplus from Kc. 3,016.9 million
to 431.2 million or to 14.3 per cent of the 1929 level. The 1927 and
1928 figures were very similar to those of 1929: the export surplus
was Kc. 3,070 million in 1927, and Kc. 3,233 million in 1928. The
year 1930 also ended with a substantial export surplus of Kc. 2,397
million from the trade with the Danubian countries; the export surplus in 1931 was Kc. 1,303 million.

The significance of this export surplus will be seen by comparing
it with the total foreign trade balance.

In Kc. million

	1927	1928	1929	1930	1931	1932	1933
Balance with the Danubian Countries	+3,070	+3,233	+3,016.9	+2,397.8	+1,302.9	+660	+431.2
Total Czechoslovak Foreign Trade Balance	+2,174	+2,016	+511	+1,759	+1,349	−144	+23

In each of the years 1927 through 1930 the export surplus derived
from the Danubian trade was greater than the total export surplus;
it was used not only to cover the import surplus with other parts of
the world but also for other purposes in the balance of payments.

This situation was the outcome of historical development. Czechoslovakia (and Austria to a smaller extent) supplied the Danubian
countries with industrial goods. However, Czechoslovakia (even as
part of Austria-Hungary) had never been able to absorb any considerable part of the Danubian agricultural surplus since her own
intensive agriculture supplied her major needs. In the period of
multilateral trade her export was partially paid for by the surplus
export of the Danubian countries with other nations, or, as was the
case before the crisis, by means of their foreign credits. The export
surplus to Austria and to a much smaller extent to Hungary may be
partially explained by the deficit in other items (dividends, profits
from investments, various commissions, and tourist traffic) of her
balance of payment with them. We should also mention the fact that
Austria served as a major reëxport point of Czechoslovakian goods,
particularly to Southeastern Europe.

This entire trade structure changed when the system of bilateral
trade relations based on clearing agreements was introduced. Its effect
upon the Czechoslovakian export to the Danubian countries was

even more severe than the economic dissolution of the Austro-Hungarian monarchy. From 1925 to 1929 Czechoslovakian exports to the area represented approximately one third of her entire export trade (33.1 per cent in 1927, 31.6 in 1929); they dropped to only 22.9 per cent in 1933, and to 20.3 in 1934, or by nearly 50 per cent and have not increased since that time. On the other hand, the proportion of her Danubian imports changed relatively little: 19 per cent in 1925, 17.3 per cent in 1929, 18 per cent in 1932, 15.8 per cent in 1933 and 16.9 per cent in 1935.

Czechoslovakia concluded clearing agreements with Yugoslavia, Austria, Bulgaria, Greece, and Rumania in 1932 and with Germany in 1933. The reasons for introducing clearing agreements with the Danubian countries were always the same: "to insure a settlement of Czechoslovak claims at least in the extent of Czechoslovakia's imports of goods from those countries making limited payments." [5] She could not, of course, gain any advantage through clearing agreements with those countries with which she had had export surpluses in the past. This was one of the chief reasons for her clearing agreement with Germany, which she concluded in order first to reduce and finally to remove her import surplus with that country. That surplus was thought to be too great a burden upon her balance of payments. In 1929 the deficit amounted to Kc. 1,029.8 million and in 1932 to Kc. 774.5 million; by 1933 it had been reduced to Kc. 165.3 million.

The profound change in her trade relations with the Danubian countries compelled Czechoslovakia to reorganize her trade abroad. The reorganization could be effected, of course, only through a long-run development. As already mentioned, Czechoslovakia's exports to the Danubian nations, which had formerly amounted to one third of her total exports, were limited after 1930 to the extent of her imports from them, plus export as a countervalue of various financial payments (as in the case of Austria) or as new credit on investment.

The chief and permanent basis of her Danubian trade was the balancing of exports against imports. In order to export goods to the clearing area and receive payment for them Czechoslovakia was obliged to import the same amount of goods from that area. Since, with the exception of Austria, the greatest part of the export commodities of the Danubian countries were agricultural products, Czechoslovakia's import possibilities were not great enough to support any-

[5] *Annual Report* of the National Bank of Czechoslovakia for 1933, p. 42.

thing like the pre-1930 volume of export. Needless to say, her policy of high agricultural protection had further reduced these possibilities. Thus her exports to the old markets were suddenly and sharply curtailed, with very limited prospects of a new expansion so long as the system of multilateral trade was not reëstablished.

The chief problem was where and how to find the new markets necessary not only to provide employment for her industrial workers but also to enable her to maintain the equilibrium in her balance of payments. The loss of the Danubian markets affected particularly the old light industries exporting mass products. There was little chance of finding export possibilities in other parts of Central Europe, and definitely no chance of receiving an export surplus in free exchange. Czechoslovak exports to Germany declined from Kc. 3,973 million in 1929 to only Kc. 1,045.8 million in 1933 (a fall of 73.7 per cent); exports to Poland dropped from Kc. 887.7 million in 1929 to Kc. 158.6 million in 1933 (a drop of 82.1 per cent). It was clear from the beginning that the only possibility of an export expansion was through a new geographical orientation replacing, if possible, the losses sustained in Central and Southeastern Europe by export to the more distant free-payment countries. In addition it became necessary for Czechoslovakia to change her former trade deficit with the free countries to an export surplus. This was essential, for otherwise she could not purchase raw materials from overseas.

It was, of course, no easy task to carry out this plan especially under the circumstances after 1931. It called for a reorientation of production, and for speeding up the process of shifting from cheap to high-quality products, which could be exported to distant markets on a competitive basis. Price adjustment was an indispensable condition for any possible export expansion in the free markets. However, even after three years of deflationary attempts, Czechoslovakian prices, calculated in gold, were invariably much higher than those of her competitors and of the free market countries.[6] Even if deflation had been technically possible it would have been politically and psychologically impossible for Czechoslovakia to persist in this direction.[7]

Deflation was counteracted not only by a reverse tendency inherent

[6] "The difference between the purchasing power of the Kc at home and abroad measured in gold, manifested itself as a brake upon our exports to the so-called sterling bloc." *Ten Years of the National Bank of Czechoslovakia*, p. 175.
[7] See the author's *Devaluation Experience in Czechoslovakia: Separate Memorandum on the Problems of Monetary Stabilization*, Paris, 1936, pp. 223–231.

in the financial policy of the state but also by the commercial policy of controlling imports, particularly of agricultural produce. The prices of agricultural goods, so far as they were successively detached from the world-market movements, did not follow the world price movement. Prices of exported goods on the free markets had to be adjusted. A higher level of prices of goods exported to the clearing countries had developed, reflecting monetary overvaluation of these currencies and the fact that there had ceased to be real competition in these markets. This tendency continued throughout the entire period—one price system for the free countries and another for the clearing countries.[8]

As in the other Danubian countries, exporters demanded subsidies to enable them to compete on the free markets. The government, however, did not wish to admit the prevalent system of multiple rates for foreign exchange. Czechoslovakia preferred to maintain the transfer of all legitimate current payments abroad and to avoid the creation of blocked accounts which could be sold in the foreign markets or used for the so-called additional export with a substantial disagio. The monetary authorities were very anxious to prevent a disagio of the Kc. on the foreign markets; they succeeded in keeping a real rather than a fictitious monetary parity. This was the reason for permitting the so-called compensation transactions to be used actually only as an exception to the general rule. When the volume of such compensations or additional exports increase the radius of the transactions concluded on the basis of parity declines, the currency is devalued in fact.

Czechoslovakia chose the method of open devaluation, pegging its new parity again to gold. The law of February 17, 1934, reduced the gold content of the Kc. from 44.58 mg. of fine gold to 37.15 mg., that is, by one sixth. The purpose of this devaluation, which was not accompanied by inflation, was to remove the existing disparity between world and internal prices and therefore improve the competitive position of Czechoslovak exports. This was important particularly for exports to the free markets, where there was prospect of expanding trade. On the other hand, export possibilities into the clearing countries, always greater than the payment ability of the

---

8 "The half way deflation, however, did not do away with the conflict between the internal and world price level, the consequence of which was a crisis to export." Annual Report of the National Bank of Czechoslovakia for 1934, p. 9.

importing countries, did not depend primarily upon price adjustment.

Following the devaluation, Czechoslovak foreign trade began, indeed, to move upward. The problem of price adjustment, however, retained its importance. If export expansion were to remain as a permanent policy, the full effect of devaluation on the level of prices must be avoided. The wholesale price index rose from 647 at the moment of the 1934 devaluation to 711 in the spring of 1936, or about 10 per cent in two years; the greatest part of this increase occurred in the first year following the devaluation. However the index for industrial materials and products during the same period rose only 5 per cent (from 667 to 702), whereas the wholesale foodstuff price index advanced from 636 in February, 1934, to 717 in September, 1935, and 718 in March, 1936, an increase of 12½ per cent. The foodstuff price increase may be explained largely by the activities of the Grain Monopoly introduced in July, 1934, "to raise the low level of prices of grains and foodstuffs and to offset the fluctuation of prices, as far as possible to stabilize prices.[9] After the introduction of the grain monopoly, the next step was to improve prices of animal products protected by quantitative import restrictions. Though there was no reason to expect that agricultural prices would fall to a level anywhere near the world market prices quoted after the outbreak of the crisis, the protection of agriculture provided much greater help than prior to it. Czechoslovak agriculture retained its degree of intensity throughout the years of the crisis and the volume of production was actually increased.[10] The prices of important agricultural products became subjected, in large measure, to direct price regulation.

More difficult was the situation of industrial goods, particularly at the time of the market fall of prices on the export markets. Domestic prices of industrial goods could not be fully protected from foreign competition by quantitative import restrictions, especially from the "free" countries. Since Czechoslovakia was trying to increase her export to these countries her use of import restrictions against them was definitely limited; otherwise she would face retaliatory measures and

[9] Annual Report of the National Bank of Czechoslovakia for the Year 1934, p. 93. The Grain Monopoly organized by virtue of government decree No. 137 (1934) was required to purchase grain of domestic origin from the farmers, import grain, flour, and mill products as well as feedstuffs, sell to the first buyer the grain purchased and imported, and sell domestic as well as foreign fodder and export grain to foreign countries.
[10] See the author's *Czechoslovak Economy during the Crisis*, Prague, 1937 (in Czech).

a loss of markets in which she had won an increase in exports and an export surplus. Whereas price development in the agricultural sphere followed the line of great protection from foreign competition, became managed and inflexible, exporting industry continued to meet with strong competition abroad, under heavy price pressure. Consistent price adjustment was obviously handicapped.

The price problem was affected by still another factor. Two series of prices developed in the export field, one for the free markets and one for the clearing countries. The latter were higher in general, for reasons already mentioned; in addition, the fixed exchange ratio in some clearing agreements operated to overvalue foreign currency, with the effect of an export premium which served as an incentive for export and raising prices. In order to speed up the liquidation of frozen clearing balances, current payments with some countries (Rumania, for instance) were gradually transferred from inelastic clearing parities to the elastic framework of sliding rates in accordance with the momentary status of the balance of payments.[11] Nevertheless the rigid parity system was maintained in some clearing agreements, especially with Germany—still the greatest single buyer of Czechoslovak goods; the overvaluation of the Rm. and the payment of high prices for exports to Germany resulted. We find, therefore, that prices for exports to the clearing countries were prevailingly higher than on the free markets; as, even in 1937, the latter represented two fifths of the total export, the difficulties of price adjustment were augmented.

Before the first year after the 1934 devaluation was ended there was a vigorous call for a further step in the same direction or for the attachment of the Kc. to the sterling bloc.[12] The argument was frequently voiced that the degree of devaluation was too small to remove the disparity between the level of prices in Czechoslovakia and in other countries. After the devaluation of the remaining gold-bloc countries in September, 1936, the second devaluation was carried out in Czechoslovakia on October 9, 1936. The gold content of the Kc. was again reduced from 37.15 to 31.21 mg. of fine gold. Taken together, the two reductions effected a 29.99 per cent decrease in the

11 *Ten Years of the National Bank of Czechoslovakia*, p. 202. Annual Report of the National Bank of Czechoslovakia for the Year 1936, pp. 31-32.
12 See the author's "L'Economie Tchechoslovaque depuis la devaluation monetaire," *Revue d'Economie Politique*, Paris, 1935.

original gold content of the Kc., or a devaluation to 70 per cent of its external value.

The tripartite monetary declaration by the United States, France, and Great Britain may be considered as one important reason for the second devaluation. It was interpreted as being the first step toward eventual stabilization of currencies and the removal of the more serious obstacles in the way of foreign trade.[13]

It is certain that the new devaluation brought the Czechoslovak price level nearer to that of other countries of similar economic structure and again eased the position of the export industries.[14] It should be added that throughout the whole period the National Bank followed a very careful credit policy and the government financial policy also remained conservative, in spite of the growing financial demands of the armament program. Among all the countries with foreign-exchange and -trade control Czechoslovakia was most successful in her efforts to bring about a step-by-step adjustment of her price level to that of the free countries. It was done under generally very difficult circumstances, which were aggravated by the existence of quantitative import control and also by the regimentation of a large part of the agricultural price structure.

The task of the Czechoslovak foreign-trade policy was extremely difficult, and yet industrial prosperity and employment depended very largely upon the maintenance and expansion of exports. The following figures should indicate the magnitude of the problem. The value of exports to countries without exchange control fell in 1933 to 37 per cent of the 1929 level, or from Kc. 7,312.5 million to 2,708.4 million, but exports to countries with exchange control dropped to only 23.9 per cent (clearing countries 23.4 per cent) or from Kc. 13,184.4 million to only 3,146.2 million, of which the figures for the clearing countries were Kc. 11,518.9 million to 2,700.4 or a decrease of Kc. 8,818.5 million. In 1929 the clearing countries absorbed more than 56 per cent of total exports.[15]

13 *Ten Years of the National Bank of Czechoslovakia*, p. 191.
14 The index of wholesale prices in terms of gold was 55.6 in March, 1938, as against 63.6 in the same month of 1935. The index in Great Britain in March, 1938, was 55.2; in the United States, 49.4; France, 47.6; Belgium, 54.3; Sweden, 53.4; Germany, 77.1; Italy, 58; Austria, 67.8; Poland, 59.1. The yearly average of the wholesale index (1929 = 100) was 77.2 in 1935; 77.4 in 1936; and 82 in 1937 or an increase of less than 6% in the first year after the new devaluation (calculated in Kc.).
15 By 1933, total imports had declined in value to 29.2% of the 1929 level. Imports from countries without exchange control fell to 33.1%, from those with control to 26.4%.

For reasons already indicated there was little immediate prospect of a substantial increase in exports to the clearing countries as long as the basis of foreign trade continued to be clearing and bilateral balancing of payments. Therefore the greatest efforts had to be devoted to the job of increasing exports to countries without exchange control, and especially to those without trade barriers. Accordingly, Czechoslovak exchange-control policy was adapted to this end throughout the whole period. Payment in free exchange was guaranteed for all imports from countries without exchange control. So far as any restrictions were imposed, the reason was to protect domestic production, especially agriculture. In her relations with the free countries, Czechoslovakia was very anxious to preserve the validity of the most-favored-nation clause—which best suited her economic structure—and to keep an orderly working exchange-payment system.

The foreign-trade policy, the adjustment of prices through devaluation, and a systematic export policy [16] were all designed to carry out the extremely difficult shift in exports needed to replace losses in the clearing countries. After 1933 foreign trade began to increase. Exports went up from Kc. 5,923 million in 1933 to 7,287.5 million in 1934, 7,946.6 million in 1935, and, after the second devaluation, to 11,981.6 million in 1937 or 58.4 per cent of the 1929 figure. Imports increased from Kc. 6,125.2 million in 1933 to 6,391.5 million in 1934 to 6,743.2 million in 1936 and then to 10,966.3 million in 1937, or 54.9 per cent of the 1929 value. In some years foreign trade increased more than world trade but on the whole the Czechoslovak share of world trade declined. More time and more stable conditions in general would have been needed to replace the loss of neighboring markets by exports to more distant ones. The Czechoslovak share of world trade amounted to 1.50 per cent in 1937, against 1.74 per cent in 1929, the share of exports was reduced from 1.84 to 1.60 per cent, that of imports from 1.66 to 1.39 per cent.[17]

No great change took place in the composition of exports. Finished goods retained their leading position with 71.8 per cent of the total

16 No direct export subsidies were given and that indirect support which was given, by permitting private compensation with free countries or so-called additional exports, were very strictly limited in amount; by far the greatest part of foreign trade was carried on at the official rates of exchange. The government did try to help exportation by organizing and subsidizing export insurance, by granting government guarantees for special types of exports (eg. foreign government orders); furthermore, some indirect taxes—sales tax, coal tax, transport tax—were reimbursed on exported goods.

17 League of Nations, *World Trade,* 1937, p. 25.

in 1937 as compared with 71.3 per cent in 1929; the nine-year average
was 71.8 per cent. There were, however, some changes in the structure of imports. The relative importance of raw materials showed a
rising tendency during these years, increasing from 49.1 per cent in
1929 to the highest figure in the whole period since 1920 when it
reached 57.4 per cent in 1937; the nine-year average was 50.8 per cent.
There was no great change in the importation of finished goods—
31.2 per cent in 1929 and 29.7 per cent in 1937, with 30.4 per cent
the average for the period. However, the imports of livestock, foodstuffs, and beverages fell from 19.4 per cent in 1929 to 12.9 per cent
in 1937, with an average of 15.7 per cent for 1934–37. Exports of foodstuffs and beverages also declined, from 11.4 per cent of the total in
1929 to 8.1 per cent in 1937, with an average for the period of 7.7 per
cent (in 1937 exports to Germany increased).

Thus the period is characterized by a basically unchanged export
structure; in imports, an increased share of raw materials and a reduction of agricultural imports, and a minor decline in the importation of finished goods. The importance of industry is clearly illustrated by these figures. But great structural changes took place in the
geographical distribution of Czechoslovak foreign trade, especially
export trade. The figures in Table 10 give very eloquent evidence of
these changes.[18]

Countries without exchange control increased their share in
Czechoslovak foreign trade from year to year throughout this period.
Against Kc. 13,184.4 million worth of exports to the exchange-control
countries in 1929 the free countries obtained only Kc. 7,312.4 million, but in 1937 the latter received Kc. 6,246.1 million and the
former only Kc. 5,725.3 million. In other words trade with free-
exchange countries increased from 35.7 per cent to 52.2 per cent of
total exports, while trade with exchange-control countries decreased
from 64.3 per cent to 47.8 per cent (with the clearing countries alone
it declined from nearly 57 per cent to 38.9 per cent). In 1937 exports
to the free-exchange countries reached 85.4 per cent of the 1929 ex-

---

[18] Similar figures comparing imports for 1929 and 1937 show the following decline (in
million Kc.).
  Total imports: 19,961.2 to 10,965.5.
    From countries without exchange control: 8,314.5 to 6,114.2 (to 73.5%);
    From countries with exchange control: 11,647.7 to 4,851.3 (to 41.7%);
    From clearing countries: 9,182.2 to 3,864 (to 42.1%);
    From Germany: 5,003.1 to 1,700.7 (to 34%).
  Cf. also *Bulletin of the National Bank of Czechoslovakia*, 1938, p. 23.

TABLE 10

MOVEMENT OF CZECHOSLOVAK FOREIGN TRADE IN THE YEARS

1929 AND 1933–37 [a]

Year	Imports in Millions of Kc.	Index 1929 = 100	Exports in Millions of Kc.	Index 1929 = 100	Trade Balance in Millions of Kc.
COUNTRIES WITHOUT EXCHANGE CONTROL					
1929	8,314.5	100.	7,312.4	100.	—1,002.05
1933	2,750.9	33.1	2,708.4	37.	— 42.4
1934	3,272.9	39.4	3,129.6	42.8	— 143.3
1935	3,416.2	41.1	3,426.5	46.8	10.3
1936	4,316.2	51.8	4,193.9	57.4	— 116.2
1937	6,114.2	73.5	6,246.1	85.4	131.8
COUNTRIES WITH EXCHANGE CONTROL					
1929	11,647.7	100.	13,184.4	100.	1,536.7
1933	3,680.1	26.4	3,146.2	23.9	66.1
1934	3,108.7	26.7	4,150.2	31.5	1,041.4
1935	3,322.3	28.5	3,991.6	30.3	669.3
1936	3,598.7	30.9	3,814.1	28.9	215.4
1937	4,851.3	41.7	5,725.3	43.4	874
CLEARING COUNTRIES [b]					
1929	9,182.2	100.	11,518.9	100.	2,336.7
1933	2,475.3	27.	2,700.4	23.4	225.
1934	2,444.2	26.6	3,532.4	30.7	1,088.2
1935	2,662.5	29.	3,293.8	28.6	631.3
1936	2,883.1	31.4	3,224.5	28.	341.4
1937	3,864.1	42.1	4,659.8	40.1	795.7

[a] Annual Report of the National Bank of Czechoslovakia, 1937, pp. 50–51.
[b] Germany, Austria, Hungary, Rumania, Yugoslavia, Greece, Bulgaria, Italy, Turkey, Spain, Latvia, and Estonia.

port value, indicating an absolute increase in view of the lower level of prices in 1937. New markets were won in free countries not only in Europe but also overseas, for example, the United States became with 9.3 per cent of total exports the second largest buyer of Czechoslovak goods, and while 84.2 per cent of total exports went to Europe in 1929 the figure for 1936 was 76.7 per cent—thus the share of the rest of the world rose from 15.8 per cent to 23.3 per cent.

Of first-line importance in the geographical readjustment of Czechoslovak trade was the change in the position of the Danubian countries and Germany. The share of the former (Austria, Hungary, Yugoslavia, Bulgaria, and Rumania), in per cent of the total, was:

Year	Export	Import
1929	31.6	17.3
1933	22.9	15.8
1934	20.3	13.5
1935	22.8	16.9
1936	21.8	15.7
1937	20.3	15.2

or a decline of 11.3 per cent of total exports, or by about one third, while imports declined only 2.1 per cent. The change in Germany's position was also very great. Exports to Germany (excluding seaports) declined from 19.4 per cent of total exports in 1929 to only 13.7 per cent in 1937, and imports declined from 25.1 per cent to 15.3 per cent. Exports to the two markets declined from more than 50 per cent of the total to only 34 per cent.

The greatest increase in exports took place in the trade with the sterling area and the United States, from 23 per cent in 1929 to 31.2 per cent in 1937; further, the exports to France, Belgium, the Netherlands, and Switzerland (the old gold bloc), increased from 7.4 per cent to 13.9 per cent of the total exports and the export to "other countries" (mostly overseas) went up from 6 per cent to 12 per cent.

The whole, undoubtedly, represents a remarkable success for Czechoslovakia's foreign-trade policy, and speaks well for the flexibility of her industry and its adjustment to the changed conditions which called for a transformation of the structure of both trade and production. But if trade with the free countries reached the 1929 level or even surpassed it, it still could not replace the losses suffered, particularly the old markets of Central and Southeastern Europe. The time was too short to effect a greater shift and to achieve the fuller employment of Czechoslovak export industry. In spite of this remarkable export development, the unemployment figures remained high. The annual average of unplaced applicants for work which reached a peak in 1933 with 738,300 unemployed—about 25 per cent of the total number of workers—declined slowly to 622,700 in 1936 and to 408,949 in 1937. The index of industrial production (1929 = 100) fell to 60 in 1933 and only recovered slowly to 70 in 1936 and 96 in 1937. The corresponding figures for Great Britain (86, 106, and 124), for Austria (63, 80, 106), and for Italy (74, 94, 100) show the slower tempo of the Czechoslovak recovery, especially before 1937. In that year the effects of the second devaluation, the increased momentum of armament, and (in the first six months) the improvement in world economy all made themselves felt. Still the national income in 1937 was only Kc. 66.7 billion or 74.1 per cent of that of 1929.[19] But no full employment was possible without a further recovery of foreign trade.

Not only had the large favorable trade balance, for several years the backbone of the Czechoslovak balance of payments, disappeared, but the whole structure of the balance of payments was altered by the system of bilateralism and clearing. There was, in fact, one balance for the countries without exchange control, working on the old multilateral basis, and a separate balance for each of the clearing countries. Only in the first area was it possible to offset an unfavorable balance arising with one country by using the favorable balance vis a vis another country. No such offset was possible in the clearing area. In fact there developed two foreign market spheres with different prices, two trade balances, and two balances of payments. The main effort of Czechoslovakia was to orient her trade towards the free sphere, to emancipate it from its dependence upon the clearing area, with its higher prices, which became economically controlled and later dominated by Germany.

Although Czechoslovakia's position as a debtor country substantially improved because of the great export surpluses, up to 1931, she still had to make payments especially to the free countries, while she herself had claims on some of the clearing countries. The existence of two distinct balances of payments had a serious effect upon the equilibrium of her foreign settlements. Czechoslovakia again achieved an export surplus (after a deficit only in 1932 of Kc. 144 million), which was always greatest right after the devaluation (thus, 898 million in 1934 and 1,005.8 million in 1937). The total export surplus in the trade balance for the years 1933–37 was Kc. 2,706.[20] But dividing this surplus according to the countries with which it was acquired

---

[19] *Bulletin of the National Bank of Czechoslovakia*, 1939, p. 34.
[20] In the period January–September, 1938—the last period of free Czechoslovakia—there was a great improvement in this respect. The total export surplus amounted to Kc. 1,628.8 million, and that with the countries without exchange control went up to 670.5 million, the highest ever achieved and that with the clearing countries to 913.1 million. Annual Report of the National Bank of Czechoslovakia, 1938, p. 28.

gives the following picture: She had for these years a net deficit of Kc. 160 million in trade with the countries without exchange control (in the one year 1929 it was Kc. 1,002 million); with the clearing countries, she had a surplus of Kc. 3,082 million (in 1929 alone, Kc. 2,336.7 million). Her balance with the countries without exchange control had very much improved but the difficult problem of the balance of payments remained.

Out of the favorable balance with the clearing countries, the adverse balance in the free markets could not be paid; for the purpose of the balance of payments these two areas had to be kept separate.[21] Czechoslovakia not only had to import raw materials from the free countries but she had to make various payments to them. Besides payments to Austria and to a minor extent to Hungary based on various claims—income from investment, commissions—the main part of payment for her debt service and other purposes was owed to the free countries. The income items in her balance of payments, such as railway transit traffic, emigrant remittances, and tourist trade, suffered under the impact of the crisis. The amount of these various payments can be illustrated by the following figures giving the payments allocated and actually made to foreign countries for the years 1933–36 (according to the internal statistics of the National Bank).[22] For patents, licenses, insurance, pensions, agencies abroad, and dividends, an amount of Kc. 2,300.5 million was paid; payments for service on, and the sinking funds of, public and private long-term loans, interests on private credits, and repayment of advances totaled Kc. 2,697.7 million; and the withdrawal of foreign deposits, purchases of securities abroad, and inheritances totaled 1,023.2 million—or the three groups together Kc. 6,021.4 million. A substantial part of this payment went to the free countries with which Czechoslovakia did not have an export surplus. It was possible to meet these current deficits only because, first, surpluses from previous years were available and, second, because special funds were raised for this purpose. After 1931, compulsory offerings to the government of foreign assets were repeatedly ordered, which meant the liquidation of foreign securities, or even other assets. These measures gave the National Bank new

[21] Throughout this period Czechoslovak export claims in clearing countries amounted to about Kc. 2,000 million. Report of the National Bank of Czechoslovakia, 1938, p. 33.
[22] Ten Years of the National Bank of Czechoslovakia, pp. 207–9.

funds amounting to Kc. 800 million. It should also be noted here that Czechoslovakia was the only one among the countries of this region whose balance of trade did not improve, but, in fact, deteriorated considerably as compared with the previous period.

It was difficult for Czechoslovakia to be more liberal as to foreign exchange control in her relations with the clearing countries as long as she was unable to bring about a large permanent improvement in her balance of payments with the free countries or at least to obtain a substantial foreign loan to help her through this difficult period. On the contrary she was compelled to introduce a system of export licensing in order to put a brake on the export of raw materials and semimanufactures to the clearing countries. Raw materials purchased in the world markets and semimanufactures were sold, often at unduly high prices, to the clearing countries, which did not have the foreign exchange necessary to buy them on the free market. Thus for the sake of the balance of payments it was necessary to interfere with such a long-established export trade as that in wool and cotton yarns with the Danubian countries, at the cost of reduced employment in the textile industry.[23]

The strain could be removed either by achieving a direct improvement in the balance of payments with the free countries, including the big creditor nations—a change that in 1938 Czechoslovakia was well on the way to effecting—or by discarding the system of clearing and reverting to multilateral trade, with the payment for imported goods in free exchange guaranteed. Of all the countries in this part of Europe Czechoslovakia achieved the greatest shift in foreign trade. Her exports to European exchange-control countries and Germany declined from 61.8 per cent of the total in 1929 to only 41.9 per cent in 1937, whereas her exports to the free countries increased at the same time from 38.2 per cent to 58 per cent.[24] This new orientation could not, however, compensate in so short a period for the losses suffered in the old markets.

Czechoslovakia, after two devaluations, maintained the stability of

[23] To the extent that some of these countries allowed export of their products only against free exchange—not for blocked accounts—there was one important difference: They restricted the exportation of their own products as for instance Yugoslavia, copper; Bulgaria, wheat; Rumania, oil; whereas Czechoslovakia restricted the export of semimanufactures in which the value of imported raw materials represented the greatest part of the price paid.

[24] League of Nations, *Report on Exchange Control*, Geneva, 1938, p. 53.

her monetary unit and continued to pay all her foreign commit-
ments.[25] There were no multiple rates for her currency and no fictitious parity. And, lastly, she steadily tried to extend the number of
countries with whom a system of free payments could be reëstablished. It can be said that together with Austria she formed a bridge
between the free countries and the clearing countries, which were
falling more and more under German influence and control. These
two spheres met in her foreign payments, with the sphere of free payment continually taking a greater share of the total. Czechoslovakia
would not have objected to, or presented any substantial difficulties
for, the lessening or removal of foreign-exchange control, assuming
that the neighboring countries, especially Germany, could have been
persuaded to change the whole system.

AUSTRIA

The structure of Austria's balance of trade and of payments was
very different from Czechoslovakia's. Throughout the postwar period,
Austria maintained a large import surplus, which in 1929 amounted
to S. 1,075 million, or 32.9 per cent of the total import S. 3,263 million). Her exports at that time totaled S. 2,188 million in value. The
average deficit for the four years 1926–29 was S. 1,055 million; in 1930
it was S. 847 million and in 1931 S. 870 million. The total-foreign-
trade deficit for the period 1925–31 amounted to S. 5,937 million (or
$836 million). This shows in itself that Austria's balance of payment
must have contained large credit items other than income received
from export to pay for the great import surpluses.

As we have seen, Austria was a creditor nation, especially in relation to the Danubian and neighboring countries. Besides income
from foreign investments she possessed other credit items, such as the
large transit trade in Vienna, tourist traffic, transit traffic, various services of the Austrian banks and insurance companies, and invisible
export resulting from tourist traffic. Though these items were large
they were not sufficient to cover the permanent, substantial foreign-

---

[25] "The impartial observer will have to admit that the organization of foreign exchange
control and the measures necessary for its successful functioning have not in general
failed in Czechoslovakia." Andreas Predöhl, "Memorandum on the Experiences of
Countries Applying Foreign Exchange Control," in *The Problems of Monetary Stabilization*, The Carnegie Endowment and the International Chamber of Commerce, Paris,
1936, p. 265.

trade deficits. The remainder of these deficits were paid from Austria's new long- and short-term foreign credits, and from the export of capital which, in most instances, took the form of selling Austrian foreign investments. This so-called repatriation of domestic capital from abroad occurred most frequently in the Austrian-Czechoslovakian sphere: Czechoslovakia purchased those shares of her domestic firms which were in the hands of Austrian banks and private individuals. Economically this signified that Austrian consumption on the whole exceeded her income from domestic sources and from foreign investments—a situation made possible partially at the cost of her foreign assets and partially by means of foreign credits. With this in mind it should be apparent that Austria did not need foreign credits to such degree as they were needed by the agricultural countries for purposes of development. In spite of this general economic situation, total adjustment of the Austrian economy to the new postwar conditions was delayed. She became a debtor of the Western countries, while retaining her position as creditor with her neighboring states. The greater proportion of her foreign-trade deficit resulted from commerce with them. In the year 1929, for example (and it showed no great change over previous years), we find that Austria had an import surplus of S. 679 million with Czechoslovakia, Poland, Hungary, Rumania, and Greece, and an export surplus of S. 47 million with Bulgaria and Yugoslavia. More than 63 per cent of the total deficit of S. 1,074 million therefore originated in trade with those countries with which she held the position of a creditor nation and from which she could expect to receive regularly not only income from investments but also substantial amounts from other titles. Her deficit with Germany amounted in the same year to S. 334 million and her surplus with Italy to S. 75 million. Austria's balance of trade with this group of countries, which later formed the bulk of the clearing countries, showed a deficit of S. 894 million or 83 per cent of her total import surplus. The trade deficit incurred with the rest of the world in 1929 was S. 181 million or approximately 17 per cent of the total deficit. The countries maintaining the greatest export surplus with Austria were Germany, with a surplus of S. 334 million, Czechoslovakia with S. 295 million, Poland with S. 185 million and Hungary with S. 167 million. Germany's position in this respect was different from the other countries mentioned. In dealing with them Austria was able to use her different current items in the balance of payment to cover the deficit to a much greater extent than in her relations with Germany. The German investments in Austria were probably not lower than Austrian investments in Germany.

The 1931 crisis (the overt manifestation of which was the bankruptcy of the Austrian Credit-Anstalt on May 8, 1931) reacted rapidly upon the economy of Austria, changing her entire position. During the year 1931 alone, one billion schillings were withdrawn from the country (a sum equal to the entire amount of short-term foreign obligations held by the Austrian banks in 1931.[26] In spite of new short-term credits and the standstill agreements arranged for the greater part of the remaining short-term bank debts in August, 1931, Austria found that she must introduce foreign-exchange control, and did so on October 9, 1931. This measure came rather late, for the flight of capital had already reached substantial amounts.[27] It soon became evident that Austria would be unable to meet all foreign obligations for imported goods and other claims. The National Bank resorted to the institution of various blocked accounts, which obviously merely increased the danger to monetary stability, especially during this initial period of exchange control, by imposing a very unsatisfactory, supervisory mechanism.

In spite of this basically unstable and threatened monetary position, Austria attempted to maintain the old gold parity of the schilling. There was very little hope that an efficient policy of deflation could be carried out to keep pace with the international price movement.[28] The most feasible method of improving the balance of payments was to reduce the import surplus. However, the schilling, on the old parity basis, acted as an import premium, and exports declined more rapidly than imports. Austria favored the conclusion of clearing agreements. This is perhaps understandable from her point of view: as a country possessing a large import surplus, she expected thereby to improve her balance of trade. In some of these agreements her expectations were not fulfilled. The overvaluation of the schilling stimulated imports and reduced exports and new balance accumulated.

[26] H. S. Ellis, *Exchange Control in Central Europe*, pp. 52–53.
[27] For a detailed analysis of the Austrian exchange control see *ibid.*, pp. 27–73.
[28] *Ibid.*, p. 33; Ellis notes that price equilibrium with the gold countries, such as America, persisted until September, 1931. Later the official party quotations did not correspond to the development of the price level as compared with the price development in countries without exchange control.

During this impasse the National Bank willingly permitted an increasing amount of private compensation, concluded on the basis of a premium for foreign exchange and thereby recognizing the devaluation of the schilling. Importers of raw materials who otherwise could not obtain foreign exchange were ready to pay higher prices, and thus the export industry was aided.

Step by step, private compensation became the normal method of buying and selling foreign exchange, creating a new foreign exchange market. By the end of 1932 normal trade was conducted entirely through private clearing, which operated at a rate of 22 per cent below legal parity. The schilling was devalued in fact. The National Bank approved all transactions that were concluded and carried out on this basis. In contrast with Czechoslovakia, Austria proclaimed no formal devaluation or a new definition of the schilling in gold. The devaluation was officially recognized only indirectly when, on April 30, 1934, the Austrian National Bank revalued its gold reserves at S. 6,000 to the kilogram of gold, increasing the old rate of S. 4,715. This meant a devaluation to 78.2 per cent of the old parity or a premium of 28 per cent for gold. This new parity, established by means of private compensation, was maintained throughout the entire period. Unlike Czechoslovakia, Austria did not follow the gold-bloc countries and Italy in their 1936 devaluation. The favorable economic development and the improvement of foreign trade were responsible for this decision, but later events were to prove that it was not entirely correct or wise.

Having arrived at a new external value for the schilling in 1932 and 1933, Austria was then able to work toward the consolidation of the foreign-exchange situation, the restoration of an orderly functioning system of foreign payments and a new equilibrium in the balance of payments.

By 1933 the deficit in her balance of trade had been substantially reduced, and further reductions were made during the following years. This was largely the result not only of her foreign-trade policy, of the system of quotas and many restrictions, but also of the lowered purchasing power of the country. The import surplus for the years 1933-37 amounted to S. 1,510 million—a yearly average of S. 320 million. This was indeed a profound change as compared with the preceding period.

The improvement in the balance of trade was based mainly upon a reduced import. Attempts to expand exports were less successful. In 1933 exports fell to S. 764 million—35 per cent of the 1929 value in schillings—and increased steadily after that date at a slow tempo, reaching 39 per cent of the 1929 value in 1934 and 43 per cent in 1936. The considerable rise in 1937 reflects the general improvement in world trade. In that year exports amounted to S. 1,217 million or 55 per cent of the 1929 value (of the total increase of S. 265 million in 1937, more than S. 150 million went to the clearing countries).

In 1933, Austrian import declined to 36 per cent of the 1929 figure; in 1935 it increased to 37 per cent and in 1937 to S. 1,454 million, that is, only 45 per cent of the 1929 value. Austria's participation in world trade was reduced from 1.12 per cent in 1929 to 0.93 per cent in 1937; imports fell from 1.29 per cent to 0.99, exports from 0.93 per cent to 0.87 per cent.[29] These figures also indicate the improvement of the Austrian foreign trade deficit.

There was no such great structural change in the geographical distribution of foreign trade in Austria as in the case of Czechoslovakia. This may be explained by Austria's position as creditor to the Danubian countries and by her large import surplus derived from trade with them. These factors largely determined the geographical division of her foreign trade during this time of clearing agreements and foreign-exchange control. In view of this position she was not, like Czechoslovakia, compelled to shift her exports from this part of Europe to more distant markets. Europe's share in Austria's exports remained practically unchanged; it was 89.8 per cent in 1925, 89.5 per cent in 1929, 89.7 per cent in 1933, 89.6 per cent in 1936, and it was not until 1937, during a year of great trade expansion, that it dropped appreciably to 86.1 per cent.

From the point of view of bilateral trade and clearing agreements with the Danubian agricultural countries her position was better than that of Czechoslovakia, since she imported a greater quantity of agricultural products from them. In 1937 about 27.8 per cent of her imports consisted of livestock and foodstuffs. In spite of steadily increasing agricultural production, Austria was only 75 per cent self-

---

[29] League of Nations, *World Trade in 1937;* Austria's export in gold dollars amounted in 1937 to 44% of the 1929 figure import to only 35% of 1929 import. *Statistical Yearbook,* 1938–39, League of Nations p. 219.

sufficient in foodstuffs in 1937 as compared with the almost complete self-sufficiency of Czechoslovakia in staple products.[30]

Austria's import from the agricultural Danubian countries (Hungary, Rumania, Yugoslavia, and Bulgaria) amounted to 18.6 per cent of her total import in 1929, and this increased to 23.9 per cent in 1937; her export to these countries for the same years was, respectively, 21.4 per cent and 22 per cent of the total. (Greece purchased 1.4 per cent of her export in 1937 and supplied 1 per cent of her import—no great change as compared to the 1929 figures.) However, during this same period imports from Czechoslovakia to Austria fell from 18.1 to 11 per cent of the total, from Poland from 8.9 to 4.6 per cent; while the percentage of exports to Czechoslovakia declined from 13.5 to 7.2 of the total, and to Poland from 4.8 to only 4.4 per cent.

When we consider the above-named countries as one unit—and Austria held the position of creditor nation with each of them—we find that their share in the Austrian imports in this period fell from 46.6 to 40.5, and in exports from 40.4 to 37 per cent. The drop in export was due to reduced export to Czechoslovakia; the decline in import was the result of greatly reduced imports from Czechoslovakia and also Poland. But the relative position of the Danubian agricultural countries in the Austrian foreign trade was not only maintained but actually advanced, particularly in the import bracket.

Germany's share in Austria's export did not change—15.7 per cent in 1929 and 14.8 per cent in 1937; her participation in the import field declined from 20.8 to 16.1 per cent. As a result of special treaties Italy's share in export increased from 9.0 to 14.2 and in import from 3.7 to 5.5 per cent.

Austria's export to all these countries taken as a whole in 1937 was 63 per cent of her total export, as against 65.1 per cent in 1929. Her imports from them declined from 71.1 per cent in 1929 to 62.1

[30] *Weekly Report* of the German Institute for Business Research, 1939, No. 5-6, p. 17. In 1937 Austria imported 459,353 pigs and 30,325 horses. She was able to meet nearly all the domestic demand for meat which contrasted sharply with the preceding decade when the local livestock industry supplied only one-half of that demand. Her dairy industry had increased to the extent that she now had an export surplus in this field, whereas in former years she had imported considerable quantities of dairy products. *Ibid.*, Supplement, March 25, 1938, p. 2.

Production of wheat in 1931–35 in terms of percentage of the 1925–29 figures was 116%, of rye 116%, of potatoes 111%, and of meat 92%. After that date further expansion was realized. League of Nations, *World Survey, 1935–36*, p. 54.

per cent in 1937 (chiefly a reduced import from Czechoslovakia and, to a smaller extent, from Germany).

These figures prove that there was no substantial change in the territorial distribution of Austrian export and that nearly two thirds of her exports went to the clearing countries.[31] She was less successful than Czechoslovakia in gaining new markets for her industrial products, though it might have been assumed that many of the specialized products of Austrian industry would have found a good market abroad. The export figures do not, of course, include purchases made by foreign tourists in Vienna, amounting to large sums. If the unnecessary and certainly harmful reduction in mutual trade between Austria and Czechoslovakia had not taken place as a result of the protectionist tendencies in both countries, the relative position of the Central and Southeastern European countries in Austria's foreign trade would have remained practically unchanged.

Austria succeeded in cutting down her import surplus from S. 1,074 million in 1929 (32.9 per cent of total import) to S. 236.8 million in 1937 (only 19.4 per cent of total import). An analysis of this surplus in relation to its territorial division will clarify this point further, especially in reference to the balance of payments. In 1937 the Austrian balance of trade with the above-mentioned group of debtor countries showed an import surplus of S. 173 million (in 1936, when the total import surplus was S. 295 million, the deficit realized with this group amounted to S. 188 million). Austria had a sufficient income from various other items of the balance of payments at her disposal for the payment of these imports. She was not obliged to make payment in free exchange, but on the other hand, neither could she receive payment in free exchange for any possible surplus in the balance of payments with these countries. The very nearly permanent position of Austria's credit balance in the clearing accounts with these countries in the last years indicates that the bilateral balance of payments with them would have allowed for an even greater import surplus from them, and would have permitted mutual trade expansion. Austria's import surplus with Germany in 1936 was S. 58 million, in 1937 S. 54 million; on the other hand her export surplus with Italy

[31] The League of Nations *Report on Exchange Control*, p. 53, gives the percentage of Austrian export to other than European exchange control countries as 35.7% in 1937 as compared with 31.9% in 1929.

amounted to S. 70 million in 1936 and S. 93 million in 1937. Her large credit balance in the clearing account with Germany showed that, in this instance also, Austria was able to settle her import deficit without paying in foreign exchange.

Taking this entire group of clearing countries as one unit, we find that Austria's import surplus amounted to S. 196 million in 1936 and to S. 134 million in 1937, as compared with S. 894 million in 1929—a decline to about one sixth. Austria's deficit with the rest of the world was S. 119 million in 1936 and S. 104 million in 1937, as against S. 281 million in 1929—a drop to about 37 per cent. Austria carried out a much greater reduction proportionately in her deficit with the clearing countries and with her debtor nations than with her creditor countries. She believed that she had solved the problem of equilibrium of the balance of payments because the appreciably reduced deficit in her trade with the free countries was offset by income from various services, especially transit traffic, tourist traffic, and transit trade,[32] which, of course, had to be drawn upon also for foreign debt service.

The movement of the gold and foreign-exchange reserve of the Austrian National Bank reflected the improvement in the balance of payments. The second half of 1932 and of 1933 saw the lowest ebb (between S. 190 and 200 million); the first rise, in 1934, reached S. 287 million in December. It allowed for the successive liquidation of the foreign blocked accounts, which was nearly completed during 1934, and beginning with May, 1935, Austria renewed, after three years of moratoria, full transfer on all funded foreign liabilities. She was able, also, to carry out the principle of remitting payment for all legitimate claims. The total amount of Austrian foreign debts in foreign currencies, calculated in schillings, was substantially reduced; this resulted chiefly from the devaluation of the pound, of the dollar (the dollar devaluation accounted for a reduction of S. 568 million) and of the gold-bloc currencies; further reduction of the debt burden came from the conversion of the 1932 League of Nations Loan from 6, 6½, and 7 to 4½ per cent. The foreign-debt service, which required more than S. 250 million in 1932, was reduced to less than half of this figure.

In spite of the renewal of the foreign-debt service and of the deficit in foreign trade the development of the gold and foreign-

[32] *Weekly Report* of the German Institute for Business Research, March 25, 1938, *Supplement*, p. 4.

exchange reserve was favorable; it reached S. 400 million at the end of 1937, not including rather large amounts which were not a part of the legal reserve. Though a consistent flight of capital resulted from uncertainty of political prospects, the reserves continued to increase. This favorable development of the Austrian balance of payments made possible the steady relaxation of exchange control. But it is not accurate to speak of a free exchange system in Austria, as is frequently done.[33] Austria, also, operated two systems of control, one in her relations with the countries with exchange control and one with the free countries. The control allowed for no payment in free exchange with the countries in the first area; it prohibited the use of the proceeds of import from a clearing country for payment in free countries. Further, all payments abroad were subject to the license issued by the National Bank.

Obviously Austria was obliged to follow an extremely liberal course in the matter of exchange control if she wished to maintain Vienna's intermediary business position in the Danubian Valley. This was particularly true in the transit reëxport trade, and in the insurance and banking business.

On the whole she succeeded, within a relatively short time after the first years of her unsettled position in foreign exchange, in reestablishing an orderly system, which afforded reasonable security and in which foreign confidence could again be placed. Her conservative financial policy, aiming at a balanced budget, and the firm credit policy on the part of the National Bank should have contributed to the readjustment of the domestic price level to that of the international markets. However, this policy lacked the support of price development in trade with the clearing countries; the price-determined free sector represented the smaller fraction (substantially smaller than in Czechoslovakia). Though Austria attempted to abandon the principle of fixed parities and to leave exchange rates to the free agreement of trading parties she was not wholly successful. Accordingly, the ratio Rm. $1 =$ S. 2 was retained in the clearing with

[33] H. S. Ellis, *op. cit.*, p. 47: "Austria's withdrawal from all but rudimentary exchange control constitutes a unique chapter in monetary history"; and p. 57: "Nevertheless, the exchange control laws were never revoked and some of their provisions were still enforced such as . . . of remitting abroad without permission of the National Bank." And he concludes that what had been achieved was, in fact, simple exchange control to prevent capital flight. To this we should add the whole clearing system. Therefore this simple exchange control was applicable only to the smaller sector, *i. e.*, trade with the free countries.

Germany, which was only slightly below the legal fictitious parity of the reichsmark.[34] Again, the entire clearing area traded on a higher than world market level of prices. Further, the development of agricultural prices was another obstacle in the way of a greater price adjustment. The general level of wholesale prices in gold (1929 = 100), which was 65.6 in March, 1935, rose to 67.8 in March, 1938; during the same period the Czechoslovak index declined from 63.6 to 55.6 [35] and that of Switzerland from 61.2 to 54. (The wholesale total price index declined, in schillings, from 130 in 1929 to 113 in 1937; the cost-of-living index fell from 111 to 105.) It is possible that a further devaluation carried out simultaneously with the gold-bloc countries, Czechoslovakia and Italy, would have brought about a fuller and more rapid price adjustment.

Industrial production in Austria recovered to a greater degree and more quickly than her export trade. The great reduction of imports acted as a stimulant to the creation of new industry and to the expansion of existing plants. The index of Austrian industrial production, including capital and export goods only (1929 = 100), reached its lowest level of 61 in 1932, rose to 86 in 1936 and to 106 in 1937 (the Czechoslovakia index at this time was 96).[36] The number of unemployed to receive relief was rather great in 1929 (the monthly average being 164,000); it increased to 329,000 in 1933 and declined to 232,-000 in 1937—or an increase of only 68,000 over the 1929 figure.

On the whole, Austria made great progress in economic recovery and in economic adjustment, particularly in 1937. Her task was made more difficult by the fact that the process of a real adjustment was delayed until after 1931 when it should have been started immediately after 1922. Moreover, during the years immediately preceding the Anschluss many persons both in and outside [37] of Austria were very doubtful as to her political future, and Nazi propaganda and activity increased from day to day. This was certainly not the atmosphere to

---

[34] At the old rate of exchange the Austrian price level was considerably beneath the German price level. This is admitted even by the German Institute for Business Research in its *Weekly Report*, No. 11–12, 1938, p. 24.

[35] League of Nations, *Report on Exchange Control*, 1938, p. 51.

[36] Established by the Oester Institut für Konjunkturforschung. League of Nations, *World Production and Prices*, 1937–38, p. 44.

[37] As early as 1933 we find this statement in *The Economist* (April 8, p. 721): "Without the creation of a Danube Federation it is merely a question of time for Austrian independence to fall victim to Hitlerite Germany." Similar statements were made from various sources throughout the whole period.

encourage new investments or a long-term economic program, particularly in Vienna, where the Jewish element, so prominent in business, became extremely apprehensive of the Nazi menace. Bearing these factors in mind we may more readily appreciate how much was actually achieved.

Austria would certainly have welcomed a return to multilateral trade and the abandonment of clearing agreements. However, since her trade with the clearing countries represented more than 60 per cent of her total trade it was very difficult for her to free herself from all the clearing limitations, especially when nearly 30 per cent of her export went to the two large clearing countries of Germany and Italy. She was less successful than Czechoslovakia in shifting her export to free countries. She continued to be more dependent upon her neighbor markets and Central and Southeastern Europe. Those markets (including Poland and Switzerland), absorbed nearly 70 per cent of her export. But in spite of this close relationship and her position as creditor, in 1937 her import from the agricultural countries of the area was only 56 per cent of her 1929 import (S. 361 million rather than S. 641 million). In contrast, Czechoslovakia's import from these countries in 1937 was 62 per cent of the 1929 amount. In view of the greater proportion of Austrian agricultural import and her more favorable commercial relations with Hungary one would have expected that her relative share would have remained at a higher level. There is no doubt that agricultural protection resulted in the reduction of import and the decrease of Austrian export. This link was clearly evident in the clearing-agreement system. In general a further devaluation of the schilling and a more liberal financial and credit policy at home could have been instrumental in improving the situation still further both in foreign trade and in domestic production.

8

MONETARY ADJUSTMENTS IN THE AGRICULTURAL COUNTRIES

IT WAS very difficult for the agricultural countries to effect a clear adjustment of internal prices or of the external value of their national currencies. As explained in the previous chapters, there was a tendency to maintain higher prices of agricultural products in the domestic markets than in the export market, although these products were a major type of exports. At the same time the prices of industrial goods increased as a result of the growing policy of protection. The problem of foreign debts was not settled and the existence of various foreign blocked accounts was an added obstacle in the way of stabilizing the exchange rates.

The idea of monetary adjustment through devaluation was avoided because, among other reasons—the desire to avoid the psychological repercussions and the effects of increasing the burden in terms of national currency of foreign obligations expressed in foreign currencies —it was thought that "the difficulties of export are mostly of such a character as cannot be removed by the change in the exchange rates." [1] Greece, was, in this respect, an exception. Higher exchange rates were regarded as a premium which should, in time of crisis, make possible the export of commodities that otherwise could not compete in foreign markets. A system of compensation export premia was introduced about 1932 in the four countries: Hungary, Rumania, Yugoslavia, and Bulgaria. Exporters of certain commodities which could not be sold abroad without subsidies obtained a foreign-exchange premium, which generally was paid by the importers of raw materials. This was, in fact, an external devaluation of the national currencies concealed by the term "compensation premium" and limited at the beginning to specified commodities or to exportation to particular countries. However, it was discovered very soon, that under such a system the greatest part of exports come to require compensation premia, that is, a higher price. Exportation with a premium tends to become the rule, exportation without it, a rare exception; and such a general in-

[1] Annual Report of the National Bank of Hungary, 1932, p. 14.

troduction of compensation premia—in the later stages not linked with any particular transaction—is identical with a depreciation of the external value of the national currencies. It was several years—generally not before 1935—before the confused and unsettled exchange rates were reorganized into a somewhat orderly, working system. Hungary and Bulgaria retained throughout this period the fiction, as did Germany, of keeping the old parities although their currencies were in fact depreciated. We shall limit ourselves to a brief survey of these monetary adjustments.

HUNGARY

The extremely comprehensive and strict system of exchange control built up by Hungary became a powerful instrument of government intervention not only in matters of foreign trade but also in the whole internal economy.

When exchange control was introduced, it was emphasized, as in other countries, that its ultimate aim was the maintenance of the pengö—parity. The policy was carried out energetically and with determination, yet as early as the second half of 1932 the unfavorable developments in the clearing accounts, the shortage of raw materials, and the increasing export difficulties, because of the high prices in Hungary, called for a change. A remedy was sought in the organization of a special compensation system; a "Compensation Office" was established to set up a list of commodities that could not be exported without a compensation premium and to determine the size of the premium required to make exportation possible. Eighty per cent of the foreign exchange received from subsidized exports was supplied to raw-material importers who furnished the premium and agreed not to increase the prices of industrial goods.[2] In addition, a system of so-called additional export premia was also introduced. In cases where, because of the relatively high domestic prices, certain exports could not be marketed abroad, the National Bank permitted the purchase of such goods out of the pengö balances of foreign exporters arising from sales to Hungary, and later also out of blocked short-term credits and other claims. This meant in effect the repayment of foreign debts at even substantially lower rates.

These compensation export premia were varied according to coun-

[2] *Ibid.*

tries and articles. Different compensation premia were permitted for different commodities and markets, because, it was asserted, the differences between prices in Hungary and those abroad varied according to countries and articles.[3] Introduced first in trade with the free-exchange countries this system was soon expanded to include the clearing countries also. It meant, of course, the complete disintegration of the external value of the pengö. Compensation rates, additional export rates, various secret rates granted in special cases became a part of the daily foreign-trade practice. As H. S. Ellis wrote aptly "literally thousands of rates came into being." [4] Nevertheless in spite of such export subsidies and a very determined effort to increase Hungarian exports to the so-called free markets, exports to the clearing countries increased from 57 per cent of the total in 1932 to 68 per cent in 1933 and 79 per cent in 1934.[5]

The whole system of multiple pengö rates became increasingly complex and more and more difficult to organize and supervise. Hungary made clearing agreements even with a number of countries which did not have exchange control. The share of her trade which was free of such exchange restrictions was therefore very small. The rates always showed a tendency to go up, and the danger arose that the steady expansion of the system of premia might undermine, as it was put, "the purchasing capacity of the pengö." One of the inevitable effects of this system of subsidies was, of course, that a product with a high cost of production, as measured in terms of an international standard, enjoyed a relatively large premium, while a smaller premium, or no premium at all, was paid on a commodity with a low cost of production.[6]

Toward the end of 1935 Hungary developed a simpler and more orderly system of premia, in a threefold division: [7] (a) A uniform premium to be applied to that segment of transactions involving foreign exchange of unlimited availability—exchange of the so-called free

[3] See Governor B. Imredy's "Address to the Annual Assembly of the Hungarian National Bank," *Annual Report,* 1936, pp. 28–30.
[4] Ellis, *Exchange Control in Central Europe,* p. 84.
[5] Figures from the Annual Report of the Hungarian National Bank, 1932, 1933, 1934.
[6] To a certain extent this system was similar to the German export subsidies, paid from a special fund; but with this difference: that the German subsidy fund was raised from a sort of general turnover tax and not from a higher price paid for the *devisen* needed for raw material imports.
[7] Imredy's "Address," p. 28.

countries; this premium was 50 per cent for exports and a 53 per cent surcharge for imports, that is, the equivalent of a devaluation of 35.5 per cent. (b) A uniform but somewhat lower premium (38 per cent for exports and 41 per cent for imports) was established for the countries which had clearing agreements with Hungary; these included France, Belgium, Switzerland, and Turkey. (c) In commerce with certain countries having foreign-exchange restrictions similar to the Hungarian, the compensation of the received means of payment or of the goods themselves was introduced which should have meant an approach toward the establishment of a balanced situation according to the natural laws of economic life. There was no economic reason for not calling these countries, representing the greatest part of Hungary's foreign trade, clearing countries too, for this kind of compensation was virtually another name for clearing. The rates applied to Germany were 18 per cent and 19 per cent, to Austria 10 per cent and 13 per cent; with other countries they were fixed only for a specified period or for a certain volume of trade and changed often *ad hoc*.[8] This step aimed at the unification of the premia, or something similar to a clear devaluation of the pengö, but at the same time it allowed greater flexibility than would have been possible with open devaluation.

There is no doubt that the new measures improved Hungary's foreign trade. Nevertheless the situation still remained complicated. The full devaluation—the 50–53 per cent premia—applied to only a very small fraction of Hungarian foreign trade. In 1936 the free foreign exchange obtained from exports amounted to only 17.3 per cent of the total.[9] More than 80 per cent of Hungary's total foreign trade was, at that time, subject to clearing or compensation. Furthermore, the premia, particularly in the trade with countries having exchange control, changed frequently, and the real rates in many of the compensation transactions were not even known, but there are many indications that they were not always the same and that special motives may have brought about the granting of higher premia. A further indication of the irregular nature of the situation was the fact that the

[8] The rates for Italy were 40% and 43%, for Czechoslovakia 40% and 41½%; after the 1936 devaluation the rates for France and Switzerland were increased to 50% and 53%, the same as for the other freely convertible exchanges, for Italy to 47% and 48½%, for Czechoslovakia to 45% and 46½%. The increase of the premia was to have substantially counterbalanced the effects of the devaluation of these currencies. Annual Report of the Hungarian National Bank, 1936, p. 10.
[9] Ellis, *op. cit.*, p. 121.

ratios between the various exchange rates of foreign currencies as expressed in pengös did not correspond to their parities on the international exchange markets.

The new system remained in operation throughout the period; Hungary refused to carry out an open devaluation or to establish a new parity, but instead officially retained the gold pengö. Although the 1935 reform of the compensation system brought more clarity and more order into the whole foreign-exchange organization, it did not completely remove the multiple rates nor did it restore that security and confidence which is essential to the smooth functioning of foreign trade. The whole system was far from simple, and it did not give promise of any long-term stability.

As a consequence of the Hungarian foreign-exchange policy there was less emphasis upon the adjustment of the domestic prices to the international markets than upon an effort to overcome the difference between the internal and foreign prices for Hungarian exports. In fact, throughout this period the general level of wholesale prices in terms of gold remained not only much above the level in the free-exchange countries but also above that of the exchange-control countries. In March, 1935, in Hungary this index was 70.2 (1929 = 100) against 57.6 in Rumania; in March, 1938, the Hungarian figure was 77.7, the Rumanian, 56.8. In 1935 the index of Hungarian export prices in gold was 65.2 (1930 = 100) while that of Yugoslavia was 52.9; the corresponding figures for 1936 were 59.7 and 57.1 respectively.[10] In 1937 the Hungarian cost-of-living index in terms of pengös exceeded the 1931 level. In order to effect a real adjustment of prices a further devaluation of the pengö would have been necessary. In spite of the de facto devaluation the pengö remained overvalued. Hungary could hardly have reëstablished a system of trade free of clearing and quotas without a thorough readjustment of the whole price structure.

BULGARIA

The chief aim of exchange control in Bulgaria, as elsewhere, was to avoid a devaluation of the external value of the leva.[11] The Bulgarian

10 League of Nations, *Report on Exchange Control*, 1938, pp. 51 and 50.
11 A. Tchakaloff, head of the Research Department of the National Bank of Bulgaria, and Dr. S. Zagoroff give the following argument against devaluation: There was no reason to hope that a devaluation could increase confidence in Bulgaria's economic position. An increase in foreign debts in leva would have been a considerable burden upon

balance of trade in 1929–31 was more favorable than that of other Danubian countries; the value of exports declined only 3 per cent in 1930 as compared with 1929 and 6 per cent in 1931 compared with 1930. The general wholesale price index dropped from 3,304 in 1929 to 2,206 in 1931 and to 1,730 in 1933 or to 53 per cent of its 1929 level. There was a real fall of prices. Until June, 1933, the official exchange rate of the leva was applied to all transactions, but at that time the National Bank began to approve private compensations in foreign trade transactions. The reason for these compensations was the same as in other countries—to overcome, by paying a higher price for foreign exchange, the difference between domestic and foreign prices and in this way to facilitate the export of Bulgarian goods.

Originally compensation was allowed for only a very limited number of goods.[12] The list of commodities for which compensation agreements were allowed was steadily expanded while the amount of premia tended to rise continually. Exports were very often initiated by the importers who needed foreign goods. A special feature of the Bulgarian system was that the exporter was compelled to surrender to the National Bank at the official rate a certain percentage of the foreign exchange; this was to be used in the service of foreign debts and other payments abroad.

The introduction of exchange premia helped to increase Bulgaria's exports and her foreign trade in general. With the expanding volume of compensation transactions the National Bank, in August, 1934, issued a special set of rules which illustrate the working of the system. Export commodities were divided into four groups according to the conditions of payment. The percentage of foreign exchange to be delivered to the National Bank was fixed at from 50 per cent for goods which could be marketed abroad with relative ease down to 20 per cent and 30 per cent for some other goods; for still other exports, which were very difficult to sell abroad, no surrender of exchange to the National Bank was required. The premia applied to the total proceeds. The percentage of the foreign exchange to be surrendered to the National Bank determined the real rate of premium. In 1936 the four lists were replaced by a single list covering an enlarged field of goods

the public finances. The fear that devaluation would tend to destroy the balance of the government budget rather than to improve the balance of payments prevented the use of such a policy. (From International Institute, *Le Contrôle des changes en Bulgarie*, 1939, p. 51.)

[12] *Ibid.*, p. 16.

subject to private compensations. The National Bank was, in effect, authorized to license imports either within or in excess of the normal quotas and to permit the payment of commercial and financial debts against the exportation of Bulgarian products or against other claims abroad. Under the new arrangement the percentage of free foreign exchange to be turned over to the National Bank at the official rate varied greatly. The National Bank endeavored in June, 1936, to stabilize the exchange premium and fixed a maximum of 35 per cent (a 26.5 per cent devaluation).

Thus the introduction of the system of premia was identical with an unofficial and partial devaluation of the leva. It was not, however, a uniform devaluation, but a complicated system of multiple rates, whose chief aim was the expansion, or maintenance, of exports by a type of subsidization. The rates of premia depended both upon the kind of foreign exchange involved—a higher premium being paid for free than for clearing exchange—and also upon the kind of export in question.

In various sectors of the balance of payments, divided according to countries and commodities, the parity of the leva was determined differently, but an attempt was made to stabilize the disagio (exchange premium) within each sector.[13] Nevertheless, it would be extremely difficult to determine the ratio of the devaluation of the leva. The premium paid on the British pound in 1936 and 1937 was 33 and 37.5 per cent, respectively. There was, of course, a different, generally lower, level on the clearing exchanges.

Bulgaria concluded clearing and various payment agreements not only with the countries with exchange control but also with Switzerland, Holland, France, Belgium, Sweden, and Finland,[14] so that the proportion of payment in free exchange was small. Throughout the whole period between 70 per cent and 84 per cent of the foreign trade was paid for in clearing accounts. The exchange premia in this segment of the balance of payments varied, and for the reichsmark, in which nearly one half of the total foreign trade was paid, there was no premium.

Bulgaria maintained the fiction of the old parity, and had a complicated system of multiple rates which were not adjusted among them-

---

[13] Tchalakoff, *op. cit.*, p. 52.
[14] See Constantin N. Bobtcheff, "Reglementation du commerce et politique commerciale en Bulgaria," (1939), p. 66. Tchakaloff, *op. cit.*, p. 65.

selves so as to agree with the quotations on the international exchange markets. It was relatively easy to carry out a strict system of exchange control: the structure of the economy was simple; foreign trade was concentrated in the hands of a rather small number of businessmen; and large segments of the trade were handled by cooperatives or even under direct government supervision. Exchange control with all that it implied, including the system of premia, became an instrument of a completely and absolutely managed foreign trade. Nevertheless, the multiple exchange rates with their potential frequency of change prevented the establishment of an orderly system of foreign payments; there existed a great deal of flexibility but not enough confidence in stability. An open devaluation of the leva relative to all currencies starting with the highest rate of indirect devaluation [15] (35 per cent premium) was considered a necessary prerequisite for the return to a free system of foreign trade and a smoothly functioning system of foreign payment.

RUMANIA

Rumania was the last of the Danubian countries to introduce exchange control—nearly a year after the other countries had done so. She hoped that, because of her substantial export surplus and the strong reserve position of the National Bank, she would be able to retain a policy of free exchange. However, this optimism was not justified by subsequent developments. The withdrawal of foreign credit, the problems of price adjustment, internal credit and bank difficulties, and the volume of foreign debts induced her to establish exchange control, but not, perhaps, until it was already too late. She could not prevent numerous frozen foreign accounts for imports and other claims, which arose as a difficult problem at the very beginning of the control.

Rumania, too, aimed at the maintenance of the legal parity of her currency.[16] However, she did not succeed in organizing a simple, efficient and smoothly operating system of control. In particular she failed

---

[15] Tchakaloff, *op. cit.*, p. 25. The general level of wholesale prices in terms of gold increased in February, 1938, to 62.7% against 59.9% in March, 1935, or by more than 14%. League of Nations, *Report on Exchange Control*, 1938, p. 51.

[16] Even in the 1934 Annual Report of the National Bank of Rumania there is the remark: "The Bank continued during 1934 the policy of maintaining the legal stability of the leu. We consider this policy one of the chief tasks of our activity." *Bulletin*, National Bank of Roumania, 1935, p. 58.

to maintain payment in free exchange to those countries without exchange control, but, on the contrary, concluded clearing agreements with a number of them—France, Switzerland, Holland, Belgium—and arranged a payments agreement with Great Britain and clearing agreements with Poland and Italy at a time when both of these countries belonged among those nations paying in free exchange. Although in most of these agreements Rumania secured payment for a specified percentage of her exports in free exchange—to be used partially for the service of Rumanian debt in these countries—the system proved to be advantageous neither for the expansion of foreign trade nor for the improvement of the monetary situation. Throughout the whole period the Rumanian exchange-control system was one of the most complicated, with very frequent changes; consequently it did not furnish the stability and confidence needed for foreign trade.

In the later years of this period, political instability and sudden radical changes of regime—extreme in some cases, as in the Goga period—made the situation even more complex. The flight of capital could never really be stopped and was relatively more serious than in some other countries. The feeling of political instability, the policy of economic nationalism directed against foreign investment (that is, against the oil industry), the policy toward minorities, such as the at first concealed and later overt antisemitic measures, and the rather inefficient controlling mechanism all worked in the same direction.

Comparatively soon after the establishment of exchange control there arose a shortage of various raw materials and imported industrial commodities. The supply of foreign exchange did not increase and the export surplus decreased in 1933 and, especially, in 1934. The exchange restrictions, originally less stringent than in some other countries, increased steadily in severity without any visible improvement, and the price adjustment was inadequate and too late. From January to December, 1934, the wholesale price index rose from 1,860 to 2,096 but the average value of one ton of exported goods fell in 1934 to 1,538 lei against 1,614 lei in 1933. "Industrial production recovered because of the lack of foreign competition due to the import and exchange restrictions" with an increase of prices as an accompanying feature.[17] Various steps were taken to improve the foreign trade situation, but constant and sudden changes,[18] which were some times retro-

[17] Roumanian National Bank, Annual Report for 1934, *Bulletin*, 1935, p. 53.
[18] There were no less than 25 changes in the restrictions upon foreign trade and the exchanges during 1934 and 1935. See *The Balkan States*, Oxford, 1936, p. 89.

active, made it extremely difficult. Uncertainty prevailed, not only as to long-term contracts but even as to regular foreign trade.

In April, 1934, a fund for financing exports was created at the National Bank to be raised out of fees and levies amounting to 10 per cent of the value of certain goods imported under quotas. The fund was to be used to help expand the export of mineral oil, wheat, and timber, in particular to the free countries. Later a new order ruled that imports from countries with which Rumania had a trade deficit were not to exceed 60 per cent of the value of exports to those countries. The foreign exchange not surrendered to the National Bank at the official parity (40–60 per cent of the exchange received) could be sold as an import certificate. These certificates soon went to a discount which tended to increase continuously. In June, 1935, a new principle was laid down: according to it the total foreign exchange obtained from exports was to be surrendered to the National Bank, and at the official rate; but to encourage export the Bank was to pay a premium determined by the difference between prices at home and abroad, by general market conditions, the foreign exchange situation, and so forth.[19] To obtain the funds necessary for the payment of these premia the National Bank charged an agio of 44 per cent for all foreign exchange for importation (this did not apply to Austria, Hungary, and Poland).

A new order issued in November, 1935, brought a general simplification of the rates of premium, but the obligation to surrender the total value of exports was retained. The National Bank had been authorized to pay the exporters a uniform premium and to charge the buyers of foreign exchange a uniform fee in excess of the official exchange rate.[20] Under this authority the export premium was fixed at 38 per cent, equal to a devaluation of the leu of 27.5 per cent. This simplification of the exchange premia and charges was a great advance but the system still remained complicated: exporters of mineral oil and its products had to pay into the States' Export Fund a tax amounting to 12 per cent of the value of their exports; thus for them the rate of devaluation was only 20.6 per cent, while importers of all goods had to pay into the same fund a tax of 12 per cent of the value of their imports, thereby raising their rate of devaluation to 33.3 per cent.

The devaluation of the leu was officially recognized, indirectly, when the National Bank was directed to pay, beginning June 1, 1936, a 38

[19] Roumanian National Bank, *Bulletin,* 1935, pp. 203–4.   [20] *Ibid.,* pp. 403, 468.

per cent premium on gold as defined in the monetary law (1 leu =
0.00652 grams of fine gold instead of 0.009, a devaluation of 27.5 per
cent).[21] The foreign-trade balance improved substantially in 1935 (a
surplus of 6,080.7 million lei against 446.5 in 1934), but the great increase in exports went to the countries with blocked foreign exchange,
59.86 per cent [22] of the total compared with 45.25 per cent in 1934.

Although this last exchange-control regulation was identical with
open devaluation, it was not uniformly applied; in practice the rate
of devaluation was higher for importation than for exportation. To a
certain extent this may have increased the protection of domestic industry but it also increased the prices of imported goods. It was expected that this would suffice to overcome the difference between
domestic and foreign prices, but the so-called economic export subsidies remained, the most important being that for wheat. To avoid
a new disintegration of the external value of the leu and the differentiation of the exchange rates it was intended to eliminate compensation
transactions, with but very few exceptions, but this was not accomplished. Compensation was to be limited to commodities which were
not regularly exported in the past and which could not be exported
under the current exchange premia plus the economic subsidies. A
very complicated system was set up to ascertain that the exports were
additional. The goods, both imports and exports, eligible for compensation under the new order were limited to those specified upon
official lists. Furthermore, a percentage of the foreign exchange obtained for exports had to be surrendered to the National Bank; the
rest was to be compensated, that is, sold in the market at the market
rate.[23] This, of course, meant higher exchange rate for the import of
some essential commodities, and the system of multiple differentiated
rates was continued. Naturally the exporters tried to prove the necessity for obtaining additional export premia and the importers, faced
with insufficient supplies of raw materials and other goods were willing to pay higher prices for foreign exchange, for they could still make
a profit in the protected domestic market. The lists, therefore, were
continually changed and expanded, in particular at the time of growing German influence, with tendency to raise prices in the Rumanian

21 In November, 1936, the gold reserve at the Bank was revalued, and the Bank paid additional subsidies—in order to encourage the domestic production of gold, particularly in
small mines—amounting in 1938 to a total premium of 83 per cent (a rate of devaluation
of more than 45 per cent).
22 Rumanian National Bank, *Bulletin*, 1936, p. 7.   23 *Ibid.*, 1935, p. 365.

market. By July, 1938 [24] when a new list was issued the number of export items included had been increased to 135, and the highest proportion of foreign exchange to be surrendered was fixed at 30 per cent with the majority between 10 per cent and 20 per cent. The same list included 123 import items. In addition, 30 per cent of the free or strong foreign exchange obtained from the export of cereals and seeds could be sold on the free market at the market rate or could be used for the payment of financial claims—a further guarantee of a high exchange rate.[25] On the import list were practically all overseas raw materials, metals, colonial products, chemicals, and machines.

The goal of the policy of stabilizing the premia on the free exchanges at 38 per cent, namely the achievement of a uniform exchange rate and the stabilization of the external value of the leu, was not attained. There were always some exceptions, which very soon disrupted the whole system. The existing multiple rates for the leu continued with two chief groups of rates: those with the free-exchange countries and those with the exchange-control countries with whom the rates were established on a different basis. But even in the commerce with the free countries there was not only the 38 per cent premium rate but, as shown, also different rates in the compensation transactions. In 1936 these transactions amounted to about one third of the value of exports to the free countries. If we also take into account exports with economic subsidies, in particular wheat—the subsidies were paid chiefly in the trade with the free sectors—we arrive at the conclusion that the official devaluation premium of 38 per cent applied only to a small part of the exports to these countries; the major part obtained higher rates. And on the Bucharest exchange market the position of the leu was judged from the compensation rate on the dollar, pound, or Swiss franc, which fluctuated according to the general economic and political situation—not to mention the rate on the rather extensive black market. It would be extremely difficult to calculate the external value of the leu during this period, but it is certain that the official depreciation based on the premia of 38 per cent was soon surpassed.

Thus Rumania, although devaluing at the end of 1935, failed to achieve currency stability, and to relieve permanent pressure upon her currency. She was also unable to bring about a new price equilibrium, especially with regard to the important agricultural prices. This may

[24] *Ibid.*, pp. 270–72.
[25] International Institute, *Le Commerce Exterieur de la Roumanie,* Paris, 1939, p. 14.

seem surprising especially in view of the favorable balance of trade and rich resources of this country. The opinion can be sustained that a consistent program carried out by an efficient organization could have succeeded in ordering and stabilizing the Rumanian exchange situation with the necessary price adjustment—assuming, of course, a political development within Rumania which would have served as a basis for the necessary confidence.

YUGOSLAVIA

Yugoslavia's foreign exchange control was more consistent, efficient, more stable—on the whole avoiding multiple rates with free exchanges —and perhaps more successful than the Rumanian. There are many reasons for this more favorable development. Yugoslavia made definite efforts, especially in the years before 1936, to attain a new equilibrium and to adjust its price level. A strict budget and credit policy would tend to work in this direction. A very important factor in the price development in Yugoslavia was the fact that that country did not, until June, 1936, control imports by means of quotas, differentiating arbitrarily among various goods to be accepted as imports. And when quota control was introduced it applied chiefly to imports from the free-exchange countries. Yugoslavia did not go as far as Rumania or Hungary in the valorization of the domestic prices of staple agricultural exports. The level of prices fell until 1935. The wholesale price index (yearly average) declined from 100.6 in 1929 to 64.4 in 1934,[26] while the level of wholesale prices in terms of gold (1929 = 100) declined to 48 in March, 1935, or to the lowest level among any of these countries. But the policy of price adjustment was not pursued consistently and in the years 1937 and 1938 prices increased [27] more than on the world markets, reaching a level of 61 (gold, 1929 = 100) in March, 1938. The development of the exchange rates reflected this movement of prices.

However, Yugoslavia was unable to avoid the creation of rather large blocked foreign accounts of both commercial and financial origin, thus making it more difficult to keep the exchange rate stable and uniform. Furthermore, she concluded clearing agreements not only with countries with exchange-control but also with free-exchange countries, such as Switzerland, France, Belgium, Holland, Sweden,

[26] Index established by the Research Department of the National Bank of Yugoslavia.
[27] League of Nations, *Report on Exchange Control*, p. 51.

expecting to reduce the pressure on her exchange by improving her balance of trade with them.

Exchange control was not sufficient to save the country from currency depreciation. The rate of the dinar weakened after a few months of control and as early as the fall of 1932 a dinar disagio developed. After a period in which exchange premia fluctuated, tending to rise and varying among the different countries, the National Bank declared, in April, 1933, a uniform premium of 28.5 per cent on all currencies, including those covered in clearing agreements. This meant a devaluation of about 22.5 per cent. It was a very important step, and consolidated the monetary situation as far as possible.

The official exchange premium obviously was more important for the sector of foreign trade with the free-payment countries, but these represented only 25 per cent of Yugoslavia's total trade. In the sector of trade subject to clearing, the rates were not always fixed according to the quotations on the foreign-exchange markets, and, although the Yugoslav National Bank attempted to introduce some degree of flexibility in these rates too, it did not achieve great success.[28]

It would be expected that the 28.5 per cent premium would be the real and only rate quoted for foreign exchange. Yet as early as April, 1934, free quotations for the £ were admitted on the Yugoslav exchange. This quotation was stabilized and kept at about 238 din. = £1, or a premium of 47.8 per cent (a devaluation of 32.5 per cent) (against 206 din. = 22.5 per cent devaluation). This higher quotation had the following practical effect upon foreign trade: exporters were obliged to surrender a specified proportion of their foreign exchange to the National Bank at the official rate. The remainder they were allowed to sell on the market at the market rate. With the existing higher rate in the market, reduction of the percentage of foreign exchange to be surrendered to the National Bank would enable exporters to get a higher average rate for their export proceeds. The increase in the proportion of foreign exchange which could be sold on the free market at a rate higher than the official premium indicated a slight further devaluation of the dinar.[29]

[28] S. D. Obradovič, *Le Politique commerciale de la Jugoslavie*, p. 62. Among these attempts should be mentioned: compensation loans with a discount on the trade under the clearing agreement with Greece; and 10–20% fluctuations in the reichsmark rate at certain periods.

[29] The National Bank of Yugoslavia was authorized on February 15, 1935, to reckon its reserves, for the purpose of calculating its reserve ratio, at 28% above the balance sheet value; but not until October 5, 1939, could it revalue them on the basis of the market price. League of Nations, *Statistical Year-Book, 1940–41*, p. 180.

Until July, 1934, the relation was: 80 per cent to be surrendered, 20 per cent to be sold on the free market—average price for the £ = 212.4 din.

After July, 1934, it was: 60 per cent to be surrendered, 40 per cent to be sold on the free market—average price for the £ = 218.8.

In August, 1935, the ratio was changed to 50 per cent to be surrendered, 50 per cent to be sold on the free market—average price £ = 222 din.

Later, in relation only to rising prices 33⅓ per cent was to be surrendered, 66⅔ per cent to be sold on the free market, average price £ = 225 din.

And after December 1, 1938, only 25 per cent was to be surrendered, and 75 per cent to be sold on the free market—average price £ = 229 din.[30] Thus instead of remaining stable the exchange premium of 28.5 per cent increased successively so that an exporter obtained for £1 an average of 229 dinars instead of the official 206. But this rate was uniform for all kinds of exports to free countries. The full market rate of 238 dinars was paid only for exchange obtained from sources other than exports.[31] Whereas the percentage of foreign exchange to be surrendered at the official rate, and with it the real foreign exchange rate for export goods, was changed, the rate of 238 to the £ on the free market was stabilized for several years. Foreign exchange was sold at this rate for the importation of some raw materials and for certain government payments abroad.

Yugoslavia was able to avoid differentiated rates in foreign trade, and black-market transactions were not extensive. Perhaps exchange control was made easier by the structure of Yugoslavia's export trade, of which 40 per cent was directly controlled by "Prisad" and Office d'Exportation [32] and great segments were carried on by the big mining corporations.

The increase in the price level in 1937 and 1938—the average wholesale price index rose to 74.7 in 1937 and to 78.3 in 1938—initiated, as was typical at this time in many countries, a demand for a further increase in the exchange premium, or, in other words, a further devalua-

---

30 Yovanovitch, *Le Contrôle des changes en Jugoslavie*, pp. 43, 44.

31 Higher rates for foreign exchange were paid officially in transactions other than foreign trade. Thus, for example, a rate of 250 din. per pound was paid for exchange obtained from tourists. A higher rate was also paid as dinars "des coupons"—the countervalue of government debt services—which could be used among other things for new investment in Yugoslavia.

32 Obradovič, *op. cit.*, p. 50.

tion. Thus it was stated, for example, that: "an autonomous monetary policy is not justified; since control has modified the mechanism of foreign trade, monetary policy moves in the opposite direction from foreign trade policy," and export subsidies and import controls—the argument continues—should be united to coördinate these two policies.[33] Pursuing this line the National Bank began in 1938 to pay 250 din. to the £ as a subsidy for the export of, at first, only a few products. It hardly need be mentioned that the granting of a higher rate, at first only as an exception, was soon extended.

Although a *de facto* devaluation existed as early as 1933, and later the disagio was substantially increased—in spite of the fact that the balance of trade was favorable in every year from 1932 to 1938 with a total export surplus of 2,736 million dinars (only 72 million in 1938)—the pressure on the exchange rate in the relatively small free sector of Yugoslavia's foreign trade continued.

A real new equilibrium of prices and of the balance of payments was not established, and it was admitted that in the event of a new legal stabilization the free market price of 238 should be taken as a base; [34] even this rate was not regarded by many as sufficient to achieve a satisfactory price adjustment. As in other countries with large clearing sectors the question of adjusting the free and clearing rates to correspond with the international quotation was not solved satisfactorily.

GREECE

In Greece, whose currency was linked to the £, exchange difficulties appeared a little later than in Central Europe, coming immediately after the pound went off gold. In an effort to maintain the stability of her currency Greece pegged the drachma without delay to the dollar at $1. = 77.05 dr., but it was impossible to avoid external devaluation. Exchange control could not prevent this. The psychological effects of Britain's departure from the gold standard produced a severe shock in the Greek economy. Greece had already felt for some time the impact of the depression in the form of reduced demand for exports, the chief products of which (tobacco, raisins, nuts, wine, currants) were regarded as luxuries or semiluxuries. The transfer problem also became serious.

[33] *Ibid.*, p. 63.
[34] Yovanovitch, *op. cit.*, p. 37; Obradović, *op. cit.*, p. 63 mentions a rate of 258 as existing *via facti*.

The structure of her balance of payments was different from that of the other agricultural countries in this area. She always had a very large import surplus, the value of imports averaged more than double the value of exports from 1923 to 1929 and the average annual deficit amounted to nearly $78 million (390 million gold fr.). In 1931 against an import of 587.78 million gold francs exports amounted to only 279.89 million gold francs (8,763.3 million dr. against 4,203.6 million dr.). A large part of this deficit was met by remittances from Greek emigrants; the sum averaged 2.7 billion drachma (176 million gold fr.) in the period 1923–29, and reached a peak of 178.3 million gold fr. in 1931. Shipping was another credit item, totaling 30.3 million gold fr. in 1931 (360 million dr. in 1929), and tourist services yielded 25 million gold fr. in 1931. But the service of the public debt was a further large debit item, requiring in 1931, 124.86 million gold fr.[35] or 1,927 million dr. Equilibrium of the balance of payments was achieved only with the help of foreign credits. From May, 1928, to December, 1930, alone, such foreign assistance amounted to 6 billion dr. ($78 million) or an average yearly rate of borrowing of about 2.3 billion drachma, with the borrowing having been even heavier in the previous year.[36] Capital imports in 1931 amounted to 253.2 million gold fr.

With its gold and foreign exchange reserves rapidly declining, the Bank of Greece could not continue to meet all applications for foreign exchange. The value of imports did not decline, a flight of capital developed, and prices at home tended to rise although world prices continued to fall. Foreign-exchange applications for the importation of articles other than foodstuffs and raw materials of prime necessity were refused, but importers turned for foreign exchange to the black market, which sprang up rapidly. (The dollar rate reached 110–115 at the end of March and exceeded 130 in April.) The official index of wholesale prices rose steadily, legal parity became a fiction, and within a few months after the introduction of exchange control it was realized that "to maintain the gold standard was a vain attempt which could not succeed." [37] By the law of April 26, 1932, the gold standard was suspended and exchange control was strongly reinforced. The drachma

35 These figures are taken from J. D. Pintos, *Le Contrôle des changes en Grèce*, Paris, 1939, pp. 5, 23, 24.
36 League of Nations Financial Committee, *Report to the Council on Greece*, Geneva, July 8, 1933, pp. 15–19.
37 Pintos, *op. cit.*, p. 11.

immediately went to a discount of about 50 per cent and after some fluctuation it was stabilized at 41–43 per cent of its value before depreciation. The Bank of Greece pursued a policy of *de facto* stabilization backed, of course, by very strict exchange control and a very extensive and complicated system of import control. Beginning in September 28, 1936, after the devaluation of the remaining gold-bloc currencies, the drachma was again linked to sterling at £ = 550–560 dr.[38] The rate of devaluation remained at an average of 41.2 per cent in 1937 and 40.8 per cent in 1938.

The policy of stabilization called for restoring the equilibrium in the balance of payments. The devaluation of the drachma was certainly the most important factor in improving the balance of trade, but the government considered it necessary to go further and not only strengthen its exchange control but also regulate imports very strictly, employing quotas and other devices to that end. The deficit in the balance of trade was greatly reduced.

The whole system of import restrictions furnished a powerful incentive for the expansion of Greek industry and agriculture. Like other agricultural countries, Greece suffered from the fall in prices in the export markets (the average price per ton of exported tobacco declined from 5,302 Swiss francs in 1929 to 2,235.4 in 1932 and to 1,575.5 in 1934); [39] but the decline in the total income from agricultural exports was more than off-set in the balance of trade by the drop in the prices of Greek imports of agricultural staples.[40] As an importer of these agricultural staples Greece did not have to face the difficult problem of adjusting their prices to the world market price, and because of her import restrictions she was able to intensify her policy of expanding domestic agricultural production. The area sown to cereals increased between 1929 and 1934 by 50 per cent. Wheat production increased from a 332,700-ton average in 1925–29 to an average of 501,100 tons in 1930–34 and reached 980,030 tons in 1938–39. Obviously the need of agricultural imports declined, the purchasing power of agriculture increased.[41]

38 League of Nations, *Statistical Year-Book, 1940–41*, pp. 180, 181.
39 Royal Institute, *The Balkan States*, p. 65.
40 E. Evelpidi "Die landwirtschaftliche Krise in Griechenland," *Weltwirtschaftliches Archiv*, LI (1940), pp. 348–72, estimates that the Greek economy gained 7,248 million dr. in these years as the result of the fall in the prices of agricultural products, after deducting the losses arising from the decrease in the price of Greek exports.
41 The average income per head of the farming population, which was 3,880 dr. in 1928 reached 4,700 dr. in 1936. Evelpidi, *op. cit.*, p. 356.

But the expansion of industrial production was, relatively, even greater. Its quantitative index (1928 = 100) rose to 127.48 in 1934 and to 182.54 in 1938. To check a too rapid increase in industrial production the importation of machinery for the expansion of existing industries or for the creation of new ones was made subject to the approval of the Minister of National Economy.

Having a passive trade balance with most countries, Greece regarded clearing agreements primarily as a device for alleviating the shortage of foreign exchange and for improving the balance of trade. With this in view clearing and other types of payment agreements were arranged with various countries, including many which did not have exchange control, as France, Belgium, Switzerland, Portugal, Sweden, and Holland.[42] By the end of 1933 official clearings existed with countries accounting for more than half of the Greek foreign trade. The number of agreements increased further, until the only important markets for or suppliers of Greece which remained on a free basis were Great Britain and the United States. Export to the clearing countries increased from 69.4 per cent of the total export in 1935 to 77.8 per cent in 1937, and import from them went up from 48.3 per cent to 55.6 per cent of the total import in the same years.[43]

The volume of trade with the clearing countries increased more than that with those on a free payment basis, and whereas the balance of trade with the clearing countries showed an export surplus or a substantial reduction in the trade deficit, on the other hand the deficit in the free sector did not change much and had to be balanced by other income items.

Nevertheless the deficit was substantially reduced on the whole. By 1938 the total value of exports, in gold francs, reached 292.6 million or more than the 1931 total of 279.8 (10.149 million dr. in 1938 against 6,331 million in 1929), but imports were 172 million gold francs below the 1931 figure (14.761 million dr. in 1938 against 13.276 million dr. in 1929).

The index of wholesale prices, which had, after a rise in 1932–33, remained stable, began to go up again in the second half of 1936, and increased substantially in 1937 (more than 12 per cent). The import control contributed greatly to the increase in prices and there were

42 Pintos, *op. cit.*, pp. 4, 6–7 Annex; *The Economist*, Jan. 30, 1932, p. 238.
43 Pintos, *op. cit.*, p. 30. Some other sources give lower figures for Greek trade with the clearing countries, perhaps including only trade with exchange-control countries. The League of Nations *Report on Exchange Control*, 1938, gives the figure 47.4% of the total as the proportion of Greek export to countries without exchange control.

repeated complaints that the clearing agreements further stimulated the upward movement.

The government and the Bank of Greece were determined to maintain the *de facto* stabilization of the drachma; the official rate applied directly to only a small part of the foreign trade, since trade under the clearing agreements was carried on at different commodity prices and rates of exchange. Greece largely succeeded in avoiding multiple, differentiated rates of exchange, but pressure on her currency in 1936 resulted in several new and very stringent exchange regulations introduced in August, 1936. One of them required that private compensations, which usually resulted in an exchange premium, were to be further reduced—although they had never been encouraged.[44] Private export compensations from the beginning of the 1932 regime until January 31, 1939, totaled dr. 2,149.3 million, certainly a very small proportion of the total value of exports in these years. But we must not forget that compensation was important mostly in the free-payment sector of foreign trade. The system of multiple rates was not completely avoided, although its use was very limited.[45]

Government interference increased in Greece, just as in other countries. Foreign-exchange control and the control of foreign trade tended to spread into a kind of general managed economy. With national production generally increased and with the foreign trade deficit reduced, this system was considered by many as being advantageous for the Greek economy.[46] On the other hand there was a strong demand for the freeing of foreign trade from the clearing restrictions, and it was admitted that, as far as the production of Greek industry and agriculture was concerned, exchange control was not necessary and could be replaced by other measures. But the integration of the Greek economy in a freely functioning international trade would still have required a readjustment of production. The price problem, too, could not be regarded as settled or stabilized as long as such a large and important portion of Greek exports were dependent upon trade with the clearing countries.

Foreign-exchange control, introduced as an emergency measure to maintain the stability of the currency, became a permanent instru-

[44] Pintos, *op. cit.*, p. 31.
[45] From the Monthly Bulletin of the Bank of Greece. The premium rates showed a rising tendency in 1938, reaching 30% or more.
[46] Evelpidi, *op. cit.*, p. 372, concluded that the crisis was on the whole advantageous to the Greek economy.

ment of economic policy in these countries. Nevertheless in all of them the national currencies were substantially depreciated in various ways, and in many of them a system of *multiple, differentiated* rates arose, proving that for the most part no new equilibrium had been achieved in regard to currency, prices, or the balance of payments. For in spite of the devotion of an enormous amount of energy to this exchange and foreign-trade control, the most essential aims—the stabilization and consolidation of money and of trade—was not achieved. As already mentioned, in all these agricultural countries industrial production increased.[47] Furthermore, their balance of trade improved: the four Danubian countries achieved a permanent export surplus and Greece greatly reduced her trade deficit. Even their percentage of world trade increased contrary to the development in Austria and Czechoslovakia. (See p. 181.)

A common feature of their foreign trade was the fact that more than two thirds of it was with countries with whom clearing agreements were conducted and that Germany was the leading participant in the clearing trade area. It is therefore necessary to analyze Germany's policy and trade relations with them in order to find the explanation of various elements in the economic development of the countries in question. It should be noted in particular that the monetary situation in all these countries was still very unclear and unstable in 1933 and 1934 when Germany initiated her new foreign-trade policy.

[47] The index of industrial production (1932 = 100) gives a very clear picture of this development:

	Hungary	Yugoslavia	Bulgaria	Rumania	Greece
1929	127.1	121.		112.9	99.1
1934	126.7	109.1	98.3	139.9	127.2
1937	178.5	138.6	129.6	148.	147.7

From German Institute for Business Research, *Weekly Report*, 1938, No. 17–18, Annex I, p. 7.

9

REGIONAL ECONOMIC AGREEMENTS

ALTHOUGH the various international attempts to organize close economic coöperation between the Danubian states on a large scale never succeeded, the continuing economic pressure strengthened the demand for a special regional regime which would ease the economic situation. A preferential system was considered as one possible step toward expanding trade between the countries within this area, and it was thought that such a system could be especially useful with regard to the export of agricultural commodities for which the Stresa Conference admitted, in principle, the use of preferential duties. There remained the question to what extent a preferential organization limited to the Danubian states could actually increase the export of agricultural products, in view of the limited consuming capacity of the importing countries. But every possible mitigation of the unfavorable position of the agricultural countries was welcomed, and thus, almost simultaneously, two regional preferential systems were established—the group of the Little Entente and the Rome group. Whereas the Little Entente was an organization only between the countries of this region, the Rome group was organized and led by a major power—Italy.

THE LITTLE ENTENTE

The Little Entente, one of the first effective political structures to be created after the war in this part of Europe, consisted originally of three separate bilateral treaties of mutual [1] military assistance. They were signed in 1920 and 1921 by Czechoslovakia and Yugoslavia, Yugoslavia and Rumania, and Czechoslovakia and Rumania. The principal purpose of these treaties was to protect the signatories against an unprovoked attack by Hungary. Out of extensive close political coöperation grew the pact of organization of the Little Entente, which was signed in February, 1933. The pact aimed at the complete unification of the foreign policy of these

[1] Hanc, *Tornado across Eastern Europe*, pp. 61 and 121.

countries. It provided for the establishment of the Permanent Council of Foreign Ministers with a permanent secretariat, and it was open to other small states of Central and Southeastern Europe, a fact which was repeatedly emphasized. According to the Pact, an Economic Council of the Little Entente was to be created for the purpose of gradually coördinating the economic interests of the three states. Close economic coöperation was a specified goal of Little Entente policy, and the economic council was assigned the task of devising the means and methods of carrying it out.

The first meeting of this Economic Council in Prague in January, 1934, outlined a far-reaching program of economic rapprochement and coördination. It included intensification of the interchange of goods between the members, coöperation between the Central Banks and between the Manufacturers' Associations, unification of railway, and port traffic, and close coöperation in Danubian shipping. The most important point upon which the whole idea of economic coöperation could be based was, of course, an increase in mutual trade. To this end the Economic Council worked out a tentative program for the expansion of trade in the near future and prepared all the necessary steps. Even during the first year, 1934, the total value of trade between the three states was to increase, according to the plan, by 50 per cent and in 1935 by 75–100 per cent. (The greatest part of the trade was, of course, between Czechoslovakia and Yugoslavia and between Czechoslovakia and Rumania.) Detailed estimates of the amounts of goods involved were drawn up. It should be noted that the idea of a customs union as a means of increasing the exchange of goods was not the subject of any serious discussion at that time. It was impossible to overcome the resistance of agriculture in Czechoslovakia and of industry in the other two countries—which would have been essential to the pursuit of such an aim.

Both Rumania and Yugoslavia greatly needed industrial goods from Czechoslovakia, but the chief obstacle to Czechoslovak export was a lack of sufficient foreign exchange in these countries. After the introduction of the system of clearing payments Czechoslovak exports to them depended directly upon imports from them. Hence, by increasing imports Czechoslovakia could make greater exports possible automatically. The main problem was, therefore, to find ways of increasing imports from Rumania and Yugoslavia, whose chief exports were agricultural products and Rumanian oil and

Yugoslav metals and minerals. There was not much hope that such an increase could be brought about by a general reduction in the protection of Czechoslovakian agriculture nor was there any prospect of greatly increasing consumption. To facilitate the export of cereals and animal products by Rumania and Yugoslavia, Czechoslovakia granted both these countries preferential treatment for such goods in the form of a drawback to the respective governments of a certain amount of the duties paid on them. At the same time the importation of some agricultural products which was entirely controlled was shifted from some other markets to the members of the Little Entente. Obviously Czechoslovakia, with her widespread export markets, was obliged to proceed carefully and to take into consideration her commercial relations with other countries. Hungary was still an important potential market, at least for some goods; animal products had to be imported from Denmark, the United States, Holland, the Baltic States and Bulgaria. There was, therefore, a certain limit even to the shifting of imports with regard to their origin.

However, the total volume of Czechoslovak imports of agricultural goods was not very large. In bread cereals the country had practically attained self-sufficiency, and only small quantities of wheat were imported in years of poor harvests. The corn imports were not large enough to offset the reduction in wheat imports. In livestock and animal products there was also a strong tendency toward self-sufficiency. Thus cattle imports declined from 95,561 head in 1930 to 1,216 in 1936; and imports of hogs of less than 120 kg. in weight were 406,447 head in 1930, but ceased completely as a result of high customs duty—on the other hand the import of hogs of more than 120 kg. (fat hogs) increased from 136,505 to 289,207 head. Yet in the same period lard imports went down from 23,842 tons to 13,937 tons. It is evident that there was little possibility of expanding the imports of agricultural staples, even by a geographical shift from other sources, as long as the basic trend of agricultural policy was not changed. It is hardly necessary to add that a more liberal policy could help in increasing exports and production and, thereby, the rate of consumption, thus enabling the country to import larger amounts of agricultural products. The commercial policy in this respect was certainly not one of economic expansion; actually it worked in the opposite direction, jeopardizing the optimum level of employment, standards of living, and foreign trade. There were some attempts or plans to change the structure of agriculture,[2] measures were taken to restrict the area under wheat and to increase the cultivation of oleaginous plants, vegetables and other crops, but a change of this kind requires time.

Great efforts were made to encourage the importation of agricultural products other than the staples, particularly fruits, vegetables, wine, and poultry. But this, too, required time—to prepare the markets and to organize the standardization of the goods.

A further possible field of mutual trade expansion was to increase the import of various raw materials from Yugoslavia and Rumania. Principal among these were: mineral oil and zinc from Rumania; and copper, lead, zinc, chromium ores, pyrites, and hemp from Yugoslavia. However, Yugoslavia was not anxious to export copper against payment in the clearing accounts, and Rumania also preferred to export as much oil as possible to the free payment countries.

In its meetings the Economic Council devoted much time to the question of increasing mutual trade and to planning for it. The Czechoslovak import control supported this policy, advising importers to buy as much as possible—if the prices were convenient, that is, not too far above world market prices—from Yugoslavia and Rumania. But the fact that without greater imports no increase in exports would be possible became so generally known that private business itself tried to find various goods in these countries which had not been previously imported from them. Industry organized importation from Yugoslavia and Rumania, well knowing that this was the only way to expand exportation. No preferential duties were granted to Czechoslovak exports; in general none were needed, demand being always greater than it was possible to pay for. In 1936 a new corporation, "Centre Economique," was created in Prague to develop sources of raw materials in these countries, to increase their imports, and thus to make possible an increase in Czechoslovak exports. Even various compensation transactions were allowed, enabling industry to pay higher prices for imported commodities from these states; the increase in exports which was expected to result was to make up for such price sacrifices. During this period a new com-

[2] L. Feierabend, "Czechoslovak Agriculture," *The Banker*, London, June, 1938 (Annex: "Czechoslovakia,") p. 45.

pany, "Planta," was established in Rumania, with the purpose of promoting the production of soya beans and of exporting them to Czechoslovakia against the import of industrial goods. Obviously because the price of Rumanian soya beans was much higher than that prevailing on the world market the difference had to be paid by Czechoslovak industry out of what was considered to be its additional exports to Rumania. It was a plan similar to the German I. G. Farben soya bean scheme. A better system of collecting hides and skins was organized too, and the operating of various mines in Yugoslavia was planned. Furthermore, Czechoslovak business intended to use its better developed foreign organization to help in exporting Rumanian and Yugoslav goods.

Czechoslovak industry realized soon after the last war that a period of industrialization had begun in the Danubian agricultural countries and that it would be vain to attempt to stop it. Therefore it was considered more useful to change the structure of Czechoslovak exports to them, not relying too much on cheap and mass industrial goods, and to take part in their industrialization. This policy continued under the Little Entente and an attempt was made to coördinate the development of new industries with the general policy. In this connection, besides further expanding its participation in the textile industry. Czechoslovak industry was active in developing the chemical industry in Yugoslavia and Rumania, metallurgical and armament production in Rumania, and the shoe industry in Yugoslavia.

The Little Entente policy of expanding mutual trade achieved a certain degree of success although it fell short of expectations. Czechoslovak imports from Yugoslavia and Rumania went up from 6.7 per cent of her total imports in 1933 to 9 per cent in 1936 and 8.5 per cent in 1937. (Yugoslavia's share in these years was 3.8, 4.4, 3.7 per cent, Rumania's 2.9, 4.6, and 4.8 per cent.) Larger imports of mineral oil substantially increased the Rumanian share. Czechoslovak exports to these two countries rose from 7 per cent of her total exports in 1933 to 10 per cent in 1936 and 10.5 per cent in 1937. The Yugoslav figures were: 3.3, 5.3, 5.1 per cent; and Rumania's 3.7, 4.7, and 5.5 per cent. In absolute terms, Czechoslovak imports increased from Kc. 407 million in 1933 to Kc. 942 million in 1937, exports from Kc. 418 million in 1933 to 1,250 million in

1937, or nearly triple the former figure. Imports were higher in 1937 than in 1929, whereas exports remained much below the 1929 value.[3] These increases were proportionately much greater than the general increase in Czechoslovak trade. The favorable trade balance with these countries was paid for chiefly by the export of capital, and, with Yugoslavia, by the expenditures of a very large tourist trade. The expansion of foreign trade in 1936 and 1937 was due, among other things, to Czechoslovak armament exports. For this purpose Czechoslovak banks granted Rumania a credit of £4 million.[4] A previous armament credit to Yugoslavia was repaid in tobacco, but the huge imports of Yugoslav tobacco connected directly with the arms exports curtailed the export possibilities of other industries not only to Yugoslavia but also to Bulgaria and Greece and Turkey, because tobacco imports from these other countries could not be expanded to a like extent. It should be noted that the Czechoslovak tobacco monopoly made great efforts to help exportation to these countries by making huge purchases of tobacco from them, greatly surpassing the quantities usually bought. Thus the Tobacco Monopoly is reported to have had in 1938 stocks of Balkan tobacco sufficient for more than eight years' consumption.

The economic Little Entente was a long-range plan intended to increase economic and financial coöperation between these three countries and to prepare their real economic rapprochement. Although a customs union in the future was an aim, it was almost impossible to realize it under the circumstances prevailing at that time in all the member states. The trade between Rumania and Yugoslavia was insignificant, Rumanian imports from Yugoslavia during 1933–37 amounting to only 1.5 per cent of total imports and exports to only 0.9 per cent.

That increase in trade which did occur resulted from conscious

[3] To illustrate the development of the trade relations between Czechoslovakia and her two partners, it is interesting to compare Czechoslovakia's trade with them (figures in Kc. millions).

Imports	1929	1931	1933	1937
from Yugoslavia	340	385	230	410
from Rumania	473	567	177	532
Exports				
to Yugoslavia	1,155	832	197	596
to Rumania	770	341	221	654

[4] The Economist, July 10, 1937, p. 69.

planning and the preferential treatment granted on some agricultural products rather than from an adjustment of the national economies of the members. In spite of the basic aim neither the industrial protection of the agricultural countries nor the trend in the agricultural policy of Czechoslovakia was changed. The expansion of mutual trade was not supposed to interfere with either of these developments; and there persisted as a weakness in the whole structure the obvious fact that Czechoslovakia was not able to buy any considerable quantities of staple agricultural products during a period in which Yugoslavia and Rumania badly needed a larger and regular market.

Besides the great degree of self-sufficiency which Czechoslovakia had achieved in foods there remains to be taken into account the additional fact that she also had to import various agricultural products from other clearing countries in order to maintain trade with them. This applied in particular to Hungary, Bulgaria, Greece, Denmark, and Turkey. The exports of these countries competed with the agricultural members of the Little Entente, especially in cereals, animal products, fruits, and tobacco. The purchasing program, envisaging the importation of various raw materials from Yugoslavia and Rumania which were not previously bought from these countries, could not be carried out within a few years.

It was hoped that other Danubian countries would join the Little Entente and great efforts were made in this direction in 1937. But in the meantime the growing political power of Germany and her expanding trade offensive in the Danube area had begun to make their influence felt even among the members of the Little Entente, with Yugoslavia in particular strongly favoring close economic cooperation with Germany.[5]

THE ROME PROTOCOLS

The Rome Protocols signed on March 17, 1934, between Italy, Austria, and Hungary, provided for an increase in trade between

[5] *The Economist*, July 16, 1936, p. 355: Prime Minister of Yugoslavia Stojadinovitch declared that Yugoslavia's closer commercial relations with Germany are natural. It was necessary to unfreeze blocked marks by importing machinery and armament, and these developments were not to be taken in any way as a breach in the solidarity of the Little Entente. It remains true, however, that Yugoslav industry was becoming increasingly dependent upon German equipment and contracts.

these countries in general and for the marketing of Hungarian wheat in particular. Under the agreement the signing countries obligated themselves to facilitate each other's exports and to increase progressively the supplementary aspects of their economies. They also decided to take the necessary steps to relieve Hungary's difficulties resulting from the fall in cereal prices, and it was further agreed that Austria should be granted preferential treatment on the greatest possible number of exports to Italy. Although the purpose of the Rome Protocols was outlined merely in economic terms, there can be no doubt about their political meaning.[6] Italy contemplated a strengthening of her position in the Danube valley, where she constantly feared too great French influence and the growing importance of the Little Entente. She continued her efforts—begun many years before—to gain a firm political as well as economic position in this region.

The bilateral commercial treaties which were put into operation on July 1, 1934, should have had the greatest importance for Hungary, providing her with outlets for her agricultural surplus and granting her a higher price than that on the world market for both wheat and wheat flour. In contradiction to the Little Entente—in which two countries exported and only one country imported agricultural goods—in this case Hungary alone exported agricultural staples which were usually imported by both Italy and Austria. There should have been, therefore, a good chance of satisfying Hungary's needs in this regard. The agreement for the marketing and valorization of Hungarian wheat was rightly regarded as the backbone of the whole arrangement: Italy guaranteed to buy over a million quintals of wheat at a price assuring the producers a profit and obtained an option for another million quintals. In case she failed to make use of this latter amount, she was to pay an indemnity to make possible its sale elsewhere. At the same time Austria undertook to purchase 2.2 million quintals of wheat or wheat flour at a favorable price. The agreement was renewed every year, and in 1936 it secured an export of 3.5 million quintals of Hungarian wheat and half a million quintals of wheat flour,[7] or more than four fifths of the total wheat export.

[6] For a detailed reference see Gerhard Schacher, *Mitteleuropa und die westliche Welt*, Prague, 1936, pp. 121 ff. Hanc, *op. cit.*, pp. 131 ff. R. Schüller, "Commercial Policy between the Two Wars," *Social Research*, X (1943), 168 ff.
[7] National Bank of Hungary, *Annual Report*, 1936, p. 10.

The price paid for Hungarian wheat was, at the beginning, 16 pengös per 100 kg. for Austria and 17–18 pengös for Italy—or at least double the world-market price.[8] But by paying this higher price the importing countries retained intact their agricultural protectionism; it was only a question of shifting their imports from other countries to Hungary. Since Italy imported ten million quintals of wheat from overseas in 1933, the required shift did not present any difficult problem although she was very careful not to disturb her commercial relations with her overseas markets, in particular with South America.[9] On the other hand, Austria imported only 2.9 million quintals of wheat in 1933, 1.1 million from Hungary. Thus to take 2.2 million quintals from Hungary meant that imports from her had to be doubled.[10] The Austrian share and sacrifice in this respect was both relatively and absolutely much greater than that of Italy.

In order to induce Austria to participate in the plan, Italy conceded to her, as a reward, preferred treatment for her industrial exports to Italy, and preferential treatment was openly granted to Austria in 116 custom tariff items (34 of them not limited to quotas). In both parts of the plan, in the preferential treatment for Hungarian agricultural products as well as for Austrian industrial goods, the resolution of the Stresa Conference was referred to. No open preferential treatment was granted either for Italian goods exported to the other members or for Austrian exports to Hungary.

However, much more important than the open concessions were concealed benefits in the form of credit or transport subsidies, which were really the basis of the whole system. Ingenious measures were devised to avoid all claims arising from the most-favored-nation clause.[11] The governments were very anxious to keep the amount of the preferential subsidies in deep secrecy; no complete list of the goods enjoying these advantages or of the amount of the subsidies was ever published.

The credit or transport subsidies amounted, in effect, to an export subsidy which was granted according to an agreement between the governments. In this form Austria obtained preferential treatment

[8] Ellis, *op. cit.*, p. 111. Hantos (*op. cit.*, p. 44), indicates an even higher price of S. 20–22. International Institute, *Le Regionalisme economique en Europe*, Paris, 1939.
[9] Hantos, *op. cit.*, p. 44.
[10] *Ibid.*, p. 43: in value this increase amounted to S. 24 million.
[11] *The Economist*, Dec. 18, 1937, p. 585.

on timber, paper, woodpulp, steel, tools, leather goods; and granted preferences to Italy on exports of rice, fruits, cheese, wine, rayon, automobiles, textiles, and chemical products. Hungary did not grant preferential treatment on industrial goods, but Italy secured a reduction of some high custom duties as well as the liberalization of some quotas for her important exports, while Austria got from Hungary substantial quotas for her exports of timber, paper, and textiles.[12] Preferential treatment in the form of transport and credit facilities was provided for Hungarian wheat, flour, livestock, poultry, eggs, vegetables.[13] In summary, the purpose of the treaties was to increase the export of agricultural products, chiefly Hungarian, and of industrial goods, chiefly Italian and Austrian, between the members of the bloc with the help, for the most part, of a concerted and secret preferential regime.

The agreement between these countries, as concluded, had a reasonable prospect of success, in particular with regard to the export of Hungarian agricultural staples, for both Italy and Austria were able to provide a fairly large market. But, in addition, Austria should have been in a position to increase her exports to her partners, while Italy should have been able to increase her sales by buying more Austrian and Hungarian goods. It is difficult to appraise correctly the effects of the Rome Protocols because soon after the agreements became valid Italy's—the major partner's—economy entered a rather abnormal period. First, while preparing for the Abyssinian campaign and later during the period of sanctions in 1935–36 Italy was a great importer of many Austrian and Hungarian goods. The increase in exports to Italy was the result of this situation, whereas there was no increase in the proportion of Austro-Hungarian trade.

The share of imports from Austria and Hungary in Italy's trade

[12] Hantos, *op. cit.*, pp. 39–40. In his article "Commercial Policy between the Two Wars" (pp. 168–89), Mr. R. Schüller explains that at the beginning of the negotiations for a preferential regime between Austria and Italy he proposed that Austria should pay subsidies for her export to Italy, and that the Italian custom duties be refunded by the amount of the subsidies; Italy was to do the same for Austria. The Italians found the scheme too simple and offered a scheme providing export credit facilities instead of direct subsidies. This was the basis of an agreement reached between the governments of Austria, Hungary, and Italy (the so-called Brocchi Treaties of 1931–32, preceding the Rome Protocols), by which the total amount of the custom duties on certain goods, and part of the duties on other goods, were refunded.

[13] *Hungarian External Economic Policy*, p. 34.

tripled during the years 1934–36. Imports from Austria rose to 6.2 per cent of Italy's total imports and those from Hungary to 3.7 per cent. (S. 129.4 million or 13.6 per cent of total Austrian exports, and 65.6 million pengös or 13 per cent of Hungary's total exports went to Italy in 1936 against 9.9 per cent and 7.8 per cent respectively for 1932.) Eighty per cent of the Hungarian export consisted of wheat and cattle; 75 per cent of the Austrian was made up of timber, paper and hardware. Italian exports to Austria went up from 2.8 per cent of her total exports in 1932 to 3.5 per cent in 1936 and those to Hungary rose from 0.7 to 2.1 per cent (or 4.9 and 4.7 per cent of Austria's total imports in 1932 and 1936 respectively and 5.6 and 7.4 per cent of Hungary's). But no great change took place in the trade between Austria and Hungary. Hungary's share in Austria's exports even declined, from 10 per cent in 1933 to 9 per cent in 1937, as did her share in Austria's imports, from 11.3 per cent to 9 per cent. (Hungary's exports to Austria fell from 27 to 16.9 per cent of the total and imports from 20 to 18 per cent.) Thus in spite of the Rome Protocols, the trade between these two countries declined relatively, and increased in absolute terms (value) only in 1937 with the general increase in world trade. Austrian exports to Hungary totaled S. 96.3 million in 1935, imports 115 million; in 1936 exports were S. 94.4 million, imports 118.3 million, and in 1937 exports S. 111.2 million and imports 131.7 million, but, still this increase in value was proportionately less than the increase in Austria's total trade.

And so the outstanding change consisted of an increase in Italian imports from Austria and Hungary. Since both countries failed to participate in the League of Nations sanctions, they replaced other countries as sources of supply for various Italian imports such as timber and cattle usually obtained from Yugoslavia. This very largely accounts for the increase in their exports to Italy, but because of her situation Italy was not able to increase her exports to them. Consequently Austria and Hungary acquired a large favorable trade balance with Italy; and in 1937 Italy's import surplus in her trade with Austria was 177 million lire and with Hungary 103 million lire. The claims of the Austrian and Hungarian exporters were frozen; a part of the debt was settled by the sale of Austrian securities, among them the Italian share of the Austrian League

Loan. To overcome this difficulty Austria and Hungary were anxious to increase their purchases from Italy, but Italy, exhausted after the Abyssinian campaign and lacking foreign exchange, bought even more than in the previous years. Her import surplus rose in 1937 to 242 million lire with Austria and to 209 million lire with Hungary (out of a total import of 631 and 410 million lire from them, respectively). In contrast with the Czechoslovak position as the creditor of her Little Entente partners, Italy became the debtor of hers with only limited payment possibilities. Complaints about the unsatisfactory functioning of the Rome agreements became more frequent. The shortage of foreign exchange made it difficult for Italy to buy the needed overseas raw materials and to deliver some goods, among them, for example, cotton yarns, and she did not show any great interest in settling her debt with either partner. In the meantime Hungary ceased to be satisfied even with the wheat-export settlement. In connection with the improved wheat prices on the world market in 1936–37, Hungarian agriculture demanded that the Rome Protocols be changed to secure for Hungary the advantage of the higher world prices by replacing the sale of wheat at a fixed price by sale at the market price but with preferential duties.[14]

Then the Italo-Yugoslav political pact, concluded in April, 1937, and followed by an economic agreement, changed the whole situation. Italy granted for the import of Yugoslav timber and cattle the same preferential treatment that was enjoyed by Austria and Hungary.[15] While this agreement was directed by Italy chiefly against the Little Entente it naturally weakened the exclusive privileges which the Rome Protocols were supposed to guarantee to Austria and Hungary. The whole system of credit and transport advantages was abandoned at the end of 1937 and the open preferential duties for Austrian goods ceased to exist on July 1, 1938.

The Rome Protocols did not fulfill the hopes of their designers. Politically they could not save Austria, nor did they improve Italy's position in Central Europe; economically their chief result was a great increase in Italian imports followed by repayment difficulties. The agreements did not contribute to an adjustment of the economies of these three countries, and checked neither the increase in agricultural protection in Austria and Italy nor the growing protec-

14 *The Economist*, April 24, 1937, p. 207, and Jan. 9, 1937, p. 64.
15 Hantos, *op. cit.*, p. 47; *The Economist*, Jan. 22, 1938, p. 159.

tion of industry in Hungary.[16] The increase in Italian agricultural imports which did occur was due to a shift of imports from other countries. It was on the whole an emergency expedient, the increase in trade resulted much more from planning and preferential treatment than from an adjustment of the respective national economies.

The two preferential systems introduced in 1934 and supported by close coöperation improved trade relations between the member combines of each group. However, they were not able to expand foreign trade between all these countries and particularly to make up for the decline in the Czechoslovak-Hungarian and Czechoslovak-Austrian trade. The intertrade between the five Succession States amounted in 1937 to only about one quarter of their aggregate foreign trade.

TABLE 11

INTER-DANUBIAN TRADE IN 1937

PERCENTAGE OF EACH PARTICIPANT IN GROUP I [a] AND IN GROUP II [b]

| | TOTAL EXPORTS | | TOTAL IMPORTS | |
	Group I	Group II	Group I	Group II
Industrial Countries				
Austria	29.6	27.4	35.9	34
Czechoslovakia	20	18.5	15.5	14
Agricultural Countries				
Bulgaria	12		13.5	
Greece	11.3		24.1	
Hungary	28.8	26.8	30.9	29.6
Rumania	27.5	20.8	30.7	29.3
Yugoslavia	28.9	25.7	27.7	25.8

[a] This group includes all seven countries: Czechoslovakia, Austria, Bulgaria, Greece, Hungary, Rumania, and Yugoslavia.
[b] This group excludes Greece and Bulgaria.

Recovery of inter-Danubian trade lagged behind the increase in the total foreign trade of these countries. Neither the Little Entente nor the Rome Protocols changed the situation to any substantial degree, nor did they prove strong enough to work as a real check to the German trade offensive.

[16] Austria reduced imports of Hungarian cattle to a small quota. In order to protect her industries, Hungary limited the subsidies that Austria was allowed to pay for Austrian export. Italy granted total refunding for Austrian timber, cellulose, and steel, but was less liberal in regard to other Austrian industries. And Austria did not open her market to Italian cotton goods. Schüller, *op. cit.*, p. 169.

10

GERMANY'S TRADE PENETRATION IN SOUTHEASTERN EUROPE

GERMANY always regarded the countries of Central and Southeastern Europe as particularly important to her economic and political position. Although—until the occupation of Austria—she never regained there the economic influence and power which she had held prior to the First World War, she did not accept the new situation in these countries as permanent and she did not consider the political system established by the Peace Treaties as compatible with her vital interests. Whereas she did officially accept the settlement in Western Europe as definitive and confirmed it in the Locarno Treaties of 1925, she refused repeatedly to recognize the frontiers in Eastern and Southeastern Europe in a similar Locarno Treaty for the East. It was widely believed that she objected chiefly to renouncing a future annexation of Austria, but her real design was more far-reaching. She wanted to renew her expansion to the southeast, her Berlin-Bagdad "Drang nach Osten," and to organize a large segment of this part of Europe as a single unit under her economic and political leadership. If Germany's aims were not clearly stated at that time or were frequently even denied by the highest authorities, it was only because she did not consider her strength sufficient or the general situation opportune for executing her policy; but, as her political power grew, unchallenged by any determined or unified policy of the Western Powers, her influence in the Southeast also grew.

Germany could point out—and this line of thought found much approval in the West—that she was naturally the most important country in the external trade of Central and Southeastern Europe, and therefore that it was only consistent that her influence be greater than that of the other powers, who did not carry on a large volume of trade with this region. This argument was directed in particular against France, who did not make any great attempts to develop large-scale trade with this region although it was important to her political system. Before the severe crisis in the thirties—to which her policy of intense agricultural protection contributed substantially—

Germany made strenuous efforts to increase her sales in these markets, which were already well known to her producers and exporters. She was very successful and became the most important single trade partner of all these countries except Yugoslavia, where Italy held first place.

Germany could not support her foreign trade with capital exports, as she had done before 1914. Although she retained her old investments in Austria and Hungary and also in Czechoslovakia,[1] she lost them in the other countries, the most important being those in Rumania; and she was unable to participate in extending new credits as did the Western Powers. She had a large export-trade balance with Yugoslavia, to whom she paid a great part of reparations in kind, and particularly with Austria, Czechoslovakia, and Hungary; and a small import surplus with the other three countries. But on the whole she had an export surplus in trade and other net credits in her balance of payments with the area.

The foreign-exchange crisis changed this development; Exchange restrictions in the Danubian countries made it difficult for Germany to retain her exports there and to receive payment for them. In addition her export claims (whose total was estimated at Rm. 220 million) were blocked and frozen in several countries. To secure payment for her exports she was among the first to conclude clearing agreements with the states of Southeastern Europe.[2] It became clear to her that she would be unable to have a favorable balance of trade or of payments paid for in free exchange with the agricultural countries of this region. Furthermore her export surplus to Czechoslovakia and Austria was soon to be greatly reduced; later, especially in the case of Czechoslovakia, it was nearly removed, as a result, of the loss of the large Czechoslovak export surplus in trade with Southeastern Europe and Austria. Thus German export to Southeastern Europe could be paid for only if Germany imported corresponding amounts of goods from these countries. The same policy which Germany demanded at that time from her creditors she had to apply in her trade with these debtor countries.

In order to carry out the necessary balancing of exports with imports, Germany had to overcome two major difficulties. First, her

[1] Czechoslovakia did not utilize the right given her by Article 296–297 of the Versailles Treaty to seize all German investments in her territory.
[2] Karl Ritter, "Germany's Experience with Clearing Agreements," *Foreign Affairs*, XIV (April, 1936), 465–75.

protection of agriculture was an extremely great obstacle to the importation of farm products from those countries. Second, the German exchange-control system was organized in such a way as to make the granting of special treatment to particular countries difficult or impossible. Originally, German exchange control had been a system of allocating foreign exchange to importers in the form of a general license, giving each a specified percentage of the value of his imports in the base period, July 1, 1929–June 30, 1930. The percentages were calculated according to the expected movements of the foreign-exchange reserves. It was repeatedly emphasized that the control was only an emergency expedient, not a permanent policy, and, in particular, that it was not to be used as an instrument of commercial policy for the preferential treatment of any country. Exchange control was not to interfere with the most-favored-nation clause.[3] This principle was maintained officially even when the foreign-exchange allocations declined to 50 per cent, and later to 45 per cent, and 25 per cent (March, 1934), and even less, and in spite of growing demands to reserve exchange for essential imports.

Nevertheless some means of encouraging imports from the clearing countries were at hand and they were used. One method was the granting of preferential import quotas to those commodities subject to an import-permit system. This applied originally only to the corn monopoly, but by the end of 1933 the import-quota system embraced most agricultural products,[4] and on March 22, 1934, it was extended to all industrial raw materials and semifinished goods. In this way it was possible to give special preferential import quotas to the products of Southeastern Europe. The preferential custom treaties signed with Hungary, Bulgaria, and Rumania could not be put into operation because third parties—countries enjoying the most-favored-nation clause—would not agree; but Hungary's import quota for cattle granted in the same treaty was retained.[5]

Another method lay in the so-called additional export agreements or barter agreements which sought both to expand exports and at the same time to liquidate frozen accounts. A large transaction of this sort was concluded in 1932 in Greece by the Reemtsma Ciga-

[3] See Harold Lossos, *Bilanz der deutschen Devisenbewirtschaftung*, Jena, 1940, pp. 11 and 38; H. S. Ellis, *Exchange Control in Central Europe*, pp. 158 ff.
[4] See Lossos, *op. cit.*, p. 41; Kurt Häfner, "Zur Theorie der mengenmässigen Einfuhrregelung," *Weltwirtschaftliches Archiv*, XLI (1935), 219.
[5] Robert W. Krugmann, *Südosteuropa und Grossdeutschland*, Breslau, 1939, p. 79.

rette Manufacturing Company. It provided for large purchases of Greek tobacco to be paid for 70 per cent by German export balances blocked in Greece and 30 per cent by Greek purchases of German products.[6] This transaction started the expansion of Germany's trade with Greece based upon huge tobacco imports. The same company in 1932 also arranged for the purchase of large quantities of Bulgarian and Turkish tobacco to be paid for partially out of blocked German balances.[7] As a rule, permission to trade on a compensation basis was granted whenever it helped to liquidate frozen German export balances. A special trade organization also arranged to increase imports of Rumanian corn and Yugoslav prunes, walnuts, and so on, and in 1933 an agreement was concluded for the importation of Bulgarian vegetable seeds as the result of an arrangement with German vegetable farmers.[8]

After the conclusion of the general clearing agreements the number of barter transactions was reduced; the importers of goods from the clearing countries had no exchange-quota difficulties, but the customs duties remained unchanged.

Like Czechoslovakia, Germany also had to maintain and even increase her imports from these countries, if her exporters were to be paid for their goods. In view of the total volume of Germany's imports it should not have been difficult to cope with this problem especially since these countries still offered good export opportunities —and the emphasis was still upon exports at that time.

Until 1934 trade with these countries declined as follows: German exports to Hungary, Rumania, Yugoslavia, Bulgaria, and Greece went down from Rm. 585 million in 1929 (4.6 per cent of total German exports) to Rm. 353.9 million (3.1 per cent) in 1931 and to only Rm. 154.3 million (2.8 per cent) in 1933. German imports from the same countries declined from Rm. 516.1 million (3.8 per cent of total German imports) in 1929 to Rm. 316.3 million (4.9 per cent) in 1931 and to Rm. 198.5 million (4.7 per cent) in 1933. Whereas exports to these countries declined both absolutely and relatively (that is, more than total German exports) the share of imports from them increased, relative to total German imports, as a

[6] Banque d'Athenes, *Bulletin èconomique et financier*, June, 1932, p. 2041.
[7] Dr. Kurt Kroymann, *Clearing und Kompensation in Aussenhandel*, Hamburg, 1935, p. 44. On the whole this company liquidated about Rm. 22.3 million of German balances through its tobacco purchases up to the end of 1933.
[8] R. W. Krugmann, *op. cit.*, p. 82.

result of the efforts to maintain a volume of imports sufficient to pay for German exports.[9] In 1933 German exports to these countries were smaller than to Czechoslovakia alone.

As early as 1932 the previous export surplus with these countries was changed to an import balance of 34.5 million and in 1933 of 44.2 million. Since then Germany has always had a passive trade balance with them.

The "New Plan" introduced in September, 1934, completely changed the policy: the emphasis was shifted from export to import, Germany exported chiefly in order to be able to pay for her imports, whereas prior to this time she imported in order to be able to export.

[9] Germany's exports to Czechoslovakia declined from Rm. 657.6 million in 1929 to 166.1 million in 1933 or from 4.9% to 3.3% of total exports; imports went down from Rm. 480.3 million to 121.7 million or from 3.6% to only 2.9%.

Germany's exports to Austria dropped in the same period from 3.3% to 2.5% and imports from 1.5% to 1.4% of the respective totals.

11

POLICY OF THE NEW PLAN TOWARD
SOUTHEASTERN EUROPE

THE NEW PLAN was closely coördinated with the political and other aspects of the Nazi program and integrated the exchange-control system and the commercial policy with Germany's totalitarian armed economy. It introduced complete import and export control coupled with exchange control, which became the most important instrument in commercial policy. Although the most-favored-nation clause of existing commercial treaties retained formal validity, virtually all of its real significance [1] was lost. Complete planning and rationing of imports was begun and only the most urgently needed goods were to be imported; naturally first among these were raw materials and foodstuffs, so far as they could not be produced in Germany.

In addition to this control of the commodities to be exported and imported, the New Plan also set out to change the territorial distribution of Germany's foreign trade, and succeeded in bringing about a great shift in the countries of origin of German imports and in the distribution of German exports. The whole idea of multilateral trade and international division of production was abandoned, and in its place the idea of the exchange of commodities between supplementary economies was advanced and pursued. Germany was not greatly interested in trying to expand her trade with countries with similar economic structures, such, for example, as Western Europe, which prior to 1932 took nearly one third of German exports and provided her with a very large export balance.[2] It was argued that countries of similar economic structure do not offer great opportunities for an extended trade. On the contrary, Germany expected to be able to increase her trade greatly with countries whose economic structure complemented her own, that is, countries that exported raw materials and agricultural products. There she saw good prospects of developing resources and of getting more supplies.

[1] H. Lossos, op. cit., p. 45.
[2] See Andreas Predöhl, "Die sogenannten Handelshemmnisse und der Preisaufbau der Weltwirtschaft," Weltwirtschaftliches Archiv, LII (1941), 193–222.

There were, of course, other considerations involved in the whole plan, for it was from the very beginning, as must be clearly understood, a part of the greater program of economic preparation for war. Gemany wanted to conserve foreign exchange as much as possible. She made great efforts to buy from countries with whom she had clearing or similar payment agreements. Bilateral trading was one of the basic principles of the whole scheme, and by using her bargaining power as a large potential market, Germany endeavored to establish her system of bilateral balancing of trade wherever it was possible and of advantage to her. She stated repeatedly that she would buy only from countries willing to take her goods. "It is not possible to buy from countries with low prices but only where there are available balances." [3] This reorganization of trade was also based on various aspects of the direct military demands of the coming war. It was highly desirable to be able to obtain the maximum volume of supplies from Southeastern Europe, which could be reached by land during a war.

Thus the armed economy, introduced in 1933, requiring huge supplies of raw materials and greater food imports, quickly changed German commercial policy by transforming it into a totalitarian trade policy. The purpose of foreign trade was not to export in order to provide employment but to import those things necessary for the war economy and to provide the required payment by planned and, whenever necessary, subsidized export. The idea of multilateral trade and international price competition was replaced by bilateral treaties and clearing agreements wherever possible and advantageous. [4]

Germany was not willing, however, to accept a balanced trade with those free-payment countries with whom she had previously had an export surplus, and the financial interests of Germany's credi-

[3] H. Lossos, op. cit., p. 97.

[4] Dr. Schacht and several other leading German officials nevertheless continued to claim that bilateralism was forced upon Germany. Dr. Schacht said: "The extreme system of bilateral trade treaties was forced upon us by our foreign creditors. The new plan was brought about by a serious state of affairs into which Germany was forced by foreign countries. The unusual in the new plan lay only in the fact that it was freed from all preconceived theoretical teachings and in the fact that it made use of all practical measures which could be of assistance. If anything smacks of the miraculous in the new plan it is again only the fact that under National Socialist leadership it has been possible for German organization to develop in a very short time the entire apparatus of import supervision, export control and export promotion." German Institute for Business Research, Weekly Report, Dec. 1, 1938, No. 47–48, Supplement: "Finance Miracle and New Plan."

tors in these countries furnished a welcome support to the Nazi demands. Generally, greater importance was attached to trade with countries exporting primary products than to trade with highly industrialized countries. And it was only one step from the practice of promoting trade with countries of complementary economic structures to the doctrines of "living space" and "Grossraumwirtschaft."

In spite of the growing need of raw materials and foodstuffs—there were repeated complaints about the scarcity of various foods—the policy of autarky and self-sufficiency in food was consistently pursued throughout the whole period. The concept of trade with complementary economies did not include any adjustment of the German economy to those of the other countries nor any change in the level of her prices, which were far above world-market prices. She put into effect a system of complete control over the importation of all significant goods, designed not only to divorce the reichsmark price of imports from the price on foreign markets but also to prevent great variations in prices on the domestic market. The volume of total imports was controlled by an import-permit system, requiring a special license for each transaction; agencies controlling the trade in particular goods were empowered to buy goods from the German importers and resell them at officially fixed prices. They could also attain the same result by charging variable license fees and special internal taxes on imported goods.[5] Thus the trade-control authorities were able to eliminate the danger that a fall in the price of imports could affect production of similar goods in Germany.

In organizing import control under the New Plan, the previously existing commodity boards were taken over (the oldest of these, the Corn Monopoly was established in 1930; it had been extended in 1933 to cover virtually all agricultural imports) as were several supervisory offices (Überwachungsstellen) controlling industrial raw and semimanufactured materials. Under the decrees of September, 1934, ten additional supervisory offices were created and these, with the eleven already in existence and the four agricultural monopoly boards, were given jurisdiction over the importation into Germany of all categories of goods.[6] Organized in this way, foreign-exchange control became a normal instrument for determining and regulating the composition of German imports in the most minute detail, including the origin and destination of goods. It was this detailed and comprehensive

[5] See Kurt Häfner, op. cit., pp. 219–20.   [6] In 1939 there were 28 such offices.

control which made it possible for Germany to carry out great changes in the composition of her imports and to shift for them, to countries which were preferable for various reasons.

As a result of the New Plan the importance of trade relations between Germany and Southeastern Europe greatly increased. These agricultural countries had a surplus of raw materials and foodstuffs, thus complying with the new theory of trade between countries with complementary economic structures. They were accessible by land—which was important in case of war. They did not represent one political unit capable of negotiating with Germany on a strong political and economic basis; their bargaining power was weak, relative to the trade possibilities which Germany was able to grant them. Furthermore, they possessed no such control over their own economies and trade as the totalitarian organization of Germany. This, too, weakened their bargaining position.

Because she was a large potential buyer of the staple exports of these countries, Germany could have gained economic and perhaps political concessions even in regular commercial treaties negotiated under more normal circumstances. How much greater then were the opportunities to expand her influence when, on the one hand, her trade was centrally planned and directed toward clearly defined ends and, on the other, the countries in question were suffering acutely from the effects of the economic crisis. They faced many problems: the threat of monetary instability, difficulty in balancing government budgets, loss of export markets, extremely difficult problems of adjusting prices to those on the world market, and even scarcities in many consumer goods. To all this must be added the fact that —after many disappointments—they had no great hope of obtaining help in the form of concerted international action by the Western countries, who still paid far more attention to Germany than to Southeastern Europe. One could hardly imagine better circumstances for the launching of Germany's economic offensive to the Southeast.

Germany's first move was to take large quantities of surplus stocks off the hands of the producers of Southeastern Europe, paying prices about 30 per cent above the ruling world-market prices.[7] It should, however, be noted that during this period Germany dis-

[7] Royal Institute, *Survey of International Affairs, 1936* (A. J. Toynbee, "Germany's Drang nach Südosten"), p. 527.

played only a secondary interest in staple commodities which could compete with her own production.[8] Not until 1937 did she import, for instance, large quantities of bread cereals from the Balkans, but during the whole period she tried to increase her fodder and fat imports as much as possible. It was her definite policy increasingly to purchase from Southeastern Europe raw materials and foodstuffs formerly obtained from overseas. The higher prices received by producers and exporters were a great incentive to an expansion of trade with Germany that was evident as early as 1934. Furthermore, Germany's credit was better in this part of Europe than elsewhere. The whole trade was carried out under clearing agreements. Exporters to Germany did not obtain free foreign exchange, as in the free markets, but, instead, got credits in the clearing accounts which could not be used generally but only for certain expenditures within Germany permitted by the foreign-exchange control.[9]

However, Germany's large purchases soon resulted in her developing import surpluses and consequently large debit balances on the clearing accounts with these countries. Thus in her great need of foreign exchange she succeeded in getting a kind of forced loan from countries which were themselves very short of capital. At the end of December, 1934, German debts in all clearing accounts already totaled Rm. 450 million, the greater part owed to the countries of Central and Southeastern Europe. In March, 1935, this debt reached Rm. 567 million.[10] However, this did not stop the expansion of German purchases. On the contrary, employing her policy of paying higher prices, Germany made great efforts to increase the volume of imports from the area in her effort to bring about the greatest possible shift in the sources of origin. These efforts were aided by her policy with regard to the exchange rates between the mark and the clearing currencies. Germany did not devalue her currency, but maintained the fiction of the original gold parity; she usually de-

[8] "The Economic Independence of Southeastern Europe," German Institute of Business Research, *Weekly Report*, Feb. 19, 1940, No. 5–6, pp. 14–19.
[9] As an exception, for a number of years Germany granted Bulgaria payments in free exchange of 10–20% of her exports to Germany, but later this too was suspended. Hungary and some other countries were given permission to import from Germany coffee and some other overseas products imported into Germany under some of her barter transactions. On the other hand, Germany resold on the free markets various goods bought in clearing transactions, often at prices below those demanded by the producing countries. Later she had to commit herself not to reëxport without the consent of the countries of origin.
[10] *The Economist*, Dec. 3, 1938, p. 485; Lossos, *op. cit.*, p. 90.

manded that the rate of exchange between the mark and the other currency in question be firmly fixed on this basis in the clearing agreement—although this fictitious legal parity was of little use in trade with the free-exchange countries. However, in view of the fact that the internal purchasing power of the reichsmark indicated a gradually increasing devaluation, acceptance of the German demand was paramount to an admission of an overvaluation of the mark or a devaluation of the other currencies in relation to the mark. Nevertheless, Germany succeeded to a great extent in imposing upon the clearing countries a higher value of the mark than was justified by its domestic purchasing power, which meant relative devaluation of the other currencies and at the same time lower prices in marks for Germany's imports. Even Czechoslovakia and Austria accepted in principle this demand in their treaties with Germany. The agreements with Bulgaria, Hungary, and Rumania also provided for fixed rates of exchange between the mark and their currencies. However, during the whole period Bulgaria was the only country in which the rate remained unchanged from the original parity of 1 rm. = 33 leva, although exchange premia up to 35 per cent were granted on other free currencies. Because of the high exchange premium, imports from other countries could not compete with imports from Germany. The overvaluation of the mark made Bulgaria's monetary policy dependent upon Germany's.[11]

In spite of German insistence upon the old parity she was induced to make some concessions. For example, in trade with Hungary the basic rate was fixed at 1.36 pö = 1 rm., but to this a premium was added by an agreement between the National Banks of both countries. For the most important commodities this premium was 18–19 per cent (equal to a rate of 1.60–1.61 pö = 1 rm.) or a much lower premium than on the pound or the dollar.[12]

Thus, while Germany admitted a devaluation, in her trade with Hungary, it was not considered sufficient in Hungary, where the mark was still believed to be overvalued in terms of the pengö.[13]

In Rumania the National Bank tried to discourage exports to Germany and to reduce Rumanian balances blocked in the Reich by

[11] *The Economist*, June 4, 1938, p. 537.   [12] *The Economist*, Nov. 14, 1936, p. 310.
[13] Mark Mitnitzky, "Germany's Trade Monopoly in Eastern Europe," *Social Research*, VI (1939), No. 1, 35.

allowing exporters to sell their clearing marks in the open market, except for two quotas of 10 per cent each, which the Bank reserved the right to purchase at a fixed rate. The experiences with the system of fluctuating rates were not satisfactory. Contrary to German expectations the sale of clearing marks on the free market did not prevent the mark from depreciating; in 1936 it fell as low as 33–34 lei per rm. Germany insisted upon a fixed rate and under this pressure the official rate of exchange for clearing marks was fixed in 1936 at 37.5 lei per rm. and was increased in December, 1937, to 38–39 lei per rm. Germany's demands to increase the value of the mark became a permanent feature of her commercial negotiations with Rumania.

In the earliest clearing agreements with Yugoslavia the official parity of the mark (1 rm. = 17.60 dinars) was the accepted rate of exchange. However, the accumulation of large balances in favor of Yugoslavia—exceeding 300 million dinars in April, 1935, caused the introduction of private clearings, by which importers could purchase the claims of Yugoslav exporters directly in the form of clearing checks. With this arrangement the private clearing rate went down to 12.50–14.50 dinars although the nominal official rate remained stable at 17.42–17.62. Here again Germany persistently demanded that the mark rate be raised and stabilized, but, of all the countries of Southeastern Europe, Yugoslavia was apparently the most independent on this point, a fact which can probably be explained by her more consolidated foreign exchange policy. In contrast, the Bank of Greece fixed and maintained the mark rate at between 36 and 43 drachmas, a rate which could not have been maintained without the constant help and intervention of the Bank.

On the whole the mark was overvalued relative to all these currencies, and this necessarily influenced not only their trade with Germany but also their internal price development and their foreign trade in general.

It might seem that Germany, having an import surplus, would be interested in a low rather than a high rate of exchange, for the overvaluation of the mark functioned as an import premium tending further to increase the import surplus. But Germany was not at all opposed to having an import surplus with clearing countries. On the contrary, one of the aims of her policy was to develop an import surplus and to use it as an instrument for expanding trade with these countries.[14] She wanted importation to lead exportation; the overvaluation of the mark served this purpose well.

This artificial mark exchange rate made the paying of higher prices, in terms of the respective national currencies, easier than would have been the case had the rate been allowed to fall to a more normal level. But still Germany very often paid prices even in overvalued marks which were higher than those on the world markets. "She paid excellent prices, usually higher than the world market quotations. They corresponded to the internal price for agricultural products of Southeastern Europe so that economic and social repercussions were avoided." [15] Thus Germany developed a consistent plan for purchasing those commodities which she wanted to import in her effort to replace imports from distant sources or from those requiring payment in free exchange. It was her deliberate policy to encourage the accumulation of balances in favor of other countries because this gave her very strong weapons to use in obtaining concessions for German exports and especially for knitting firm economic ties with these countries, which it was her ultimate goal to include within her empire.

It was plainly stated that "Since German purchases increased at a far greater pace than the demand for German goods, the other countries acquired considerable clearing funds with the Reichsbank, which soon accumulated to larger sums than were necessary to pay for the current import of German industrial goods." [16] Continuous complaints about the embarrassment caused by these blocked accounts was clear evidence of such a development. At the beginning of May, 1936, for instance, German debts on clearing accounts to Greece were about Rm. 40 million, to Hungary and Yugoslavia Rm. 25 million each, to Rumania 18 million, and to Bulgaria about 10 million (Czechoslovakia's balance was Rm. 62 million),[17] and in 1937 Yugoslavia's claim rose to Rm. 36 millions—certainly substantial amounts for these countries. Germany, of course, did not stop her purchases, but tried instead, with varying success, to induce these countries to increase production regardless of the cost to them of various commodities usually purchased overseas, such as textiles

[14] H. Lossos, *op. cit.*, pp. 74, 77.

[15] "The Economic Independence of Southeastern Europe," German Institute for Business Research, *Weekly Report*, Feb. 19, 1940, No. 5–6, p. 36; S. D. Obradovič, *op. cit.*, p. 36.

[16] "The Economic Independence of Southeastern Europe," p. 17.

[17] *Financial News*, June 4, 1936.

and oleaginous plants. The only possibility of using the export proceeds was to increase imports from Germany; the accounts were to be settled exclusively within the framework of bilateralism. Germany was unable to supply her trading partners with raw materials, various other overseas goods, or, frequently, even with adequate amounts of manufactured consumers goods. Under these circumstances a new argument was conceived and presented: Whereas Germany's need for raw materials and other goods was described as being unlimited, the ability of these countries to buy and consume Germany's industrial products was inadequate, because of their low level of economic development. This Germany viewed as a "straitjacket" which had to be broken for it inhibited the flow of her vital imports.[18] The way to correct this was to extend and develop their economies and to make new investments by buying German machinery. It was further argued that German goods for direct consumption could hardly be absorbed in sufficiently large quantities to liquidate the clearing balances. In 1936 Dr. Schacht made a special trip to sell this proposition to the Balkan nations and to induce them not only to maintain but to increase their exports to Germany.

What was the attitude of these countries concerned? Germany's large purchases were certainly welcomed as a great source of relief, especially for agriculture, and the high prices paid by German buyers provided numerous supporters for this kind of trade. Thus new vested interests were created among politically influential groups (peasants and farmers) who were not familiar with the intricacies of the clearing-payment system and who had formerly known Germany as a powerful trade partner with well-established credit. To them, exportation to Germany was a way out of the depression and as such was to be defended and maintained. Therefore, when the clearing situation became unbalanced and the volume of blocked claims increased it was extremely difficult to attempt a remedy by reducing exports to Germany, if no alternative outlets for the export surpluses were available. Nevertheless, nearly all these countries tried this method. In 1937 Rumania limited the export of petroleum and petroleum products to Germany against clearing credits to 20 per cent of her total exports to Germany. Yugoslavia, similarly, prohibited the export of copper except for free exchange, and Hungary, like other countries, tried to find other markets, especially in Great

18 H. Lossos, *op. cit.*, p. 83.

Britain. However, the loss of the Italian market to Yugoslavia and Greece during the period of the League of Nations sanctions was an important factor in causing them to augment their exports to Germany, the only country willing to buy all the available goods.

If they were to be paid for such exports these countries were obliged to increase their imports from her—increased exports were followed by increased imports, not always voluntarily. Their government orders, which were sometimes very important, were placed in Germany even at prices higher than elsewhere. In addition, imports from other countries were shifted to Germany, frequently through the use of exchange control or the import-permit system.[19] Thus imports from Germany increased at the expense of other countries, particularly the free countries and Czechoslovakia and Austria; and Germany pursued her aim of gaining dominance in the trade of these countries first by obtaining a key position in their export trade and then by gaining progressively greater influence over their imports.

Germany delivered a great number of industrial products, both consumer and capital goods, but she followed no rigid or consistent price policy. Where she had to expect foreign competition she offered her products at lower prices than other suppliers, using a system of export subsidies, but where such competition was not taken seriously she asked for higher prices than could be obtained in other markets. This was true particularly of chemicals—for example, dyestuffs and pharmaceutical drugs—tools, special machinery, optical materials, and most products subject to international cartels. There were constant complaints against the high prices asked by the German exporters who thought they already had a monopoly. Later, when shortages were increasing in Germany, there were also frequent complaints about the long delivery terms and the inferior quality of German goods.

The fact that these countries were compelled to buy goods of mediocre quality, manufactured with substitutes, indicates the lower value of the marks they received. But it would be wrong to assume —as it is often stated and quoted—that aspirin, cameras, and harmonicas formed a major part of German exports. An example of the

---

[19] Largely for the purpose of carrying out such a shift of imports Yugoslavia introduced in June, 1936, an import-permit system which authorized the National Bank to refuse import licenses for some very important products from non-clearing countries. S. Obradović, *op. cit.*, p. 30.

contrary is seen in the following import figures in 1936: from Germany Hungary obtained 70 per cent of her total machine imports; Yugoslavia, 50.4 per cent; Rumania, 35 per cent, and Bulgaria, 80 per cent.[20] After all a large foreign trade designed to establish firm links with these countries could not have been built up by exporting goods which were largely useless to the importing countries. However, the agrarian countries soon became aware of the importance and danger of their trade relations with Germany, but there was a conviction among them that they were forced into it by the general economic and political situation which was beyond their control or influence.

The following figures [21] show how in the period up to 1937 Germany succeeded in expanding her trade with these agricultural countries.

TABLE 12

GERMANY'S FOREIGN TRADE WITH THE AGRICULTURAL COUNTRIES OF SOUTHEASTERN EUROPE [a]

YEAR	EXPORTS		IMPORTS	
	Millions of Rm.	Per Cent of Total Exports	Millions of Rm.	Per Cent of Total Imports
1929	585.0	4.3	516.1	3.8
1933	154.3	2.8	198.5	4.7
1934	170.6	3.9	248.2	5.6
1935	252.6	5.9	319.1	7.7
1936	374.9	7.9	386.9	9.2
1937	555.7	9.4	574	10.5

[a] Hungary, Yugoslavia, Rumania, Bulgaria, Greece.

As the above figures show the value (in rm.) of German imports from these countries in 1937 exceeded that in 1929, whereas total German imports in that year reached only 40 per cent of the 1929 level. Taking 1933 as 100, import in 1937 from Southeastern Europe was 282, export 283. This increase in trade with Germany largely accounts for the increased share of these countries in world trade.[22] Between 1929 and 1937 their share of world imports rose

[20] R. W. Krugmann, op. cit., p. 164.
[21] "Trade Relations between Germany and the Southeastern European Countries," Weekly Report, German Institute for Business Research, Supplement, March 4, 1938.
[22] League of Nations, World Trade, 1937, p. 25.

from 2.04 to 2.13 per cent and of exports from 1.90 to 2.69 per cent and of total world trade from 1.98 to 2.42 per cent, a development contrary to that in Czechoslovakia and Austria. The percentage figures in the above tabulation are typical of the shift in German trade carried out during this period to conform with the requirements of the New Plan. At the same time German imports from all industrial countries declined from 35.4 per cent of total imports in 1929 to 27.8 per cent in 1937, while those from other countries increased from 64.6 to 72.2 per cent. And, as Dr. Schacht boasted,[23] it was possible between 1934 and 1937 to increase imports of ores by 132 per cent, of petroleum by 116 per cent, of grain by 102 per cent, and of rubber by 71 per cent, whereas imports of finished goods were decreased by 63 per cent. In the light of this development the increase in imports of particular commodities from Southeastern Europe is even more significant.

The figures in Table 13 [24] indicate how the share of Southeastern Europe in Germany's total import of particular commodities had already increased by 1937 as compared with 1929.

This growth in the share of Southeastern Europe was indeed important from the point of view of German imports, but how much more important were these exports for the small countries, under the difficult market conditions abroad!

There has been much discussion about terms of trade during this period; and it has been stated that Germany's terms of trade were less favorable than they would have been if she had devalued her currency, adjusted her price level, and continued to trade on the traditional basis. Of course, such measurements are very difficult in general and in the case of Germany particularly so because of her complicated trade and foreign-exchange policy, and because it is almost impossible to know what the terms really were. Without a knowledge of all the pertinent facts, which are not yet available, it would be difficult to pass any definite judgment with regard to Germany's terms of trade with Southeastern Europe during this period. She often paid, even in marks, higher prices in these countries than it would have been necessary to pay on the world markets in free exchange. But this was exactly the critical point. In order to obtain the required free exchange it would have been necessary to sell adequate exports in these markets,

[23] German Institute for Business Research, *Weekly Report,* Dec. 1, 1938, No. 47–48, pp. 5–6.
[24] Based on official German foreign-trade statistics.

TABLE 13

PERCENTAGE OF GERMANY'S TOTAL IMPORTS OF PARTICULAR COMMODITIES

	1929	1937
Wheat	2.4	36.9[a]
Barley	37.4	80.5
Corn	6.8	32.9
Eggs	17.3	24.3
Non-tropical fruits	24.5	35
Meat—meat products	7	35
Cattle	9.6	18.8
Pigs	0	21.0
Lard	0.1	31.0
Tobacco	47.8	61.3
Timber	24.5	35
Bauxite	37.2	62.1
Lead ore	2.9	28.9
Copper and copper alloys	3.3	5.6
Hemp and Flax	1.1	11.4
Tropical fruits	6.1	11.3

[a] In 1935–39 the average of the total export from Rumania, Hungary, Yugoslavia, and Bulgaria was: wheat and wheat flour, 1,889,000 tons; corn, 1,013,000 tons; barley, 306,000 tons. This was equal to 37.2% of the total deficit of European imports in wheat; to 19.3% in corn; and to 23.1% in barley. Foreign Agriculture, Washington, D.C., 1940, No. 12, p. 707.

but because of her high level of prices, calculated in terms of the fictitious mark parity, she was able to export to them only by granting large export subsidies. In her trade with Southeastern Europe subsidies were not generally necessary, therefore the amount of the subsidies saved in this way can be deducted from the higher prices she paid for such imports. Furthermore, she managed to obtain higher prices at least for a part of the exports in question. Several German statements try to prove that her terms of trade, as a result of careful planning, were at least as favorable as those of other industrial countries,[25] and

[25] Dr. Fritz Meyer has made the following calculation of the terms of trade for the leading industrial countries (a value of more than 1 indicates that the price of imports rose more than the price of exports; less than 1 means the opposite).

	1930	1935	1937
U.S.A.	0.91	0.79	0.82
Germany	0.93	0.80	0.82
Great Britain	0.92	0.85	0.87
Italy	1.04	1.00	0.95

Thus German terms of trade according to Dr. Meyer were equal to those of the United States! See his article: "Die Sicherung der autonomen Wirtschaftsentwicklung im Bereich der Aussenwirtschaft," *Weltwirtschaftliches Archiv*, LIII (1941), 349.

that her planned economy—working through the commodity boards and similar agencies—prevented the higher price of imported goods from having any effect upon production costs or the cost of living.[26] But even if the terms of trade had been less favorable with this area than with the free countries, the sacrifice was certainly only a very minor item in the costs of the German armed economy.

There is a second question: what were the terms of trade of the agricultural countries of Southeastern Europe with Germany? Here again there is not sufficient factual evidence for a considered answer. We can, however, point out simply that these countries on the whole obtained higher prices from Germany than elsewhere and that they were not charged correspondingly high prices for their imports from Germany, although the quantity and kind of goods available were restricted and their quality was not always the best. Again the hypothetical question can, of course, be raised: If they had adjusted exchange rates and price levels to meet the world market would they have been able to obtain better terms of trade? But the problem must be analyzed within the framework of the total effects of the trade with Germany upon the national economies of the countries concerned, for it is a greater problem than the mere question of terms of trade or of whether in return for their exports these countries received an adequate and appropriate volume of imports. First it can be stated that the increased exports to Germany caused increased economic activity in general, giving rise to a favorable export multiplier effect, and certainly contributed to the recovery of the distressed national economies. But to what extent did the trade with Germany stop or change the process of readjustment which had been in progress since the beginning of the crisis? To what extent did it delay a badly needed integration of these economies with the world economy? Did it not even reverse this desirable trend and lead them instead into the autarkic German economic system with all its consequences? The extent to which the high prices paid by German importers affected the whole price structure of the countries in question depends, obviously, upon the proportion of the total exports of important commodities that went to Germany. Very often the portion sold to Germany was decisive, influencing the price of the total available stocks.

26 See an instructive description of this policy in "Deutsche Preispolitik und Weltwirtschaft" in *Vierteljahreshefte des Institutes für Konjunkturforschung*, 1938–39, No. 3, pp. 333, 351.

Although various systems for governmental control of import and export existed, they were not as effective as was Germany's centralized totalitarian control, and, in particular, they had no comprehensive equalizing system for preventing the increase in prices of the exported goods from spreading over to the goods on the domestic market. Thus the higher prices obtained from Germany, resulting in part from the overvaluation of the mark but also in part from the higher mark prices, spread from one commodity to another; the whole level of prices was raised thereby, but most important was the rise in export prices.[27] Because of this rise in prices the price levels of these countries were divorced even more from the world-market system. The problems of adjusting to world-market prices and of exporting to the free markets to obtain foreign exchange, which was vitally needed for some purposes, became increasingly difficult. Restrained by their clearing trade with Germany and desiring to avoid greater and more general direct devaluation, they resorted to all kinds of subsidies and exchange premia to support their exports to the free exchange countries. The higher the prices which Germany paid, the greater these difficulties became and the more acute grew the need for export premia. The devaluation of currency, admitted and accepted in the case of the mark, did not remain confined to it but spread in relation to other exchanges so that a concealed devaluation gradually took place.[28] This was one of the main reasons for the unstable monetary conditions in Southeastern Europe. The purpose of German policy, to detach this whole area from the world market and to include it in the German economic sphere, became clearer every day in spite of the continuous attempts of the countries involved to mitigate the growing danger. It was undoubtedly Germany's aim to be of decisive influence in the whole economic development of this region. To achieve this, it was necessary for her to have a key position in their export trade and for their exports to continue to be of primary importance for their whole economies. And as an official German source stated: ". . . this is more or less the case in Southeastern Europe

[27] I do not think that any great inflationary effects originated from the advances made by the Central Banks to the exporters on their clearing balances in order to shorten the period that they were forced to wait for their export proceeds. This was done in Yugoslavia, in Greece (where a short term government loan was issued to mobilize these balances), and also in Czechoslovakia. Of course the exchange rate of the mark was definitely supported by these advances.

[28] League of Nations, *World Economic Survey*, 1938–39, p. 205.

which owes its relatively great economic stability during the economic crisis to Germany's readiness to purchase its foodstuffs and raw materials." [29]

[29] "Changes in the Problems and Possibilities of German Foreign Trade." *Weekly Report* of the German Institute for Business Research, Jan., 1939, No. 1–2, p. 6.

12

THE INCREASE OF TRADE WITH GERMANY

GERMAN purchases under the clearing agreements and the overvaluation of the reichsmark were the instruments used to make the trade of Southeastern Europe dependent upon Germany by detaching it from the world-price structure and thus forcing it into the German living space. The degree of success of this policy depended economically upon the economic strength, policy, and foreign-trade relations of the countries selected to be the victims of German trade aggression. A stronger position was held by countries with some products readily marketed abroad, and by those which diligently tried to effect an adjustment of their price level or which enjoyed special preferential treatment with other countries.

Bulgaria, even before the crisis, carried on larger trade with Germany than did the other countries: in 1929, 29.9 per cent of her export trade and 23.2 per cent of her import trade was with that country. By 1933 these figures had already risen to 36 per cent and 38.2 per cent, respectively, Germany being her greatest trade partner. In the commercial treaty which was put into operation in February, 1933, Germany granted Bulgaria reductions and consolidations for 33 import tariff items. At the same time, Germany's demand for specialized agricultural products fitted in very well with Bulgaria's program for changing the structure of her agriculture from the production of staples to diversified and intensive agriculture; she succeeded better than the other countries in bringing about such a shift. Germany asked particularly for fat and textile fibers, agreeing to be a permanent buyer of any quantities offered and to pay remunerative prices. Of course, she was in a good position to fulfill this last condition because of the overvaluation of the clearing mark.

Bulgaria's main export products did not compete with German agriculture,[1] and during the whole period the production of complementary crops increased. The acreage of soya cultivation increased from 2,500 ha. in 1934 to 17,000 ha. in 1937. Sunflower acreage went

---

[1] The share of cereals in Bulgaria's exports in 1936 was only 13.8%; that of fruit 9.4% (in 1938, 17.5%); of eggs 11.9%; of hides and skins 3.6%; tobacco 46.6%. For details see M. Deyanowa, *Weltwirtschaftliches Archiv*, LI (1940), p. 430.

up to 166,000 ha. in 1938 against only 19,500 in 1925. Poultry production was also intensified and fruit production, including canning, was extended. Cotton production more than tripled in four years, hemp production reached 3,305 tons in 1936; the area of flax was increased by 500 per cent. It was not difficult to place all the available surpluses in Germany. A new company, "Vitaminosa," bought the whole soya crop, paying guaranteed high prices. In 1937 export to Germany absorbed 43.1 per cent of the total, imports from her 54.1 per cent (in 1936 these figures were 47.6 and 61, respectively). Thus Germany is seen to have gained a completely dominant role in Bulgaria's trade. On the other hand, Italy failed to gain any increase in trade with Bulgaria, in spite of the commercial treaty of 1934 which granted Bulgaria tariff concessions on numerous items and preferential treatment for poultry, eggs, and corn flour, together with a quota for cattle and the guarantee of the annual purchase of a specified amount of tobacco.[2]

The bulk (about 90 per cent) of Bulgaria's exports to Germany consisted of tobacco, nontropical fruits, eggs, meat and meat products, hides and skins, and, after 1937, wheat.

Bulgaria, like other countries, had to accept permanent large credit balances in her account with Germany (about 400 million leva on the average), a great part of which was spent on arms.[3]

Greece's position was similar, in that her agricultural surpluses did not compete with production in Germany, and consequently could always find a good market there. Germany gained a firm position in this market by large tobacco purchases, which represented about two thirds of the total Greek export to Germany. For Greece and Bulgaria the situation on the world tobacco market had a direct bearing upon their trade relations with Germany and their dependence upon her. The fact that after the last war Balkan tobacco did not regain its market in Great Britain and could never obtain any share of it worth mentioning definitely weakened the position of these countries.

Greece's exports to Germany in 1929 amounted to 23.2 per cent of the total and in 1933 to 17.9 per cent, her imports, 10½ per cent and 11½ per cent, respectively. Italy was her second largest European

2 Bobtcheff, *Reglementation du commerce*, p. 57.

3 "Most of Bulgaria's 10 million RM credits in Germany is to be spent on arms and an additional order for £2.5 million has been placed for artillery," *Daily Telegraph*, London, June 18, 1936.

customer, taking 18.3 per cent of her total export in 1929 and 14 per cent in 1933. The imposition of sanctions against Italy greatly affected Greece's trade with that country, her exports declining to 5.9 per cent in 1935 and in 1936 to only 1.8 per cent of total exports. But Greek exports to Germany, supported by this development, increased to 29.7 per cent in 1935 and to 36.4 per cent in 1936. Although Greece demanded very high prices from Germany and refused to pay in free exchange for various raw materials and semifinished goods, she did not solve the problem of the abnormal growth of trade with Germany, with all of its political, economic, and social implications. In 1937, Greece still sold 31 per cent of her total exports to Germany and obtained 27.2 per cent of her imports from there. Tobacco, tropical fruit, wine, and bauxite made up about 80 per cent of Greece's exports to Germany, however hides and skins, iron ores and pyrites were also important. Although her dependence upon Germany was great, it was not as decisive as in the case of Bulgaria, because of the large volume of trade with other countries particularly the United States and Great Britain. These two countries together always took more than 25 per cent of Greek exports.

Hungary's position in regard to wheat and some animal products was certainly improved as a result of the Rome agreements, but she still suffered greatly from the loss of much of her export trade, in particular to Czechoslovakia. She needed additional large markets for her staple products. This need was met to a large extent in a new agreement concluded with Germany in 1934 which provided import quotas for several important items. Government committees were established to coördinate the mutual trade and the quotas were steadily expanded. In 1937 large quotas were granted for cereals (both bread and fodder), dairy products, fruits, vegetables, and wine. Although she did not follow Bulgaria (and, to a certain degree Rumania) in changing the structure of her agriculture according to the German demands,[4] Hungary, nevertheless, succeeded in meeting Germany's demand for additional supplies of meat, cattle, lard, and poultry.

Under these circumstances exports to Germany increased rapidly, rising from 11.4 per cent of total exports in 1933 to 23.9 per cent in

[4] R. W. Krugmann, op. cit., pp. 79, 118, 119. In October, 1933, Germany concluded an agreement providing for the production and delivery of linseed. She committed herself to buy the yield of 600 per cent of the area previously devoted to linseed and to pay a price 45 per cent above the world market price. But production increased only a very little—just enough for domestic consumption. The whole project failed.

1935 and 24.1 per cent in 1937; imports also rose, from 20 per cent in 1929 to 26.2 per cent in 1937. Soon the adverse trade balance changed to a surplus; but it could not be used for the purchase of raw materials as was formerly the case, for Germany had ceased to be a transit country for overseas purchases. Furthermore, the increased export to Germany reduced the surplus available for export to other markets, where free exchange could have been obtained.[5]

Exports to Germany generally commanded the high prices especially needed for slaughtered animals and other food products for which Hungary could not obtain satisfactory prices elsewhere. When it is realized that, in 1937, 54 per cent of Hungary's exports went to Germany, Austria, and Italy, all of them paying higher prices than were available elsewhere, the enormous influence of German purchases upon the whole Hungarian economy becomes apparent. Throughout this period the free-exchange countries took only 20–25 per cent of Hungary's exports, the largest share, about 8 per cent, being that of Great Britain. A shift to Germany as a source of imports was only the logical consequence of this development. Very soon Germany came to make her influence felt even with regard to the kind of new industries that were to be established in Hungary.[6]

In 1937 Hungary supplied Germany with lard, bauxite, meat and meat products, vegetable and legume, cattle, wheat and corn imports. Other important articles were fruit, eggs, poultry, and seeds.

The position of Rumania and Yugoslavia in their trade with Germany was somewhat stronger due, chiefly, to their greater economic resources.

In petroleum and its products Rumania had a commodity which could always be placed on the world market—at the prices quoted there. This provided the country during this period with more than 40 per cent of her total exports, by value. The fact that by far the greatest part of the petroleum industry was owned by very important foreign concerns certainly strengthened the Rumanian trading position. Furthermore, Rumania's exports of cereals was always oriented toward the West because of the availability of sea transport. Western European countries usually purchased between 25 and 30 per cent of Rumania's cereal export, Great Britain alone taking about 11 per

5 *The Development of Hungary's Foreign Trade*, p. 42.
6 *The Economist*, June 20, 1936, p. 673.

cent. Rumania also obtained a certain, although not decisive, help from her treaty with Czechoslovakia; in 1937 her exports to this country exceeded those of 1929.

Her customary large exports to Germany were hard hit by the German trade barriers and declined from 27.6 per cent of total exports in 1929 to only 10.6 per cent in 1933. They began to recover in 1934, chiefly by reason of compensation transations, and moved up again after a new treaty was concluded in March, 1935, so that Germany accounted for 16.7 per cent of total exports in that year and for 19.2 per cent in 1937. The decline in Rumanian exports to Italy during and after the period of sanctions—a factor in which was a large volume of claims blocked in Italy—contributed to the rise in export to Germany, which showed an increase from 3,855 million lei in 1936 to 6,054 million lei in 1937. Imports from Germany also increased, accounting for 29.8 per cent of the total in 1937 as compared with 24.1 per cent in 1929. Although Germany's share in Rumania's foreign trade was not greater in 1937 than in 1929, it was nevertheless very important to Rumania.

Germany insisted with great energy that Rumania shift her agricultural production to fodder and oleaginous plants if she wanted to maintain her trade with the Reich. A special company created by I. G. Farben undertook the task of expanding soya production. To this end contracts were concluded with as many as 70,000–100,000 peasants, under the terms of which the company granted advances and agreed to buy the whole crop at prices fixed beforehand.[7] By 1937 the acreage under soya had already increased from 1,465 ha. in 1934 to 97,451 ha. The price steadily mounted until it reached several times the world-market quotation. The production of sunflowers and rapeseed increased similarly. Germany tried to encourage export by paying higher and higher prices; the average price for 100 kg. of goods exported to her ran from Rm. 8.38 in 1936 to Rm. 12.21 in 1937.[8] This special incentive was designed to help overcome the difficulties arising from the large clearing balances in Germany, which were liquidated for the most part only by the delivery of large units (electric power plants, factory equipment, and the like).[9]

According to a Rumanian opinion the German market was im-

[7] R. W. Krugmann, op. cit., pp. 125, 139.   [8] Ibid., p. 126.
[9] German Institute for Business Research, Weekly Report, April 6, 1939, No. 13–14, p. 41.

portant because it was possible to place there numerous commodities difficult to sell elsewhere.[10] In 1937, Rumania sold to Germany 61.2 per cent of her total corn export; barley, 57.4 per cent; rye, 21.5; oats, 18.3; wheat, 8.3. Germany also took a great share of her timber and seed exports.[11]

Yugoslavia's position was also strong, although she did not possess a single large commodity comparable to Rumania's petroleum and its products. However the position of copper and other metals, minerals, and hemp was somewhat similar, representing together 18–20 per cent of her total exports. But the geographical distribution of Yugoslav exports served as a greater source of strength, as long as trade barriers were not prohibitive, and, in addition, the Little Entente arrangement brought her exports to Czechoslovakia in 1937 above the 1929 level. In 1929 Italy, Yugoslavia's greatest customer, took 24.9 per cent of total exports; Austria, 15.6 per cent; Germany, 8.5 per cent; and Czechoslovakia 5.4 per cent. Italy imported chiefly timber, animal products, and cereals. In 1933 Italy's share still was 21.5 per cent, Austria's 21.7 per cent, and Germany's only 13.9 per cent.

In 1934 Germany's percentage of total exports went up to 15.4 as a result of the new commercial treaty of that year, in which Germany granted Yugoslavia various import concessions and, especially, conceded—through the marketing boards—higher prices for several agricultural staples.[12] Permanent committees for the coördination of mutual trade were established. In the long run "coördination" was apt to imply pressure for the adjustment of Yugoslav production to meet German needs. German purchases were welcomed as a substantial help, and the economic recovery in 1935 was regarded as a direct effect of regional influences.[13] But the sanctions against Italy were a severe blow to the Yugoslav economy, which lost nine tenths of its important Italian exports during this period (exports to Italy declined from 672 million dinars to only 137 million in 1936, or to only 3.1 per cent of total exports). The combined concessions granted to Yugoslavia by Great Britain, Czechoslovakia, and France were entirely inadequate and covered no more than 25 per cent of her export

10 *Le Commerce entre la Roumanie et les etats danubiens,* International Institute, 1937, p. 19.
11 German Institute for Business Research, *Weekly Report,* 1939, No. 13–14, p. 40.
12 R. W. Krugmann, *op. cit.,* p. 76.   13 S. D. Obradović, *op. cit.,* p. 28.

losses,[14] which were estimated at between 500 and 600 million dinars. The failure of the Western Powers to compensate smaller states for the losses they suffered because of carrying out the sanctions had, especially in Yugoslavia, definite effects, political as well as economic, and in the case of Yugoslavia, put a strain upon her relations with France.

Germany, however, continued to buy large amounts of agricultural products and raw materials needed for rearmament, making use of Yugoslavia's acute export difficulties. But the capacity of the Yugoslav market to absorb the kind of goods which Germany produced practically reached the saturation point. As a result Yugoslavia accumulated a clearing balance of more than 500 million dinars and was faced with the necessity of increasing her imports from Germany. The introduction of import control in June, 1936, was one measure designed to liquidate these debts. Another was the placing of huge government orders in Germany. First, as early as March, 1936, a contract was signed between the Yugoslav government and the Krupp firm for the renovation of rolling mills and an iron foundry in Zenica —this in spite of the fact that British and Czechoslovak bids were lower.[15] Large orders were also placed in Germany for railway materials and German firms received various other public orders. After the sanctions Germany's influence in Yugoslav markets increased. Exports to Germany went up to 26.7 per cent of total exports in 1936 and to 32.4 per cent in 1937. Exports to Western Europe and Switzerland averaged about 25 per cent (the largest single share among the free countries being Great Britain's, 9–10 per cent); those to the United States were about 5 per cent.

The fact that Germany continued to pay higher prices made it extremely difficult to export Yugoslav products to the free markets. "The exchange premium required for making such export possible complicates the supply of raw materials and threatens the monetary stability." [16] It is hardly necessary to add that once Germany had

14 J. Elwyn Jones, *Hitler's Drive to the East*, New York, 1937, p. 43. France even refused to discontinue timber imports from nonsanctionist Austria in favor of Yugoslavia. See also *The Economist*, May 2, 1936, p. 277: Great Britain offered concessions on bacon, eggs, poultry and turkey for the duration of the sanctions to the amount of 100 million dinars. The greatest blow to Yugoslavia was her loss of timber exports to Italy. They fell from 371 million dinars in 1935 to only 37.3 million. Exports to Great Britain increased from 46.4 million to only 92.3 million.
15 Royal Institute, *Survey of International Affairs*, 1936, p. 530.
16 S. D. Obradović, *op. cit.*, p. 30.

TABLE 14

DEVELOPMENT IN THE TRADE OF THE SEVEN COUNTRIES OF CENTRAL AND SOUTHEASTERN EUROPE, 1927–37

COUNTRY	EXPORTS TO GERMANY AS A PERCENTAGE OF TOTAL EXPORTS				EXPORTS IN GOLD DOLLARS IN 1937 AS A PERCENTAGE OF 1929	EXPORTS IN 1937 TO THE "OTHER COUNTRIES" a (PER CENT OF TOTAL EXPORTS)	IMPORTS FROM GERMANY AS A PERCENTAGE OF TOTAL IMPORTS				IMPORTS IN GOLD DOLLARS IN 1937 AS A PERCENTAGE OF 1929	IMPORTS IN 1937 FROM THE "OTHER COUNTRIES" a (PER CENT OF TOTAL IMPORTS)
	1927	1929	1933	1937			1927	1929	1933	1937		
Bulgaria	23.0	29.9	36	43.1	78	36	21	22.2	38.2	54.8	56	21.3
Greece	21.3	23.2	17.9	31	57	49.7	7.4	9.4	10.2	27.1	47	44.9
Hungary	13.3	11.7	11.2	24.1	56	34	17.8	20	19.6	26.2	46	35.1
Rumania	18.6	27.6	16.6	19.2	77	45.6	22.3	24.1	18.6	28.9	49	34.4
Yugoslavia	10.6	8.5	13.9	21.7	60	39.5	12.34	15.6	13.2	32.4	52	31.7
Austria	18.4	15.9	15.7	14.9	44	37	16.9	21	19.7	16.3	35	37.9
Czechoslovakia	24.1	22.9	20	15	40	60.7	20.9	24.2	19.8	15.5	38	64.2

a "Other countries" are those other than Germany, Italy, Poland and the seven included in the table.

established her influence she used it in Yugoslavia to urge increased production of the commodities she needed. It is not surprising then that the acreage of oleaginous plants increased from 7,900 ha. in 1934 to 25,000 ha. in 1937, of hemp from 30,775 ha. in 1933 to 50,000 in 1938, with Germany the chief customer for these crops. The principal items in the export to Germany in 1937 were: timber, hemp, meat, nontropical fruits, bauxite, wheat, eggs, lead ore, and copper.

From Table 14 we may derive a comprehensive picture of the position Germany won in the trade of the seven countries under discussion. It also gives some indication, in the columns showing the value in gold dollars of exports and imports in 1937 as a percentage of the 1929 figures,[17] of the degree to which these countries had by 1937 overcome the crisis in foreign trade. It further pictures their dependence upon trade with the countries of Central and Southeastern Europe, where the principle of bilateralism had made the greatest headway. To make the dependence clear, figures are given showing the percentage of total trade which those countries were able to maintain with countries other than the seven included in the table and Germany, Italy, and Poland. The aggregate exports and imports in gold dollars for 1929 and for 1937 are also included, showing that the passive trade balance of the agricultural countries, which in 1929 amounted to $137 million, was converted to an active balance of $44 million in 1937, while the Austrian passive balance was reduced from $151 million to $26.2 million in the same years.

TABLE 15

VALUE OF AGGREGATE EXPORTS AND IMPORTS IN MILLION DOLLARS, GOLD

	EXPORTS		1937 AS PERCENTAGE OF 1929	IMPORTS		1937 AS PERCENTAGE OF 1929
	1929	1937		1929	1937	
The Five Agricultural Countries	601	410	68	738	366	49.5
Czechoslovakia	606	246.3	40	590	226	38
Austria	307.9	137.8	44	459	161	35

[17] Calculated on the basis of figures from the League of Nations, *Statistical Year-Book 1938–39*, pp. 218–19. The *Year-Book* does not make clear what rate of exchange was taken as a basis for conversion into gold dollars. Thus if the Bulgarian leva, for instance, were calculated on the basis of the fictitious official parity, this might explain the surprisingly high percentage of her export.

13

THE DEVELOPMENT DURING THE WORLD
ECONOMIC RECOVERY IN 1936–37

THE STEADY INCREASE in Germany's share of foreign trade and the trade methods introduced by her intensified the discomfort and apprehension of the five agricultural countries. They began to fear economic and political dependence upon her, and at the same time they were faced with increasing difficulties in exporting to free countries to obtain badly needed free exchange. Even Hungary, politically close to Germany and selling to her as much as 70 per cent and 80 per cent of the total exports of some commodities, tried to find free markets for her goods in order to retain contact with world export prices. It can be said that all these countries were anxious to escape from the more and more demanding embrace of German trade penetration.

The chief possibility of escape lay in finding markets elsewhere. Unwilling, or feeling unable, to make the required monetary and price adjustments, they resorted to all sorts of measures to increase their exports to the free markets: They tried export subsidies, and improved and standardized production to meet the demands of customers in the free countries. As the figures show, their efforts were not without success. With the sole exception of Greece, their share of exports to Great Britain, France, Switzerland, Holland, Belgium—(markets with which they were rather familiar) and the United States increased between 1929 and 1937. Greek exports to these free-exchange countries decreased from 41.5 per cent of total exports in 1929 to 33.7 per cent in 1937; there was a very slight increase in exports to the United States (from 16.1 to 16.5 per cent) and to Switzerland. Bulgarian exports to this group rose from 16.5 to 26.6 per cent (her greatest increases being in exports to Belgium. Great Britain, and the United States). Even in 1937 this group of six free countries imported more from Rumania, Yugoslavia, and Greece than did Germany. Only in the cases of Bulgaria and Hungary did Germany have a greater share. However, the importance of this success was partially offset by their losses of exports to Italy as a result of the sanctions and the exhaustion of the Italian economy after the Abyssinian campaign.

This development weakened the position of Italy in Southeastern Europe much to the advantage of Germany. The failure of the League and the Western Powers to be more active in the economic field during and after the period of sanctions also supported the German offensive.

The hopes of Southeastern Europe for liberation from the threatening influence of Germany rose when, in 1936–37, the prices of food and raw materials on the world market improved considerably. They became able to compete, there was less need of export premia, less burden upon their exchanges and upon government budgets. Reflecting the recovery in the world economy, the value of Yugoslavian exports rose by 80 per cent, Bulgarian by 64 per cent, Hungarian by 36 per cent, and Rumanian by 96 per cent.

The new situation certainly offered one more opportunity for international action. The improvement in world prices for cereals, tobacco, timber, oil, and other products of Southeastern Europe— some prices rose by 20 per cent during the year June, 1936, to June, 1937—provided freer and better markets, strengthening the competitive position of these countries so that German offers involving political as well as economic terms could be ignored.[1] While this development strengthened the agricultural countries, it exerted a cumulative pressure on Germany. The margin between the prices offered by Germany and those obtainable in free exchange greatly diminished. "The exporting countries were able to exert stricter control over their export to Germany and to drive harder bargains over prices and exchange rates."[2] The free markets and their currencies began to exert a pull upon Central and Southeastern Europe, whose vulnerability to German economic and political penetration lessened, while the rise in prices weighed heavily upon the rigid German economy.

Appreciating the critical nature of the situation, Germany acted— using all the means at her disposal to sustain her offensive. She increased prices, speeded up deliveries, and her clearing debts declined. Early in 1937 she even reduced her customs duties on wheat, rye, barley, oats, flour, vegetable oil, and various animal fats. As a result, her share of the goods imported by these countries increased slightly but her share of exports from them fell. But all her efforts could have

[1] *The Economist*, March 27, 1937, p. 695; July 24, 1937, p. 165; June 5, 1937, p. 614.
[2] League of Nations, *World Economic Survey*, 1936–37, p. 154.

been successfully met if the Western Powers had inaugurated a vigorous and comprehensive program for the consolidation of the area, a program which could definitely have forced a change in the development of Germany, and which was within easy reach at the time. "The two great democratic powers in Western Europe with their rich resources and rich democratic associates in the West must today read the hand writings on the walls of Central Europe. The moment is ripe," wrote *The Economist*.[3]

Such a program—assuming, of course, unity among the democratic powers seconded by a majority of the Danubian states—in addition to counteracting German penetration, could have provided solutions for the most pressing economic problems of the region: Restoration of orderly monetary conditions with the stabilization of currencies and the abandonment of the complex system of multiple rates, and exchange premia. Settlement of foreign debts ceased to be so difficult a question; the total amount of indebtedness was reduced by the devaluation of the currencies of the creditor nations, by partial repayments and repatriation of debts, and by various concessions with regard to interest rates, although a far-sighted attitude on the part of the chief group of creditors, perhaps enforced by their respective governments, was still needed. But such an attitude was hardly shown, for instance, by the British Council of Foreign Bond-holders.[4] A settlement of this problem could have made unnecessary the annual negotiations between debtor governments and their creditors concerning the quotas of debt service in the subsequent years, which was a practice not calculated greatly to foster favorable trade relations.

Furthermore, abandonment of clearing agreements and the largely German-inspired principle of bilateralism needed to be closely geared to the monetary and exchange stabilization. But even the foreign-trade position was not so difficult as would appear at first glance. German penetration was not yet firmly established. In 1937 about 25

[3] March 13, 1937, p. 516.
[4] See the author's "Frozen Credit Problem in Central Europe" in *The Problems of Monetary Stabilization*, 1936, Joint Committee Carnegie Endowment and International Chamber of Commerce.

The total amount of principal outstanding of defaulted dollar bonds offered in the United States by all five agricultural countries was on Dec. 31, 1938, only $175 million. (J. W. Gantenbein, *Financial Questions in United States Foreign Policy*, New York, 1939, pp. 156 ff.) All these countries substantially increased the percentage of the regular debt service they paid.

The total external debt of the entire region was estimated at not more than £650 million for 1938. See Royal Institute, *South-Eastern Europe*, London, 1941, p. 123.

per cent of the total exports of the agricultural countries went to Germany and not more than 15 per cent of those from Czechoslovakia and Austria or not more than about 21 per cent of the aggregate exports of the whole group. Of course the reduced volume of Czechoslovak export to Germany and to the Danubian countries—also the result of the German policy—weakened her position. Nevertheless these countries supplied Germany with 14.8 per cent of her imports, the agricultural countries alone with 10.5 per cent and the Little Entente alone with 7.1 per cent. Furthermore, among the goods imported there were some which Germany urgently needed and for which she would have been required to pay free exchange elsewhere. Such were oil from Rumania; metals, minerals, and hemp from Yugoslavia; bauxite from Hungary and Yugoslavia; and fats from all these countries. But even the importation of food became generally more important as the complaints in Germany against scarcities of various kinds of foods grew in number. Germany was indeed vulnerable in her imports from Southeastern Europe. The bargaining position of these countries, *acting as a unit,* would have been far from negligible, and perhaps Germany could have been compelled to change her policy if concerted action had been agreed upon.

The problem was not to stop exporting to Germany but to take away a certain margin in various goods to break her hold at critical points; even this problem was not insoluble. Germany controlled a larger share in the exports of Bulgaria and Greece than in those of any of the other countries and this was due chiefly to her tobacco purchases. A small increase in the negligible British purchases of tobacco could have changed the whole situation at this time, but Great Britain was too slow. Only in 1939 did she begin to purchase Balkan tobacco to blend with American tobacco.[5]

There can be no doubt that there existed all the prerequisites to help in consolidating foreign trade and economy in Southeastern Europe. In 1937 Great Britain became the second largest buyer from the five agricultural countries taken together. Her share, combined with those of Czechoslovakia and Austria, was greater than Germany's, and this still does not take into account the purchases of France or of the United States. In addition there were ample oppor-

[5] See Allan G. B. Fisher, "The German Trade Drive in Southeastern Europe," *International Affairs,* XVIII (London, 1939), No. 2, 161. In 1937 Great Britain bought less than 1% of the tobacco exported from Bulgaria and Greece. Before 1914 British purchases of Greek tobacco amounted in some years to £9 million; in 1937 less than £20,000.

tunities for increasing, directly or indirectly, the purchases of some critical commodities. For example, France, Great Britain, and some other countries, perhaps including the United States, could have granted additional trade facilities and quotas for the import of Czechoslovak and Austrian industrial goods, coupled with concessions for the import of agricultural goods from Southeastern Europe into these two countries. There were various other possibilities, if boldness and determination had been shown; but, though the voices warning of the danger of German penetration became more clear, there was very little prospect of such action.[6] The Western countries, particularly Great Britain and France, were reluctant to increase their purchases from Southeastern Europe to a degree sufficient to offset the specious allurements of the German offers. France was very short-sighted even in dealing with her ally Czechoslovakia. She pursued no policy of trade expansion with her and failed to grant larger quotas even on industrial goods which did not compete with French production. The French share in the aggregate foreign trade of these countries totaled only 3–4 per cent.

On the whole, "the eagerness of the Balkan States to receive evidence of British and French interest in their trade relations was much greater than the eagerness of Great Britain and France to allow such interest to express itself in any form which required revision of other points of their national commercial policies."[7] No such reluctance was visible in trade relations with Germany—perhaps because of the greater financial interest at stake.[8] Yet Germany's trade in 1937 with countries with which she did not have any clearing or similar bilateral payments agreements amounted to only 22.3 per cent of her total import and 14.2 per cent of her export.[9] Without a fundamental change in this policy carried on by so influential a country it could hardly be expected that the countries of Central and Southeastern Europe could abandon exchange control and bilateralism. On the contrary, the principle of bilateral trade was bound to expand gradually to other countries. Only the major economic powers could have forced Germany to return to multilateral trade. But the great powers

---

[6] *The Economist* wrote on March 21, 1936 (p. 630): "The crude fact is that a German attempt to conquer and dominate Central and Southeastern Europe would sooner or later bring the United Kingdom into the lists on the Anti-German side."

[7] *Survey of International Affairs,* Vol. I, 1938, London, p. 45.

[8] For a discussion of this problem see H. J. Tasca, *World Trading System,* Paris, 1939.

[9] H. Lossos, *op. cit.,* pp. 52–53.

failed to take the initiative which in the end would have forced Germany to change her policy, and would have thus not only freed the countries of this region from her economic aggression but also prevented the strengthening of the Greater German economy essential to the virtual self-sufficiency of the Reich. Alternatively it would have forced Germany to fight both before she had undisputed access to these resources and before she was fully prepared internally. The issue could have been forced at pitifully small cost compared with the price being paid today.

Perhaps the differences of interest among the great powers and between various groups within them prevented their taking unified action. Perhaps they still did not grasp the full significance of the problem. But there is also reason to believe that, even at that time, German propaganda had already succeeded in convincing the Western countries that it was to the advantage of European and world economy and in the interests of the preservation of peace to recognize Germany's special economic interests in this part of Europe. Again, prior concern for Germany overshadowed the settlement in Central and Southeastern Europe. It is hardly necessary to add that Germany was very busy encouraging differences between the Danubian states and between various factions within them. She obviously opposed a preferential treaty concluded between Czechoslovakia and Austria in 1936 (and later extended) [10] and similarly discouraged a rapprochement between the Little Entente and Hungary and in 1937 between the Little Entente and Austria. After the lessons of the sanctions period and after seeing the lack of unity and determination between the Western Powers and their reluctance to help, the small countries realized that their future depended upon the relations between the Great Powers. And this attitude decisively influenced their policy.

Another change in the whole economic situation took place after a new world economic depression, which began in the United States in the summer of 1937 and brought with it new great decreases in the prices of raw materials and foodstuffs. Germany's bargaining power was again strengthened, at once. She expected that the Western countries would withdraw their purchases from Southeastern Europe because of the decline in business and that the countries of Southeastern Europe would be forced back all the more on their trade with Germany—a very favorable development for her in view of her

[10] *The Economist*, July 25, 1936, p. 1936. R. Schüller, *op. cit.*, p. 170.

increased import requirements.[11] Germany could continue strengthening her trade with the raw-material and agriculture countries for the demands of her armed economy were greater than could be satisfied by these countries.[12] Furthermore, she was very eager to prove to them that trade with her was stable and not subject to business-cycle fluctuations and that she was helping them by paying prices which did not depend upon the changeable world market. The growing belief that the Western Powers considered the Danubian countries a part of Germany's sphere of special interest was doubtless working in Germany's favor. But a decisive new development which had the most profound effects upon the whole problem of relations between Germany and Southeastern Europe was the annexation of Austria.

[11] German Institute for Business Research, *Weekly Report,* Supplement, May 4, 1938, p. 2.
[12] Even in the agreement with Czechoslovakia in 1937 the relation between agricultural and industrial exports had to be changed in favor of agriculture in accordance with German policy, a considerable export of wheat and flour being agreed upon.

14

GERMANY'S ECONOMIC ASCENDANCY AFTER THE ANNEXATION OF AUSTRIA

THE BRIEF PERIOD of recovery in 1936–37 thus came to an end without weakening the growing German influence in Southeastern Europe. In 1938 Germany swung over from economic to political and military aggression. The occupation of Austria, carried out without any opposition on the part of the Western Powers, only strengthened the growing belief that Great Britain and France had given Germany a free hand in Southeastern Europe, in particular, with regard to economic expansion. The world did not immediately realize the meaning of the occupation of Austria, not only for Germany's position in Central and Eastern Europe but also for Europe as a whole. In fact, there were some opinions expressed that went so far as to say that Austria would be an economic burden to Germany by necessitating increased imports of food and raw materials. Similar views were heard after the partition of Czechoslovakia at Munich, too. Yet, of course, the opposite was true, and few people realized how greatly Germany's industrial war potential was increased by the occupation of these countries.

Before discussing in detail the effects of the annexation of Austria we would like to point out here that as a result of this move Germany obtained definite economic supremacy in the Danube basin and, moreover, a springboard for further military and economic expansion. This one experience has clearly demonstrated that the economic and political balance in this part of Europe will always be disturbed when Austria belongs to any kind of a union or federation with Germany. Austria belongs to the Danubian group economically, politically, and geographically; she holds a key position for maintaining a workable balance in this part of Europe. Thus annexation has exposed problems of European magnitude.

With the incorporation of Austria the German envelopment of Southeastern Europe assumed the character of a drive toward a self-sufficient Central and Southeastern Europe under German economic and political tutelage. Germany's share in the foreign trade of this region was increased substantially by the addition of Austrian trade, which still held third or fourth place in the total trade of Southeastern Europe. In 1937 Germany and Austria together took about 47 per cent of Bulgaria's total exports, 41 per cent of Hungary's, 35 per cent of Yugoslavia's, 32 per cent of Greece's, and 27 per cent of Rumania's, or more than 34 per cent of the total exports of the whole agricultural group, and 20 per cent of the Czechoslovak exports. Italy took only 5.8 per cent and Great Britain, France and the United States together only 19.4 per cent.[1] In addition about 41 per cent of the total imports of these five countries came from Germany and Austria: Bulgaria, 58.2 per cent; Hungary, 44.2 per cent; Yugoslavia, 42.7 per cent; Rumania, 40.1 per cent; and Greece, 29.6 per cent. Czechoslovakia bought from them 19.9 per cent of her imports, while Italy's share was merely 2.9 per cent and that of the three large democracies, 16.7 per cent. Czechoslovakia bought about 7 per cent of the area's exports and supplied about 8.3 per cent of its imports.

The shift which had taken place in the import trade of these countries—toward Germany and away from Czechoslovakia—is clearly shown in the following: In 1929 Germany exported to them goods valued at $129.4 million, gold (18 per cent of their aggregate imports for the year), Czechoslovakia, $94 million (12.7 per cent), Austria $74.7 million (10.2 per cent); but in 1937 German exports to them totaled $115 million (about 32 per cent) while Czechoslovak exports were only $31 million (8.3 per cent) and Austria's $29.7 million (8 per cent). The income from Southeastern Europe's exports which, before the introduction of bilateralism, was used to pay for the imports from Czechoslovakia, served now to pay for imports from Germany, which also bought goods previously exported to other markets. This, obviously, weakened the Czechoslovak position.

The new position of Germany in Southeastern Europe was, under the existing circumstances, so strong that it was believed to be impossible for these countries to escape by normal orthodox commercial methods. "The system is tending toward a gradual freezing out from those regions of nearly all states whose trade is conducted along orthodox lines."[2]

---

1 *The Economist*, May 17, 1938, p. 355, gives the German and Austrian share of total exports for the year 1936 and 1937: 36.8 per cent and for imports 42.3 per cent. The German Institute for Business Research, *Weekly Report* (Supplement, May 3, 1938, p. 21) has for 1937 the figures 34 per cent of exports and 41 per cent of imports.
2 *The Economist*, May 14, 1938, p. 356.

Annexation of Austria resulted in a further increase in total German import requirements because of the introduction of the German policy of shifting the source of imports to neighboring countries and further because of the inauguration of an armed economy in Austria. It was to be expected therefore that the incorporation of Austria would lead to 1) a greater total volume of imports than the mere sum of the 1937 imports of Germany and Austria (Austria could at the same time help support the increased import requirements by her exportation of many commodities to these her old markets) and 2) a further expansion in the volume of bilateral trade.

The annexation also brought with it, at least for a while, a relaxation of Germany's clearing difficulties because, in contrast to Germany, Austria had considerable credit balances in her trade in Southeastern Europe. The significance of Germany's capital investment was also increased in some of these countries, for Austria still possessed various investments in Yugoslavian, Hungarian, and Rumanian banking,[3] and in the textile, chemical, food, and other industries. For example, whereas German investment in Yugoslavia in 1934 was estimated at only 55 million dinars,[4] Austria had an additional 336 million dinars invested there.

Throughout the political crisis of 1938 Germany continued her policy of intensive trade in Southeastern Europe, granting further price concessions. The Anglo-French export offensive in Southeastern Europe, starting after the London Conference in April, 1938, was not able to shatter the German position. Indeed there is not much evidence of a real offensive. In April, Great Britain bought 200,000 tons of corn from Yugoslavia (the Yugoslav price was then no higher than the world-market price),[5] at a time when the political implications of the whole development clearly overshadowed all economic considerations.

The Munich Pact removed all doubts as to the policy of Great Britain and France. After Munich the agricultural countries, though

[3] *The Economist*, March 26, 1935, p. 672, estimates the sums owed Austria in all clearing accounts (excluding the German account with the largest credit balance) at the equivalent of Rm. 65 millions.

It is to be remembered that because of the close relationships between banking and industry in this part of Europe the acquisition of banks' securities meant that much greater control over industry was obtained than would be implied by a corresponding investment in banking in the United States.

[4] *Survey of International Affairs*, 1938, p. 48.

[5] "The Breakdown of the British Trade Drive in Southeastern Europe," *Weekly Report*, The German Institute for Business Research, No. 19–22, Oct. 26, 1940, p. 68.

anxious to expand trade with the free-payment countries, were very reluctant to do anything that could be understood as being directed against Germany. By virtue of the Munich Pact Czechoslovakia became powerless militarily, politically, and economically. As far as her economy was concerned, Germany was able to dictate freely to Czechoslovakia, and the complete occupation of that country in March 15, 1939, with Slovakia reduced to a vassal puppet state, meant for all practical purposes incorporation into the German economy; this was gradually carried out.

It is obvious that the German gains with regard to trade with Southeastern Europe was much greater even than from the annexation of Austria. The German position, embracing the trade of Czechoslovakia and Austria in addition to her own, was now absolutely dominant. Nearly half of the aggregate trade of this region, both import and export, consisted of trade with these three countries. The status in 1937 and 1938 is indicated in Table 16.[6]

TABLE 16

GERMAN, AUSTRIAN, AND CZECHOSLOVAK DOMINANCE OF SOUTHEASTERN
EUROPE'S TRADE

(IN PER CENT)

	IMPORT		EXPORT	
	1937	1938	1937	1938
Bulgaria	63.2	57.8	53.7	63.5
Greece	31.5	31.9	36.7	43.1
Hungary	50.2	50.1	44.3	50.1
Rumania	53.5	55.2	34.2	36.1
Yugoslavia	53.8	50.1	43.1	49.9

In addition to accounting for these large shares of the aggregate export and import trade of Southeastern Europe the three countries in question also held a crucial position in the exports of certain very important commodities. In 1938 they took about 44 per cent of the

---

[6] The position of Italy and France in 1938 is indicated by these percentage figures.

	IMPORTS		EXPORTS	
	Italy	France	Italy	France
Bulgaria	7.5	3.7	7.6	1.5
Greece	3.4	1.6	5.2	2.9
Yugoslavia	8.9	2.9	6.4	1.5
Hungary	6.3	1.5	8.5	1.9
Rumania	5	7.7	5.3	4.7

total wheat exports of the whole region; 42 per cent of corn; 52 per cent of tobacco; 25 per cent of timber; 24 per cent of copper; 70 per cent of bauxite,[7] and a large share of all other food products, fruit, and raw materials. Thus Southeastern Europe became indeed dependent upon trade with Germany.

Like Austria, Czechoslovakia also had large balances in various clearing accounts amounting to Kc. 2,381 million [8] ($75 million at the actual rate) on June 30, 1938. Along with Czechoslovakian territory granted at Munich, Germany acquired at least Kc. 500 million worth of these balances, the greatest part of them being the debts of Southeastern Europe. She was able to use them for settling her debit balances with these countries and in the future could establish a kind of triangular trade with Czechoslovakia, exporting more to Southeastern Europe than she imported from there, thereby acquiring a credit balance to use in paying for an import surplus from that region. Germany in turn would, supposedly, maintain an export surplus in her trade with Czechoslovakia, but, of course, Germany could not supply Czechoslovakia with the products imported from overseas. She could not replace the link of the free-payment sector of the market. The old multilateral trade could not be reëstablished in this way. Furthermore, she did not have an export surplus with Czechoslovakia and, in fact, her deficit with that country mounted steadily.

Besides clearing balances, Czechoslovakia possessed various other financial claims in Yugoslavia and Rumania particularly. Acquiring control over the large Czechoslovak investments in Southeastern Europe was yet another substantial addition to the strength of the German position. Czechoslovakia had considerable investments: in the textile and chemical industries of Rumania, Yugoslavia, and Hungary; in the Rumanian metallurgical industry; in the sugar industry of Yugoslavia and Bulgaria; in the shoe industry of Yugoslavia; in the Hungarian and Yugoslav glass industry; and in the banks of Rumania, Yugoslavia, and Bulgaria. Her capital in Yugoslavia was estimated at 775 million dinars, so that after acquiring it Germany controlled 1,200 million dinars or 17.8 per cent of the foreign capital invested in Yugoslavia against 14.1 per cent held by Great Britain and 17 per cent by France.[9] She also got control of 13.4 per cent of the foreign

---

[7] Royal Institute, *South-Eastern Europe,* 1939, p. 111.
[8] Annual Report of the National Bank of Czechoslovakia, 1938, p. 33. Besides Southeastern Europe these accounts also included Italy, Germany, Spain, Turkey, and Chile.
[9] Mirko Lamer, *Weltwirtschaftliches Archiv,* XLVII (1938), pp. 501, 506.

capital in Bulgaria and the Czechoslovak share in the Rumanian metallurgical industry, which amounted to about 1,860 million lei [10] (nearly $9 million at the actual rate).

Thus with the occupation of Austria and Czechoslovakia and with complete economic control of these two countries, Germany really attained a more influential economic position in Central and South-eastern Europe than she had had even before 1914. She still held various important investments, although they were smaller than those held by the Western countries, but she also held about 50 per cent of the total trade carried out on a bilateral clearing basis—the export of some products was dependent upon sale to the area dominated by Germany to such an extent that it would have been impractical to attempt to find other markets for them. In 1938 German exports to Southeastern Europe (excluding those of Austria and Czechoslovakia) amounted to 10.3 per cent of her total exports and her imports to 9.8 per cent of the total. Germany was determined to build up this trade in the further exploitation of all the advantages offered by her new powerful position. Her offensive was greatly intensified; new methods were used, new programs outlined. From the thesis of intensive trade relations Germany went over to the theory of living space and *Gross-wirtschaftsraum*. Pitted against her enormous economic power, centrally controlled and directed, there were five weak states, not united within or among themselves. It was not difficult to guess the future trend in their relations with Germany.

Her aim was to convert Southeastern Europe into a kind of hinterland to supply her with food and raw materials,[11] to build a Berlin-Bagdad economic axis. In order to achieve this aim, Germany, immediately after Munich, launched a new campaign to increase her imports from this region. It was also a part of her plan to promote the output of primary goods and to organize the production of the whole area so as to complement more fully the German economy. She was also anxious now to fix the exchange rates finally and to stabilize the prices at which she would buy and sell and to direct the trade and resources of the region into the desired channels. All this was designed to help her to exclude other countries from the trade of this region.

10 *South-Eastern Europe*, p. 124.
11 Göring was reported to have said that economic-political expansion in this part of Europe was indispensable for the success of the Four-Year Plan. *Le Temps*, Sept. 20, 1938; quoted in *Survey of International Affairs*, 1938, p. 48.

With Bulgaria already completely dependent upon her economically, with Hungary politically tied to the Axis, and with export to Germany acting as the predominant influence on Hungarian prices,[12] Germany concentrated her new offensive primarily against Rumania and Yugoslavia. Both these countries were still trying to find markets in the West, and Germany was very anxious to obtain more of some of their products, particularly Rumanian oil and Yugoslav metals and minerals.

Only a few days after Munich, Dr. Funk, German Minister of National Economy, outlined a new program in Beograd. He emphasized that the recent political events would make possible new economic developments leading to still closer economic coöperation between Germany and Yugoslavia. No other territory could be a market for Southeastern Europe comparable to that offered by Germany and her new acquisitions. Before his trip to the Balkans, Dr. Funk had openly suggested that Germany buy the bulk of the exports of all these countries and resell part of them to other countries in return for raw materials not available in the Southeast.[13] Dr. Funk suggested in Beograd that Germany buy half of Yugoslavia's exports in return for German goods.

Furthermore, he proposed a long-period agreement for wholesale purchases at guaranteed and stable prices for a number of years. Agreements of this kind, it was argued, would afford protection against business-cycle fluctuations because Germany could—thanks to her comprehensive economic control—assure stability of prices.

The Yugoslav government did not accept this scheme, which Berlin hoped would have given Germany a position approaching monopoly of Yugoslav trade, both exports and imports. Dr. Funk proposed an even more far-reaching trade program to Bulgaria including in particular the purchase of cereals, tobacco, fruit, and pork products. But the idea of a long-term contract (twelve years) was not attractive to Bulgaria either.[14]

---

[12] The level of agricultural prices, bolstered by German purchases, could be maintained without a complete change of policy only if Germany continued her purchases and continued to supply her with industrial goods. In December, 1938, she paid 20 pengös per quintal for Hungarian wheat at a time when the price in Rotterdam was equivalent to only 8–10 pengös. *Survey of International Affairs*, 1938, p. 61.

[13] See Allan G. B. Fisher, *op. cit.*, p. 152: Germany did, in fact, resell abroad large quantities of Bulgarian tobacco, Greek raisins, and other goods against the frequent, vain protests of these countries. See also *The Economist*, Nov. 5, 1938, p. 262.

[14] Allan G. B. Fisher, *International Affairs*, XVIII, No. 2 (1939), pp. 152, 154.

Although Germany did not succeed in obtaining her original aim she began to buy Yugoslav raw materials and foodstuffs on an unprecedented scale, increasing her imports by 50 per cent even in October, 1938. With her position for making payments in clearing improved, at least for a while, by the acquisition of Austrian and Czechoslovak credit balances, she again pushed prices above those on the world market. Thus she seriously influenced the course of Yugoslav prices, making exportation to other countries increasingly difficult. On the other hand, the prices of German goods remained below the world level until they were firmly established in the Yugoslav market. Under such circumstances Yugoslavia was obliged to increase the general exchange rate for export to the free markets from 238 dinars to the pound sterling to 262 dinars per pound.[15] In other words, the new large sales to Germany were followed by a further devaluation of the dinar. A new clearing agreement was concluded, too, stabilizing the rate of the reichsmark. The National Bank of Yugoslavia was obliged to buy or sell marks at between 14.30 and 14.70 dinars per reichsmark, but by February, 1939, the rate had fallen to 13.80 and in June, 1939, the rate of 14.30 was reëstablished and it was demanded that the fluctuations of the exchange rate should cease and a firm ratio be maintained.[16]

Under the circumstances it was difficult for Yugoslavia to continue her 1938 policy of reducing exports to clearing countries, especially Germany. This was made particularly difficult by the high exchange rate fixed for the mark and because of the continuation of the policy of high agricultural prices. Germany was, of course, able to buy all Yugoslav surpluses—her war economy, in full swing, had unlimited need for the products of Southeastern Europe.[17]

A new agreement was concluded in December, 1938, with Rumania also. It had to provide means of overcoming the difficulties arising out

---

[15] *The Economist*, Dec. 24, 1938, p. 657. On July 1, 1939, a special free exchange committee was set up to further exports to free countries. A rate of 258 dinars per £ was now guaranteed for total export proceeds, whereas previously one quarter had to be surrendered at the official rate. Furthermore, one third of the export proceeds could be sold at 340 dinars per £, giving the exporter an average rate of 285 dinars against the previous 245. *The Economist*, September 2, 1939, p. 449. S. D. Obradović, *op. cit.*, p. 36.
[16] German Institute for Business Research, *Weekly Report*, July 27, 1939, No. 29–30, p. 80.
[17] In 1938 Germany bought 125,000 tons of wheat at an average price of 191 dinars per quintal. This gave the Yugoslav farmer an average price of 155 dinars for the whole crops, while the world price at Liverpool was falling at that time from a level equivalent to about 85 to one of about 53 dinars. *Survey of International Affairs*, p. 61.

of the accumulated balance of blocked marks (said to have amounted to 1.5 billion lei). Germany asked for an increase of the clearing rate of the reichsmark to 55 lei but obtained only a rise from 38 to 40.5–41.5 lei. The agreement also provided that in 1939 the commodity trade between these two countries was to be increased to Rm. 250–300 million (about 10 billion lei) or by about 50 per cent over 1938. The share of petroleum in the total export was raised from 20 to 25 per cent, and Germany renewed her right to buy 400,000 tons of wheat and 50,000 tons of other cereals.[18] The agreement further provided that Rumanian exports were not to fall below the highest level previously attained for the combined export to Germany, Austria, and the occupied part of Czechoslovakia. It was also agreed to try to assure that an equal value of goods would be exchanged between them—nothing more than a promise on paper.

Although she had a permanent debit balance in the clearing accounts, Germany tried to foster her economic penetration by extending long-term investment credits to these countries, the purpose being ostensibly to help in developing their resources: to build roads, railroads, grain silos. In particular large credits of this type were extended or promised to Yugoslavia.[19] All this was, of course, only another trick. While granting long-term credits could win Germany the support of various groups, the fact that they were not required to pay for the deliveries from Germany meant merely a delay in German payments for exports from these countries. The credits in the end were, obviously, not financed by Germany (although perhaps her exporters had to wait for payment) but by the National Banks or governments of the agricultural countries—they could not make exporters wait for payment on their exports to Germany, for this would not have fitted into the plan. No real capital export took place; this was merely another subtle device for fostering the expansion of German trade.

The countries of Southeastern Europe did not get much encouragement from the Western Powers to resist the German offensive. The only country which could quickly provide a suitable market for the goods of these countries was perhaps Great Britain, whose share in

[18] See German Institute for Business Research, *Weekly Report,* July 27, 1939, No. 29–30, p. 79; *Survey of International Affairs,* 1938, pp. 55–56; *The Economist,* Dec. 24, 1938, p. 658.
[19] Germany promised a credit of 200 million dinars for the expansion of the steel works in Zenica, 200 million for the arsenal at Kragujevac, 300 million for an aircraft factory, 200 million for a rifle factory, and so forth. *The Economist,* April 29, 1939, p. 248.

their exports was about 8.5–9 per cent of the total for the year 1936–38 and of imports 7.5–8 per cent. These proportions were, on the whole, stable. On the other hand, the share of the five agricultural countries in total British imports averaged, between 1934 and 1938, only 1.3 per cent (the highest figure being 1.6 in 1936), their share in her total exports, only 1.5 per cent.[20] Thus a very slight increase in the share of these countries in Great Britain's import trade would always have been a very important help to them. In September, 1938, Great Britain arranged an optional contract with Rumania for 400,000 tons of wheat and took only 200,000 tons.[21]

After Munich, in the fall of 1938, the Rumanian and Bulgarian kings and the Yugoslav regent went to London and complained about the German trading methods, stating that they were afraid of being economically strangled by Germany, and asking for Britain's help.[22] The British government informed them that it was interested in developing trade with this area and would be glad to use any practical means of doing so.[23] But, of course, Great Britain was not willing to imitate German methods of bulk purchases, which were possible only with government assistance. It was also pointed out that until the end of 1938 the expansion of German trade had not been at the expense of Great Britain, but of Austria, Czechoslovakia and Italy. Therefore the British were not prone to pay too much attention to competing with Germany in Southeastern Europe.[24] But behind all this attitude was the officially expressed political conviction that Germany was entitled to occupy a position of dominance there. And Dr. Funk's statement was accepted with approval that German policy would increase the productive power of these countries rich in raw materials and raise their standard of living.[25] No statement could better illustrate the whole mode of thinking underlying the appease-

[20] Great Britain bought £1 million worth of cereals from Rumania out of a total import of £76 million, and £2 million worth of oil out of £48 million worth of oil import. One third of her poultry import came from Hungary and Yugoslavia, who also furnished a large share of British imports of eggs. However, her participation in the tobacco exports of the Balkans was at a minimum. *The Economist*, Nov. 5, 1938, p. 266.
[21] *The Breakdown of the British Trade Drive in Southeastern Europe*, p. 65.
[22] *Survey of International Affairs*, 1938, p. 62.
[23] Statement of the President of the Board of Trade, *The Economist*, Nov. 5, 1938, p. 266.
[24] A. G. B. Fisher, *op. cit.*, pp. 165–67.
[25] *The Times*, Oct. 8, 1938 (quoted by Fisher, *op. cit.*, p. 155). The fact that Prime Minister Chamberlain deprecated, in the House of Commons on Nov. 1, 1938, the suggestion that Herr Funk's activities were concealing political motives fits into the whole picture. *Survey of International Affairs*, 1938, p. 64.

ment policy, allocating Central and Southeastern Europe to the German sphere of influence.

The new German economic treaty concluded with Rumania on March 23, 1939, a few days after the occupation of Prague, indicated convincingly what the real aims of the German offensive were. This treaty greatly exceeded the traditional limits of trade agreements. It was hailed in Germany as the first instance in which state economic planning had extended beyond the limits of the domestic economy, and as the first milestone in the shift from world trade to regional trade.[26] In reality it meant that the Rumanian economy had to be fully adapted and subordinated to German needs. Germany was to gain an economic monopoly instead of just a trade monopoly, for although only 35.8 per cent of Rumania's total export went to Germany, Austria, and Czechoslovakia, she was greatly dependent upon these markets for the sale of particular commodities: to them, in 1937–38, went 15.8 per cent of her timber; 12.9 per cent of her cattle; 16 per cent of her wheat; 78 per cent of her corn; 88.5 per cent of her rye; 69.5 per cent of her barley; and 96.8 per cent of her hog exports; and many other commodities always found a convenient market there.

Germany was anxious to increase these imports "in order to secure a steady supply of goods." [27] The complementary nature of the economies of these two countries provided ample opportunity for expanding trade along Nazi lines. Germany underscored the advantages of the great stability of her market, which would give the Rumanian producers security for long-term calculations. "The variety of German purchases contributes greatly to the diversification of the Rumanian economic structure"; [28] and consequently Germany was, they asserted, the ideal partner for a program of long-term development such as was provided by this agreement. This plan, it was further argued, would prove how German import interests could be brought into line with the demand of the Southeastern European countries for the organic growth and expansion of their industry and for economic security.

The plan specifically called for the development and direction of Rumanian agriculture with German assistance. Production was to

[26] "Foreign Trade and Trade Policy," German Institute for Business Research, *Weekly Report,* July 27, 1939, No. 29–30, p. 80.
[27] "The German-Roumanian Trade Treaty," *ibid.,* April 6, 1939, No. 13–14, p. 40.
[28] *Ibid.*

be shifted to fodder, fiber plants (cotton, hemp, flax), and oil seeds. Germany agreed to pay satisfactory prices for these crops and, in addition, to furnish new varieties of rare plants and to carry out a series of experiments for the production of new oleaginous seeds. Because of her almost unlimited demand for the mining products of the Balkans, Germany was greatly interested in the development of Rumania's mineral resources. To this end the treaty called for mutual exploitation of ore and oil deposits by the establishment of German and Rumanian companies and by the delivery of German machines and equipment. Germany even agreed to have the first processing, such as the smelting of ores, done within the producing country. The agreement also provided for the creation of free zones for German enterprises and shipping, the delivery of armaments and of equipment to Rumania's armament industry and for the development of transportation, timber industries, and processing plants for agricultural products. The greatest emphasis was put on those industries which prepare foodstuffs and raw materials for export and which can be considered as justified national industries.

Only when the state of economic advancement called for in the agreement had been reached would the conditions be suitable for a further drive toward industrialization.[29] In fact, Germany claimed that under the protection of exchange control the industry of Southeastern Europe had developed to such an extent that it had reached the saturation point and that consequently control of capital investment was necessary. This was really a surprising argument in view of the repeated complaints in these countries about the lack of many industrial goods, their extremely low level of consumption of industrial goods and the difficulty of obtaining raw materials abroad. But such an explanation was needed for the assertion that "this cooperative economic planning is an outstanding example of the harmony of interests with regard to all decisive economic questions between the Southeast and Germany." [30] Later we shall see some other examples of how German official and scholarly economic doctrine was always prompt in finding "pertinent" arguments and justification for any kind of economic action.

There were, of course, no difficulties in paying for the increased

[29] *Ibid.*, p. 42.
[30] The volume of industrial production in Rumania in 1938 was estimated at about 39 per cent greater than that in 1929. *Ibid.*, pp. 38 and 42.

imports from Rumania. The agreement called for extensive German credits in the form of capital goods exports which were to accelerate the development of Rumania's resources, and for a further expansion of German purchases. As a matter of fact, so far as Germany was not able to settle her import balance with exports of Czechoslovak armament and later with armaments from other sources, the National Bank or the government was obliged to pay the Rumanian exporters—again, a forced loan, to Germany, as a result of this agreement. But this did not hinder Germany from stressing that she offered the Southeastern States contracts guaranteeing their sales over a long period.[31]

[31] Weak indeed was the British answer to this so-called "Wohltat Agreement." In a new treaty of May 11, 1939, a purchase of 200,000 tons of wheat was promised provided delivery could be made at world market prices. A loan of £5 million was granted, the greater part of which was to be used for armament purchases and the rest on the purchase of public utility equipment and road construction. Further, 30% of the value of mineral oil products exported to Britain were eligible for use as dividends and salaries, a concession to British and Dutch capital. Thus, in spite of the change in the political situation when the necessity for checking German expansion was realized, and in spite of the imminent danger of war, Great Britain, like France, did not see any necessity for adopting a new foreign-trade policy to fight effectively any further expansion of totalitarian trade. It took weeks before even this new British-Rumanian agreement with its meager results was concluded.

15

THE SMALL COUNTRIES AND BILATERALISM

THERE WAS no longer the question of to what extent Germany could absorb the surpluses of these countries. The emphasis was now laid upon the problem of how far her import requirements could be met by them; her clear objective was to cover the maximum possible part of her import deficit with supplies from them. This required not only the diversion of trade but also a real adjustment of production. The schemes for the reorientation of agricultural output were obviously not directed toward the integration of this region with the world economy but toward increasing the self-sufficiency of Germany in many important commodities. It was a program of autarky for the economic empire of Greater Germany, and not one of world economic coöperation.

According to various estimates Southeastern Europe could largely satisfy Germany's peacetime needs for grains (with the exception of corn), livestock and meat, vegetables, nontropical fruit, timber, tobacco, bauxite, and mineral oil, and could make important contributions in other commodities which she had to import, such as various metals, fats, eggs, and hides and skins.[1]

Great efforts were concentrated on the production of industrial crops particularly of oleaginous and textile plants and of fodder. But in spite of the German willingness to subsidize production by every possible means not much was achieved. In 1938 soya exports, chiefly from Rumania and Bulgaria, hardly covered 10 per cent of Germany's demand (though Rumania's output reached 86,100 tons in 1939). Production of hemp fiber in Yugoslavia doubled in 1938 as compared with the average for 1930–34, but increased only slightly in the other countries.[2] Cotton production in Bulgaria and Greece, although it more than doubled in five years, was insufficient for their own domestic needs, and, in spite of various German attempts, no progress

[1] See *The Economist*, November 5, 1938, p. 269, and O. Frangeš; "Die Donaustaaten Südosteuropas und der deutsche Grosswirtschaftsraum," *Weltwirtschaftliches Archiv*, LIII (1941), 284–328; see also Krugmann, *op. cit.*, pp. 128 ff., dealing with the new orientation of agricultural production; and further various statistics in *Foreign Agriculture*, U.S. Dept. of Agriculture, No. 12, Dec., 1940, p. 707.

[2] Figures from League of Nations, *Statistical Yearbook*, 1941.

was achieved in the production of wool.[3] Practically, the only shifts realized prior to the outbreak of the war were limited to increased production of oilseeds in Rumania, Bulgaria, and, to a less extent, in Yugoslavia (not much in Hungary), and a rise in hemp production. This reality remained unaltered behind all the high-sounding schemes, and it was indeed hardly to be expected that peasants would shift to a new kind of production on a large scale as long as they obtained remunerative prices for all their staple crops.

Nevertheless, the German experts were busy explaining that a long-range program would be developed and carried out to transform the structure of Danubian agriculture, increasing its intensity and efficiency which would open the way for a higher standard of living and a strong domestic market. One writer assumed that not only all the food and fodder which Germany imported from all parts of the world could be obtained from Southeastern Europe, but in addition all agricultural raw materials.[4] The only exception according to him was tropical and semitropical crops. Germany was said to be able to absorb practically all the raw material and agricultural surpluses of the Southeast. Of course, a fundamental change in the whole economic structure of the region would be required which in turn would call for an authoritarian, regimented economy (*Wirtschaftslenkung*) on the German pattern.

As a matter of interest to indicate how these problems were discussed in Germany before the war and also to show further what the German program for this area was, we give here the content of Mr. Wagemann's proposal. He is President of the Institut für Konjunkturforschung, now an official institution. Based upon a special expert analysis by von der Decken, Wagemann assumes first an increase in yield by 50 per cent—with Western agricultural techniques a rise of 200–400 per cent would be possible but would require too long a time. The total area available for agriculture in these countries (excluding Greece) was 39 million ha.; 26 million ha. of arable land and 13 million for pasture. An increase in yield of 50 per cent would free 13 million ha. for new products. The area needed to cover the German import needs (including Austria and Czechoslovakia) was, in million hectares: 2.2 for cereals (4 million tons); 0.1 for legumes; 1.6 for meat

[3] Thus, for instance, I. G. Farben founded "Wotirag," a special company in Bulgaria for the purpose of promoting wool production. Frangeš, *op. cit.*, p. 296.
[4] Ernst Wagemann, *Der Neue Balkan*, Hamburg, 1939, pp. 77, 95.

(all calculated in acreage); 2.0 for fats; 0.5 for eggs; 3.6 for other foods.

The total agricultural imports of the Greater Reich would thus require 10 million ha., leaving 3 million for industrial crops like textile fibers and organic raw materials. This program was supposed to be carried out within 25 years. Wagemann, of course, did not attach any importance to such economic considerations as comparative cost or possible competition on the international markets (the high cost of production of soya in Rumania can be taken as an example of production made possible only by Germany's purchases at prices several times those charged for the overseas product). Wagemann equally ignored any similar change in German agriculture.[5]

With Germany's political and military strength and her special economic position in the Southeast it was only natural that her trade with these countries should further increase in 1939 as the following figures show. The percentage share of Germany, Austria, and Czechoslovakia in the trade of the five agricultural countries in 1939 and 1938 is given.

	PER CENT OF TOTAL EXPORTS		PER CENT OF TOTAL IMPORTS	
	1939	1938	1939	1938
Bulgaria	71.1	63.5	69.5	57.8
Hungary	52.4	50.1	52.5	48.1
Rumania	43.1	37.1	56.1	49.9
Yugoslavia	45.9	49.9	53.2	50.3
Greece	30	36.7	32.1	31.9

With the exception of exports from Greece and Yugoslavia, the trade between Germany and the Southeast again increased. Already Germany and the countries she controlled absorbed more than half the aggregate trade of these countries.[6]

Germany's next immediate aim, which was within the realm of

[5] *Ibid.*, pp. 77 ff. Much more realistic in regard to the possibilities of economic cooperation between this area and Greater Germany, and the autarky of the whole bloc is Frangeš, *op. cit.*, p. 308. Although favoring far-reaching and close ties between this region and Greater Germany and Italy which he suggests should be considered as one inseparable unit, he does not believe that, even assuming a great shift in production, it would be possible to attain self-sufficiency in fats in general. Nor does he see any good prospect for the production of cotton or wool and only limited opportunities in hides and skins. But he still believes that autarky of the whole bloc including Italy could be attained to a very great degree.

[6] The figures for 1939 are from the publications of the individual states as given in *South-Eastern Europe*, pp. 108–110. Germany also included Turkey in her trade offensive, where she proceeded in the same way. In 1936 she took 51% of total exports (13.6% in 1932); in 1938, 42.9% (and with Austria and Czechoslovakia 47.5%), and she de-

possibility even before the outbreak of war, was to expand her share
in the trade of Southeastern Europe to 60 per cent of the total. Great
Britain's share in the exports of the region was 8.5 per cent (less
than 1937) and in imports 6.4 per cent (less than 1937 and 1938). According to Dr. Funk,[7] Germany increased her imports from this area
during the first year of war, 1940, by Rm. 400 million over 1939 to a
total of Rm. 1.3 billion, or more than double the 1929 value.

The steady growth of German trade with this area had its effect
upon the question of payment and upon the terms of trade. Being
firmly established in these markets, Germany tried to increase the
prices of the goods she delivered; their quality deteriorated and the
delivery terms were extended; and after the occupation of Czechoslovakia she sold these countries large amounts of armament, partly
obsolete. Germany's terms of trade certainly improved. She was not
satisfied with the fact that the mark, contrary to the dollar, was not
everywhere accepted at its gold parity; consequently she tried persistently to improve the exchange rate of the mark, in order to get
cheaper supplies. She succeeded only after her great military victories.
To complete our data, we give the average rate of the mark in the five
national currencies.[8]

---

livered, together with these two countries, 51.4% of total Turkish imports. Blocked
Turkish balances in Germany totaled 10.45 million Turkish pounds at the end of 1936,
2.04 million in 1938 and 9 million in the spring of 1939. Nevertheless Germany was very
anxious to grant Turkey long-term investment credits in 1938–39 in competition with
Great Britain, and although Turkey's debtor she granted her a credit of Rm. 150
million. In 1938, 83.6% of Turkish imports were subject to clearing as were 81.6% of
her total exports.

   See Hazin Atif Kuyucak, "Exchange Control in Turkey," 1939.
[7] Walter Funk, *Wirtschaftsordnung im Neuen Europa*, Vienna, 1941, p. 19. In 1940
half of Hungary's trade was with Germany (without Czechoslovakia), more distant
markets being almost excluded. Germany took 40% of Yugoslav exports and furnished
65% of their imports; and more than half the Rumanian export and import trade was
with the Reich. Trade with Bulgaria declined, however (from 65 to 60%) in favor of
increased shares for Italy and U.S.S.R.; exports to Greece also fell off (from 30 to 24%
of the Greek imports) but imports from Greece rose (from 34 to 44% of total Greek
exports). Greek exports to the United States increased to 20% during the time prior
to the entry of Italy into the war. See Eleventh Annual Report of the Bank of International Settlement, 1941, pp. 69–70.

   Only as a matter of interest we add the figures for 1941 given in the *Twelfth Annual
Report* of the Bank of International Settlements, 1942, pp. 47 ff. According to this
source, Germany's share in the trade of Bulgaria ran to 80% (exports only); that of
Hungary to 59%, and of Rumania (January–June, 1941)—all three states being Axis
partners, satellites—to 65%. These figures do not include Slovakia, but it is not clear
whether they include the Protectorate of Bohemia and Moravia. Royal Institute, *Europe
under Hitler*, 1941, p. 14.
[8] Twelfth Annual Report of the Bank of International Settlement, 1942, p. 26.

	July 1, 1940	April 1, 1942
Bulgaria	32.75 [a]	32.75
Greece	46.50	60
Hungary	1.62	1.66
Rumania	49.50 [b]	59.50
Yugoslavia	14.80	20

[a] No change took place in the rate in Bulgaria, and only a slight change in Hungary.
[b] Raised in December, 1939.

It seemed for a short time after the outbreak of the war that the trade situation of some of these countries, particularly Yugoslavia, Rumania, and Greece (and also Turkey), might improve. This was during the winter and spring of 1940, when the "United Kingdom Commercial Corporation" created by the British Treasury began to operate with the aim of developing trade with Southeastern Europe. By preëmptive buying and by bartering overseas commodities (jute, tin, rice, tea) and so forth, regardless of world market prices, this company tried to divert goods from Germany. Obviously the proximity of Germany's great military strength put an effective brake on the actions of the Balkan states who accepted the British proposals only with great caution. Nevertheless, the existence of the possibility of trading with the British company somewhat improved the bargaining position of the region. An obvious question comes to mind: how much could have been accomplished and at what low cost had the Allies organized such a company in 1936 or 1937, when conditions for combating German penetration were so much more favorable.

With regard to the usual debits on clearing accounts the German attitude was very simple: whereas Germany was a practically unlimited buyer of all the surpluses of this region, its ability to consume most goods was not yet developed sufficiently to absorb an equal value of the goods which Germany could export. Within the framework of bilateralism the only solution was, therefore, for Germany to let her exports of consumption goods decline and for the small countries to make new investments by buying machinery, which Germany was, seemingly, prepared to deliver. Thus these countries would be compelled to use the income from exports directly for industrialization, instead of for consumption, through a kind of forced saving. And, as it was stated, thanks to their clearing assets, the Balkans became for the first time in their history, "creditor" nations.[9]

[9] German Institute for Business Research, *Weekly Report,* Feb. 19, 1940, No. 5–6, p. 20.

Another writer suggested [10] a very simple solution indeed. The Balkans could not fully utilize their balances for purchases of German goods. The best step then would be for the National Banks to buy the exporters' claims in German clearing, which would be the same as issuing currency against a purchase of gold or dollars. Continued expansion of credit would be justified as long as the country in question showed a tendency to retain credit balances with its chief supplier, Germany. Such an expansion of credit would help to stimulate economic activity. In other words, according to this line of reasoning, exportation was to help remove the lack of domestic capital not by making possible the import of the appropriate countervalue of goods, but by leading to the issue of new currency. Yes, there was never any shortage of arguments by economists, semiofficial and official experts to justify every move of German policy. Full of hypocrisy and demagogic half-truths, they tried to be useful to the regime and to earn their honors. It is often indeed painful to read such explanations and arguments, transferring into the field of economic reasoning the phrases and mentality of Nazi propaganda.

It had been stated, at an earlier date, that exchange clearing in the Danubian states had far surpassed what could have been accomplished by a Danubian Customs Union, that a kind of economic federation had been created.[11] But no such description could, in fact, be applied to the economic relations of Southeastern Europe with Germany. These countries were not permitted to sell and buy freely on the German market, their economies were not integrated with that of Germany or with each other, their trade with Germany was controlled and regimented in every detail. The advantages of a large economic unit were not attained except in very limited measure. While Germany, pursuing her own policy of self-sufficiency, did not adjust her agriculture to that of the other countries, they on the other hand were continually urged to adapt and subordinate their production to the requirements of the German totalitarian armed economy. Obviously their consumption also was subject to great distortion as a result of bilateral trade with Germany. And being step by step embraced by the German war economy, following the principle of autarky, and being more and more detached from the world economy, they were

[10] E. Wagemann, *Der Neue Balkan*, pp. 95–96.
[11] Paul Einzig, *The Exchange Clearing System*, London, 1935, p. 94. Such a statement was frequently heard.

subjected to a gradually growing exploitation. Their position was that of colonial or semicolonial states rather than that of equal members of an economic federation.

Of course, various German experts were ready to prove that the German policy was of great advantage to Southeastern Europe. On the negative side they pointed to the shortsightedness of the creditor nations during and after the crisis of 1931. They could refer to a lack of appreciation by the Western Powers of the importance of the region and to an unwillingness to help their distressed economies, an argument which could be directed particularly against France which had political ties with some countries of this region. They could also refer to the failure of the various international conferences and attempts at concerted action and were able to exploit the inconsistencies between the commercial and credit policies of the creditor nations.

On the positive side, the scope of the arguments and justifications —supported by copious statistics—was wide. They could assert that German purchases greatly helped these countries in overcoming the depression. As compared with 1929 their foreign trade by 1937 and 1938 had improved more than that of most other countries in Europe. Furthermore, Germany always paid generous prices and was anxious to help Danubian agriculture according to the plan.[12] Naturally the experts did not add that in so far as Germany actually paid more than would have been necessary elsewhere, this too was according to the plan and was only a very small item in the total cost of the German armed economy.

Another argument was that Germany helped to maintain Danubian agriculture and to diversify its production. (Except in Bulgaria where this policy had already been pursued for some time, it was really more of a program for the future than an actual achievement.) Germany had not opposed industrialization if it was kept within the limits of "organic development," which, in fact, meant that she opposed the erection of secondary industries. Up to 1937 the volume of industrial production increased—but the difficulties of obtaining foreign raw materials grew steadily, too. The national income increased everywhere although it still remained well below the 1929 level.[13] The

[12] Such was the argument of one of the leading officials of the German Foreign Office, Dr. Karl Ritter, in an article in *Deutscher Volkswirt*, No. 42, 1940.
[13] See the special series of statistics on Economic Development in Southeastern Europe, *Weekly Report* of the German Institute for Business Research, May 4, 1938, No. 17–18, p. 36.

Germans emphasized that the progress in the development of the region was due only to the expanding German economy—they neglected to add how much German protectionist policy had contributed to the depression in Southeastern Europe. They admitted that the whole expansion in this trade was the result of Germany's shifting her purchases from other countries to this region, but, again, they did not say that this was done because of the lack of foreign exchange and even more out of military expediency rather than from any desire to help the region. They also pointed with pride to the fact that in many fields Germany had secured a virtual purchasing monopoly which could be used to create economic servitude, but, it was asserted, it was not used to exert pressure on prices.[14] And while admitting that Germany held a dominant position in the foreign trade of these countries, they did not wish to believe that this, coupled with the German trade methods, infringed upon their economic independence. On the contrary, it was argued that prior to the German trade expansion these countries were completely dependent upon the world market with all its price fluctuations and uncertainties, a situation further aggravated by the lack of diversification of their production; whereas, now they had a regular buyer who purchased their whole surpluses, paying high prices and freeing them from the vicissitudes of the world markets and the business cycle. The mechanism of exchange control was regarded as an instrument to stabilize production, prices, and markets—especially when combined with bilateralism.[15] Although Germany could not immediately supply this region with overseas products, she expected to do so in the future by developing an extensive transit trade.

Of course, these experts again neglected to say that the whole development was a part of the German armed economy preparing for war, with its vast demands for all kinds of commodities. They did not point out the artificial nature of the whole structure, which had not been tried in a peacetime welfare economy, and it was never suggested that more freedom be introduced into the whole trading system. But this was the "German Order," the new solution of the problem of Southeastern Europe, which many regarded as a way out of manifold difficulties. The German economic domination certainly supported

[14] A very instructive article, "The Economic Independence of Southeastern Europe," *Weekly Report,* of the German Institute for Business Research, Feb. 19, 1940, No. 5–6, p. 18.
[15] See Dr. Fr. Meyer, *Weltwirtschaftliches Archiv,* LIII (1941), pp. 320–69.

German political and later military strength, but this economic development itself was decided on the field of politics rather than of economics. It is part of the chapter of appeasement, of allocating to Germany a special sphere of influence in this part of Europe.

Thus in 1939 before the fresh outbreak of war, Central and Southeastern Europe was subject to German economic domination to an extent greater than in 1914. These nations achieved freedom after the First World War. They survived the primary postwar economic crisis, recovered, and were steadily making good economic progress under the influence of young liberated forces and growing democratic elements. Then they had to pass through the greatest economic crisis in history and fell again under complete German domination, becoming at best her satellites, though being no poorer, altogether, in natural resources than Germany. The reasons why all this happened must be analyzed.

Various elements in the problem have been discussed here. We have seen that beginning with the peace treaties no economic program for this area was agreed upon, no measures were taken to prevent the growth of an exaggerated economic nationalism, no agricultural policy was organized to prepare these countries to compete with overseas producers and to adjust themselves to the new conditions, no policy was devised for a real development of their domestic markets.

Both before and during the crisis there was no unity among the major powers with regard to this part of Europe and very little was done to promote or enforce unity between the states of this region. These countries were too weak to resist the German economic offensive, to defend themselves against totalitarian aggression working within bilateralism. There was no help from Western Europe, which failed to unite to force Germany to change the economic policy that was part of her general policy. The great Powers did not see in time the importance of the problem. The countries in the Danube valley were unable to carry out the necessary economic readjustments. They therefore succumbed to the German drive. The key to all this must be sought in the sphere of world politics rather than merely in the domain of economics. Throughout the whole period the problem of Germany was uppermost. Only when all the facts are assembled will it be understood why these countries became, in effect, German dependencies.

In the German view, they obtained full economic security because of their relations with the Greater German Empire. There is a certain analogy between this kind of economic security and that enjoyed by German labor. Labor in Germany obtained economic security but lost all freedom; this security was supposed to provide permanent employment, but soon the level of living, real wages, working conditions, all became uncertain and deteriorated; security became identical with forced labor. The economic independence of these small states was succeeded by so-called economic security. Free but uncertain foreign markets were replaced by an assured and permanent market, which was attractive at first. Yet, before long, the real value of the income from exports became uncertain, and various onerous conditions were imposed; it became hard to distinguish between economic security and economic servitude within the big German European Empire, which resembled a colonial regime rather than a federation. This certainly was not a solution in the interests of the region, and it could not last long. It was, however, the German solution of the problems of Central and Southeastern Europe, and had been worked out as a new conception [16] even before the outbreak of the war. Yet many statesmen regarded Germany as competent to organize this difficult region and to establish order therein.

But the Nazi commercial policy demonstrated that there is no real possibility of remaining on a basis of even relatively free trade, once commerce with a totalitarian state has absorbed a large portion of a country's total trade. The lack of a similar trade organization tends to cause the acceptance of terms imposed by the totalitarian country. This fact, if recognized in time, could have helped in checking Germany's expansion and the severity of her policy. Of course it was not in conformity with the policy of the Western Powers to respond in such a way, and the smaller powers were not sufficiently strong to oppose the German policy with any prospect of success.

A survey of the causes of the economic crisis in Central and Southeastern Europe, and of the measures taken to fight them and to restore sound conditions could furnish a great deal of material for a detailed analysis of many questions of economic theory as well as of policy.

[16] The German idea of economic security to all trade partners based on carefully balancing mutual economic interests was proclaimed as winning out against the traditional situation in which a sound national policy was in conflict with the profit idea in a capitalistic economy. *Weekly Report* of the German Institute for Business Research, Oct. 26, 1940, No. 19–22, pp. 61–74.

While it is not within the scope of this book to deal with these aspects of the problem, some conclusions, referring especially to foreign-trade and foreign-exchange control, to the system of clearing agreements, and to the concept of bilateral trade are nevertheless indicated. They will be particularly appropriate because the use of exchange control and of clearing agreements as instruments of commercial policy is repeatedly brought up in proposals for postwar economic settlements.

The history of foreign-exchange control during this period has confirmed, once more, the fact that the efficacy of such measures in maintaining the external value of a currency is narrowly limited in scope. It can function, with some prospect of success, if its aim is to control various capital transactions and unnecessary and unjustified expenditures abroad. But if foreign-exchange control goes beyond this limit and is used to stop payments abroad which are legitimate and justified, such as debt service and various other financial payments and, particularly, payment for imported goods, then such a policy can succeed only if accompanied by a complete and thorough control of all foreign transactions.

If exchange control is to be used as a means of curtailing imports and supporting and directing exports it becomes an instrument of foreign-trade policy and cannot be considered a purely monetary device.[17] It belongs, then, in the field of quantitative import controls, as a sort of import permit system concealed under the name "exchange control," and as such it represents one of the crudest forms of import control, usually completely arbitrary and devoid of any system of checks and balances. If extended over a long period it cannot remain confined to the sphere of international trade but will invade other parts of the economy, influencing production, prices, consumption, and finally, if it is to be effective, requiring centralized planning. From a system of import licensing, just as from exchange control when used for quantitative import control, the way leads to a planned, entirely controlled foreign trade. It would be erroneous, therefore, to attribute the results of such a regime to exchange control alone, because in reality exchange control itself becomes only one instrument in the general management of foreign trade, with a growing tendency toward control and planning throughout the whole national economy.

Likewise, it would be wrong to conclude that an expansion of

[17] H. S. Ellis, *Exchange Control in Central Europe*, p. 319.

foreign trade was fostered by the clearing-payments agreements, which were introduced partially by countries with import surpluses to force their partners to balance the trade between them, and partially in an effort to overcome the insuperable obstacles to trade created by exchange control elsewhere. If it were stated, for instance, that the development of German trade with countries with which no clearing agreements existed was far more unfavorable than the development of trade with clearing countries,[18] it does not follow automatically that this is very closely connected with the existence of the clearing agreements. The share of countries with clearing and other payment agreements in Germany's import trade rose from 50.3 per cent in 1932 to 77.6 per cent in 1938, and in her exports from 70 to 84 per cent, thus accounting for four fifths of her total foreign trade. However, Germany's share in world trade decreased from 9.35 per cent in 1929 to 8.56 per cent in 1937 (imports from 9 to 8, exports from 9.73 to 9.15 per cent). In reality substantial increases in German trade occurred only in the case of the countries of Southeastern Europe, the Near East, and South American clearing countries; in all cases they were areas which in addition to having exchange control were considered by Germany as complementary to her in their economic structure. The increase in the share of these regions in total German trade was not the result of the clearing agreements but of a deliberate totalitarian commercial policy which used clearing agreements as a very apt instrument for its purposes. Further evidence is found in the fact that various payment agreements between Germany and certain industrial countries of Europe did not prevent their trade from declining.[19] Similarly, trade between the Rome Protocol countries or

[18] "Position of Clearing Agreements in German Foreign Trade," *Weekly Report* of the German Institute for Business Research, Berlin, Supplement, May 23, 1939, p. 2.

[19] It is interesting to compare the increase in the proportion of German trade with Southeastern Europe with the shift in her trade with other areas. From 1929 to 1938 imports from Southeastern Europe rose from 3.8 to 9.8% of total German imports; exports from 4.3 to 10.3% of the total; imports from South and Central America rose from 11.4 to 14.9%; exports from 7.3 to 11.7; with the Scandinavian countries imports rose from 7.3 to 11.4 and exports from 10.2 to 12.9%. And with the Near East (chiefly Turkey) imports rose from 1.4 to 3.8 and exports from 1.4 to 5.4%.

On the other hand, German trade with other regions declined, chiefly with these following countries. With Western Europe imports dropped from 15.7 to 11.7; exports from 26.2 to 20.8; with Great Britain, imports dropped from 6.4 to 5.2; exports from 9.7 to 6.7; with United States imports dropped from 13.3 to 7.4; exports from 7.4 to 2.8; with the British Empire countries, imports dropped from 10.6 to 7.9, and exports rose from 3.9 to 5.8; with the U.S.S.R. imports dropped from 3.2 to 0.9%, and exports from 2.6 to 0.6; with Czechoslovakia, imports dropped from 3.6 to 2.6 and exports from 4.9 to 2.6 per cent. *Weekly Report*, July 27, 1939, No. 29–30, p. 79.

the Little Entente countries did not mount as a result of the clearing agreements between them but as a result of deliberate trade planning in which various devices, including clearing, were used to increase mutual trade. In general, if clearing agreements were not supplemented by a comprehensive policy of trade expansion they automatically tended to contract mutual trade because of the application of the principle of bilateral balancing, first of trade and, soon, of the entire balance of payments. It was only a short step from clearing agreements to bilateral trade, with all its consequent evils—distortion of production and consumption, abandonment of competitive buying and selling, and, in the smaller countries, a growing dependence upon the stronger partner. Bilateral trade, which was also recommended by some German experts as a device for stabilizing the trade and production conditions of Germany's trade partners, has, in general, been openly refused and recognized as basically contrary to the idea of international exchange of commodities. And it is certainly true that "Modern civilization is based on a world economy which functions through a system of multilateral trade of a specific pattern that embraces the whole world." [20]

Experience with bilateral trade, clearing agreements and total import control (permit system) furnish unambiguous evidence that the smaller countries, in particular, should be interested in multilateral trade and in trade carried on without any restrictions applied to each separate transaction. Under a system of bilateral trade or even of extensive quantitative import control the small countries will, as a rule, have a weaker bargaining position than with multilateral trade based on the most-favored-nation clause. Either they will succumb to some big state with its greater bargaining power, or they will be induced to unite into major economic blocs. The formation of great blocs, often giving further support to the policy of protection, is thus one result of this kind of commercial policy.

[20] League of Nations, *Network of World Trade*, Geneva, 1942, p. 10

16

ECONOMIC DEVELOPMENT: THE PROBLEM AND THE PROGRAM

AN ECONOMIC program of reconstruction and development of this region, preferably on an international basis, should be an integral part of any peace settlement. Its chief aims should be economic advancement and economic integration of the backward parts of this area with the rest of Europe, and also with the world economy.

THE PROBLEM OF DEVELOPMENT

Any such program must start with an analysis of the most important economic and social problems of the region, not merely for the period of postwar relief and rehabilitation but for development over a long period. The situation in Austria and Czechoslovakia will be similar to that of other industrial countries of Europe occupied by Germany, primarily a problem of postwar relief and reconstruction and adjustment to the new world-market conditions, but the development of Southeastern Europe and the potential exchange of commodities with it on a huge scale will be of greater direct importance to them than to the other countries. At the same time both these countries, in coöperation with the Western Powers, could play very useful roles in the development of these backward areas, because of their knowledge of local conditions and their great immediate interest.

Before discussing the formation of large units, ideas of federation, it should be underscored that the main problems cannot be solved by any more formal organization itself, but there must be a real solution, going to the root of the troubles. This will be by no means easy. For the agricultural countries of Southeastern Europe the problems to be considered are very much the same as those which emerged after the last war, and even existed before it. They are the problems of *a market for agricultural exports, of population pressure, poverty, and the lack of capital.*

The feasibility of substantially raising the low standard of living has often been questioned. Do the prerequisites of broader economic

Table 17

Agricultural Production in Central and Southeastern Europe (in Percentage of World Production)

	Wheat (1938-39)	Corn (1937-38)	Oats (1938-39)	Barley (1938-39)	Rye (1938-39)	Sugar Beets (1938-39)	Tobacco (1937-38)	Colza [Rapeseed] (1937)	Sesamum (1937)	Wool (1937)	Flax Fiber (1937)	Hemp Fiber (1937-38)
Austria	0.3	0.2	0.6	0.7	1.2	1.8	0.6	0.1		0.1	0.1	
Czechoslovakia	1.1	0.3	1.9	3.0	3.5	4.7	0.8	0.7		0.4	1.4	1.2
Hungary	1.6	2.4	0.5	1.7	1.6	1.3	0.9	0.4		0.8	0.4	3.1
Yugoslavia	1.8	4.5	0.5	1.0	0.5	0.8	0.4	0.6		1.7	1.4	12.2
Rumania	2.9	4.0	0.7	1.9	1.1	1.4	0.7	2.9	0.2	0.5	1.1	6.6
Bulgaria	1.3	0.7	0.1	0.8	0.4	0.2	2.8	0.2	1.2	0.5	0.1	1.1
Greece	0.6	0.3	0.2	0.6	0.1				3.1			
Total	9.6	12.4	4.5	9.7	8.4	10.2	6.2	4.9	4.5	4.0	4.5	24.2
Germany	3.3	0.1	9.3	9.7	17.7	17.9	1.4	6.0		1.1	4.2	1.7

Table 18

Production of Metals and Minerals (in Percentage of World Production)

	Antimony (metal content) 1937	Bauxite 1937	Chromium (metal content) 1937	Copper (metal content) 1937	Iron (metal content) 1937	Lead (metal content) 1937	Zinc (metal content) 1937	Manganese 1937	Coal 1937	Petroleum 1938	Magnesite 1936	Pyrites 1937	Gold 1937
Austria	0.6				0.7	0.5	0.2	1.4			22.4		
Czechoslovakia	2.8				0.6	0.3	0.2		1.3		4.7 [a]	0.2	0.1
Hungary		13.3			0.1			0.3	0.1				
Yugoslavia	4.8	8.9	4.8	1.7	0.3	4.2	2.6	0.1			3.9	1.3	0.3
Rumania		0.3			0.1	0.5	0.4	0.6		2.4		0.1	0.5
Bulgaria		0.1	0.2					0.2					
Greece		3.4	3.4		0.1	0.4	0.5	0.2			6.6	1.9	
Total	8.2	26.0	8.4	1.7	1.9	5.9	3.9	2.8	1.4	2.4	37.6	3.5	0.9
Germany		2.3		1.3	2.8	4.6	9	7.0	14	0.2	0.8	4.0	

[a] The figure here represents exports.

activity—the natural resources, the labor, the capital—exist in South-eastern Europe? Is it possible to establish an appropriate organization? At this point it should be made clear that by a general economic development we do not mean that this area must reach the same high standard of living as was made possible in other countries by special conditions: rich natural resources, less dense population, huge amounts of capital accumulated over a long period, access to the open seas, or profits from colonies or overseas trade. But it would be defeatist to assume that with the resources available a considerable improvement is impossible.

Let us discuss the problem by examining first the resources of these countries. Tables 17 and 18 (p. 230) [1] on the greater part of the mineral and agricultural production furnish a basis for only a rough comparison between these countries and Germany.

The seven countries produce important minerals, bauxite, antimony, magnesite, lead, copper, chromium, and kaolin—and also oil—in larger quantities than does Germany. And in addition to the products listed in the tables certain others should be mentioned. Czechoslovakia, Austria, Rumania, and Yugoslavia exported large quantities of timber (nearly 11.5 million cubic meters in 1937); there are also important deposits, and large production, of lignite in most of these countries. There are other potentialities as yet unexploited. The production of minerals could undoubtedly be increased, since the search for them has not been completed; for example, new oil deposits have been recently found in Hungary (the actual yearly production has surpassed 500,000 tons), Yugoslavia, and Austria. The possibilities of electric-power production through the use of unexploited water-power facilities are great. Huge supplies of agricultural products—cereals, livestock, poultry, eggs, hops, tobacco, vegetables, seeds, hemp, fodder, and various fruits—have always been exported.

From the point of view of existing and potential resources and production, the comparison with Germany shows little reason for believing that general economic advancement is impossible. (We do not, of course, compare the resources of this region with the natural wealth of rich countries like the United States or Soviet Russia.) The comparison with Germany should be completed by an estimate of the invested capital used in production, trade, and transportation, and by a comparison of the intensity of production and the occupa-

[1] From Royal Institute, *Raw Materials*, London, 1939.

tional distribution of the population. Such a study would help to explain the great differences in national income. An analysis of the figures or income and population in Table 19 (p. 233) [2] brings out the following facts: In the period from 1925 to 1934 the population of 79 million (or less, depending upon the year taken as a basis) in the seven countries mentioned received yearly a national income of $7,252 million, gold, or in international units, 9,767 million. On the other hand, the population of 67.6 million in Germany received a total national income of $15,157 million, or 17,580 international units. If we compare the incomes in terms of gold dollars, Central and Southeastern European countries received a total national income equal to 47 per cent of Germany's; in terms of international units, their income was 56 per cent of Germany's. It follows that per capita income was far less than half that in Germany.

According to the figures in the table the lowest per capita incomes occurred in the countries with the largest percentage of agricultural population: Rumania, Bulgaria, and Yugoslavia.[3] At the other end of the scale are industrialized Czechoslovakia and fairly well-developed Austria, which can be considered advanced countries. Greece with her different economic structure and Hungary with her growing industrialization lie in between.

To illustrate further the close causal connection between the low level of per capita real income and agriculture, it is useful to take into account the relationship between the ratio of farm population to farm land and the low yield of agricultural production. The table [4] below shows clearly the very low yield per hectare in the four Danubian states, together with the high ratio of farm population to farm land.

In Western and Central Europe, the intensive cultivation of agricultural products other than cereals is carried on, and the amount of

[2] Figures for national incomes are taken from Colin Clark (*op. cit.*, p. 40); no exact comparison is possible, especially for the prewar period, but Clark's figures based on all available material indicate the fundamental trends. For the definition of international units, see p. 5, above.

[3] *South-Eastern Europe,* 1941, p. 85, gives the following average per capita income (including that received in kind as well as in cash) based on various sources: Yugoslavia (1937), £12; Hungary (1936–37), £19; Rumania (1936), £12–15; Bulgaria (1937), £14–16; Greece (1929), £16. (National currencies are converted into sterling at the ruling rates of exchange.)

[4] Figures for yield per ha. are from League of Nations Conference on Rural Life, 1939, Document No. 1, p. 16.

Figures for ratio of agricultural workers to cultivated land are from O. S. Morgan (ed.), *Agricultural Systems of Middle Europe,* New York, 1933, p. 131.

Table 19

Income and Population Figures

	NATIONAL INCOME, IN $ MILLION, GOLD, INCLUDING INDIRECT TAXES 1925–34	NATIONAL INCOME IN INTERNATIONAL UNITS Period	Units	REAL INCOME PER HEAD OF WORKING POPULATION IN INTERNATIONAL UNITS	POPULATION Period	Figures (in millions)	PERCENTAGE OF POPULATION OCCUPIED IN AGRICULTURE[a]
Germany	15,157	1925–34	17,580	646	1937 (est.)	67.6	28.9
Austria	1,040	1925–34	1,613	572	1934 (est.)	6.76	26
Bulgaria	347	1925–34	524	284	1938 (est.)	6.08	81
Greece	494	1924, 1929, 1934	922	397	1937 (est.)	7	54
Hungary	1,077	1925–39	1,205	359	1937 (est.)	9.03	53
Rumania	974	1925–39	1,471	243	1936 (est.)	19.42	78
Czechoslovakia	2,125	1925–34	2,680	455	1937 (est.)	15.22	34.2
Yugoslavia	1,495	1925–34	1,352	330	1937 (est.)	15.4	79
Total of all 7 countries	7,252		9,767			78.91	

[a] League of Nations, *Europe's Trade*, Geneva, 1941, p. 50; for Germany, Austria, and Czechoslovakia, see D. Warriner, *Economics of Peasant Farming*, Oxford, 1939, p. 20.

	Average Yield of Wheat in Quintals per Hectare (1933–37)	Number of Agricultural Workers per 100 Hectares of Cultivated Land (exclusive of woods)
Germany	22.2	34.3
Austria	16.3	22.6
Czechoslovakia	17.3	28
Hungary	13.9	28.6
Yugoslavia	11.1	40.8
Rumania	9.1	41.1
Bulgaria	11.9	58.6
Denmark	31.3	16.4
Netherlands	29.6	28.6

livestock per capita is relatively large. In Southeastern Europe, a considerably larger population is employed in agriculture per unit of arable land than in Central and, of course, Western Europe,[5] with a much lower average yield, and with much less farm capital available; the result is clear—a low standard of living and relative overpopulation. To this already unfavorable situation the trend in population growth in Southeastern Europe added a further complication. The population of Bulgaria, Hungary, Greece, Rumania, and Yugoslavia jumped from 46 million in 1920 to some 59 million in 1939.[6] And although the rate of natural increase declined after 1920 in all these countries except Greece, the excess of births over deaths [7] per thousand inhabitants in 1931–35 was as follows: in Hungary, 13; in Yugoslavia, 13.9; Bulgaria, 13.8; Rumania, 12.3; Greece, 13; Czechoslovakia, 5.8; in Germany, 5.4. With very little new land to be cultivated and insufficient industrial development this meant, of course, continual population pressure in agriculture. This problem does not exist to any significant extent in Czechoslovakia and Austria, on the whole, and it arises only to a limited extent in Hungary, which, however, has not brought about a land reform to settle the urgent matter of large estates.

General economic development has inevitably been retarded by

[5] D. Warriner, *Economics of Peasant Farming*, p. 9. "The farms of Western Europe are twice as large, carry twice as much capital to the acre, produce twice as much corn to the acre and employ only half as many people to the acre as the farms of Eastern Europe."
[6] A. Reithinger, *Das wirtschaftliche Gesicht Europas*, Stuttgart-Berlin, 1936, pp. 16–18. Reithinger predicts, from the trend of population in the thirties that the population of the Balkans and Poland will have increased by 24 million in 1960, that of the Southeastern countries by 12 million.
[7] League of Nations, *Statistical Yearbook 1937–38*, Geneva, 1938, pp. 42–43.

failure to relieve poverty and population pressure in agriculture. It is not a new problem, it is not the result of a new political situation nor of the First World War. Its origin can be traced back to the second half of the nineteenth century when the European conflict centering around the import of cereals from overseas first began. To the industrial nations of Western Europe the importation of American grain at lower prices meant an improvement in their terms of trade. The cleavage of Europe into highly industrialized Western Europe and backward, agricultural Southeastern and Eastern Europe, with Central Europe occupying a middle position, was never overcome. As a matter of fact, real income per head was higher in the economically distressed thirties than in 1913.[8] For the period 1925–34 Colin Clark cites as the average annual income per head in Czechoslovakia, Austria, Hungary, Rumania, and Yugoslavia, 386 international units against 352 in 1913; this is a rise of 10 per cent, in spite of an increase in working population from 20 million in 1913 to 22–23 million in the latter period.

AGRICULTURE

Any discussion of postwar economic reconstruction has to start with some assumptions. The first one results logically from the findings of our analysis. Now that we have arrived at the conclusion that the problem of Southeastern Europe (and also of the small countries of Central Europe) is closely interrelated with the European economy as a whole and thus also with the world economy and that its solution is vital for European stability, our next step is to recognize the need of a policy of economic integration of Continental Europe which will, it is to be hoped, substantially increase its trade with the U.S.S.R. The division of Europe into wealthy industrial regions and poorly developed, retarded agricultural areas must be gradually overcome if there is to be a reasonable prospect of success in rebuilding Europe as a whole.

Some opinions have been expressed and hopes voiced that, although Nazi policy must be entirely repudiated because of its methods and philosophy, the Germans nevertheless succeeded to a large extent in bringing about the economic unification and integration of Europe.[9] It seemed for a while, particularly before the new military

[8] Colin Clark, *op. cit.*, p. 136. [9] G. D. H. Cole, *op. cit.*, p. 83.

campaign of 1941, that in applying the same or a similar pattern throughout the greatest part of Europe the German war economy might have such an integrating influence on the monetary system and on equalizing costs of production and prices.[10] But, instead, the German policy in the occupied countries soon tended toward disintegration. For instance, whereas Germany exerted every effort to check inflation in Germany proper her policy in the occupied countries directly stimulated inflation. There has been no free trade between Germany and the other parts of Europe—except the so-called incorporated areas and Holland—and therefore no real price and cost adjustment. The only uniformity achieved or even attempted was designed to adapt all the economies to supplying armaments, food, and raw materials for German war requirements. Therefore no real economic integration in Europe can be expected from the German domination.

Yet a policy of economic integration of Europe must be worked out. It can be assumed that the general objective of postwar economic policy will be an expanding economy with growing world trade, whose ultimate purpose is to raise the standard of living. The whole European Continent—including Germany—could gain greatly from increased inter-European trade and the economic integration of the Continent, which would lead eventually to a large-scale development of the backward regions of Eastern and Southeastern Europe. If this can be achieved, it will be of great importance to the industrial countries, who are confronted with growing competition in the overseas markets and faced with uncertainty as to the postwar situation of the British economy. There is the potentiality of a really large increase in consumption in this backward area; development of the region would be the most efficient way to bring about an upswing in European trade.[11]

Any integration of the European economy must begin in the sphere of European agriculture, with the aim of completely changing its structure and of removing all the obstacles to its development. These obstacles go back to the first policy of large-scale protection, originally against overseas competition, which started in 1879 in Germany. The

10 See the author's *The New Economic Warfare,* New York, 1941, p. 179.
11 The importance of Great Britain for the Continent is evident from the fact that in the years before the Second World War it had an export surplus of $500 million yearly to Great Britain.

various measures toward self-sufficiency taken before and after the 1930 crisis were only the last step in the same policy.

A fundamental change in agriculture is one means of expanding the inter-European exchange of commodities and of providing a regular market for agricultural exports from Eastern and Southeastern Europe. We must first dispose of a frequently heard objection to the effect that if food consumption in the exporting countries increased, scarcely any surplus agricultural products would be left for export. Although it is true that food consumption in this region is extremely low [12] as compared with more developed countries, the export of foodstuffs was needed to obtain foreign exchange with which to buy essential raw materials and other goods not available at home; in order to buy the most basic necessities of life the peasants were therefore forced to sell their crops even though it meant an unsatisfactory diet. As long as these countries do not possess other exportable commodities they will remain dependent upon agricultural exports to obtain their vital imports. Furthermore, the very low level of consumption indicates that there are large possibilities of increasing production for the home market, especially in view of the very low yield in cereals, sugar beets, and potatoes as compared with other countries.[13]

Economic integration of agriculture will, of course, not be identical

[12] It is difficult to obtain reliable data on consumption per head for most of these countries, in which the statistical service was not yet organized on a satisfactory basis. Even the League of Nations' Report on Nutrition (Geneva, 1937) gives only sporadic figures with regard to food consumption in this region. We include some of these statistics (pp. 109, 226): Sugar consumption per head was in Bulgaria 5 kg. yearly, in Yugoslavia 5.5 kg., in Hungary 13.5, as against 28 kg. in Czechoslovakia, 24.6 in France, 26.1 in Germany. Consumption of milk, including cream, butter, and cheese in terms of milk, averaged in Rumania 21 gallons per head for 1930–34 and 40 in Bulgaria for 1925–26, against 83 in Czechoslovakia, 69 in Austria, and 79 in Germany for 1930–34. Consumption of citrus fruit was nearly negligible; for instance, in Rumania, 1.5 kg. per head against 18.5 in France, 11.2 in Germany, 5.9 in Czechoslovakia.

The German Institute for Business Research (*Vierteljahreshefte*, 1940–41, No. 23, p. 93) published average figures for consumption per head for various goods in Hungary, Bulgaria, Yugoslavia, Rumania and Greece, which correspond with other countries as follows in kg. per head yearly.

	The Five Countries	Germany	Czecho-slovakia	France	U.S.A.
Sugar	7	25	28	23	50
Butter	1.5	8.8	4.5	4.9	9
Meat	24	52	35	41	70
Eggs (number)	78	120	115	154	199

[13] See N. F. Hall, *Memorandum on Measures of National and International Character for Raising the Standard of Living*, Geneva, 1938, p. 51.

with the complete removal of agricultural protection, but the first step, to be efficient and helpful, should be the reduction of such protection to its 1913 level. At that time there was not such a striking difference between the level of agricultural prices in the industrial countries with protection and those on the world market. This policy of artificially maintaining enormously high agricultural prices dates from the period before and during the last crisis and is a result of exaggerated protectionism. It is evident that it was a factor disturbing the economic equilibrium of the whole world. The excessively high level of these prices must have exerted a downward pressure on the standard of living of the whole Continent but especially upon the agricultural countries. This development in the high-cost producing countries with steadily increasing protection made it clear that sooner or later a settlement between the industrial and agricultural interests decisively affecting the whole position of these countries in foreign trade would become inevitable. Germany, Italy, France, Czechoslovakia, Austria, and Switzerland were among the high-cost countries with extreme protection, and together, they accounted for 15 per cent of the world wheat production. And yet, as has been seen, they, with the Low Countries, and, for some products, also Great Britain, were the customary markets for the agricultural surpluses of Eastern and Southeastern Europe which could be regarded as complementary to their economies.

It is therefore evident that an expansion of international trade and, in particular, inter-European trade, is impossible without a reversal of the policy of autarky. Great emphasis is now being placed upon improving the standard of nutrition, which would automatically lead to an increase in agricultural production as a whole. But obviously such a policy could be carried out successfully only if there were a strong determination to reduce agricultural protection radically, and, by so doing, to increase world trade. Such a program also fits in very well with the structural changes badly needed in European agriculture, which requires a shift from energy foods to more protective foods (such as fruit, meat, dairy products, vegetables). Although production of protective foods in Western Europe greatly increased between the wars there is still much to be done in this direction throughout the entire Continent. There is no doubt that high-price countries of a relatively high level of efficiency, and whose peasants have superior technical skill and cultural knowledge, can adapt themselves more easily to the production of protective food, are better prepared for such necessary reorientation of their agriculture, than are the countries in peasant Europe with lower efficiency and which are greatly dependent upon outside aid; but these in turn will be able to supply the more progressive countries with the cereals and fodder crops needed for extending the production of cattle, pigs, and poultry.

This important program aiming at gradual integration of the European economy could be effected through the use of the usual instruments of foreign trade, supported by a comprehensive international program.

There still remains the question of whether the agriculture of the Danubian and Eastern European countries will be able to compete with overseas production in their old markets better than it did in the last crisis. This problem will not arise during the period immediately after the war, when a general shortage of food and all kinds of goods will prevail. But the experience during the period of postwar transition will perhaps be ample to indicate whether Danubian agriculture will really be in a competitive position. Should this not be fully true even after correct monetary adjustment and all other appropriate measures have been carried out, then, for a short period before such full adjustment is achieved, a solution can be found in international commercial agreements granting certain export quotas to the agricultural exporting countries of Europe. Another method might consist of an internationally supervised, gradually declining, preferential regime, strictly limited as to the period of duration. At any rate the mistake of the thirties of closing European markets to Southern European exporters must not be repeated.[14] And if the agricultural policy in postwar Europe should follow the principles just mentioned—the abandonment of the old ideas of self-sufficiency in bread-cereals which was supported during the last decade by military considerations, and the shifting, where feasible, to the production of protective foods—it would greatly help in solving the very difficult problems of Eastern and Southeastern Europe.

This represents, of course, only one side of the question, the other being the reconstruction or rebuilding of agriculture in the region

[14] D. Warriner, *Eastern Europe after Hitler.* It must be understood that there can be no solution through East Europe Federation or similar union without the possibility of finding markets for food produce in the West (p. 20).

concerned. It is clear that this task in its totality will be bigger than the shift in agricultural production in Western and Central Europe. The comprehensive program which, let us hope, will be worked out with international coöperation of experts will have to deal with the question of a fundamental reorganization of agriculture in Eastern and Southeastern Europe, with developing it and bringing it to a much higher level. It will have to include such points as much greater intensity, and greater diversification of production, the commercialization of agricultural marketing, financing and transport and the task of proper education. The low level of domestic consumption and the extremely low yield compared with other European countries illustrate both the possibility and the need of greatly intensifying production of the present type of crops. (See p. 234.) There has been very little use of farm machinery and a nearly negligible consumption of artificial fertilizers.[15] Greater production arising from more intensive methods will certainly aid any postwar shift in crop structure; such a shift will be badly needed and there will be ample opportunities for it. It will, for example, certainly be important to increase the production of fodder for the expansion of cattle, pig and poultry production which is to be expected both here and in other countries.

The need for a greater diversification of agricultural production is to be stressed. In pursuing this aim the production of protective foods must also be progressively increased in these countries, which are far behind Western Europe in this respect. In the West, about one third of the agricultural area was devoted to protective foods against less than one seventh in Southeastern Europe. Obviously the program will have to vary according to the fertility of various sections; thus the better grades of land are more adapted to the production of livestock and crop diversification than are the areas with poor soil and little rainfall. Bulgaria can serve as an example for sections with similar conditions in successful shifting to diversified production. In nearly all these countries there were some efforts in this direction although little was done in Rumania in spite of the favorable natural conditions there. The policy must embrace all suitable kinds of agriculture, and there are already various detailed programs for diversi-

15 The consumption of artificial fertilizers in all these countries was extremely low compared to other countries in Europe. After 1931 it was practically negligible in Rumania, Bulgaria, and even Yugoslavia. It reached in Hungary only 10–15% of the Czechoslovak consumption, which itself was only about one half of the consumption in France, and only 30–40% of that in Germany. A. Reithinger, *op. cit.*, p. 27; Krugmann, *op. cit.*, p. 29.

fication based on an efficient adaptation to the natural potentialities of these countries rather than on self-sufficiency, as in the German plan.[16] The opportunities for diversification are many. Wherever the required conditions exist, the production of fodder, various oilseeds, and industrial crops (such as rapeseed, sunflower seed, flax and hemp, cotton in Bulgaria and Greece) can be extended. The whole system of animal and poultry farming needs to be reorganized in nearly every respect, and a great deal can be done in many of these countries in vegetable and fruit production and in the development of canning and processing industries. Promising starts have already been made in this direction in many places. Similarly these reforms are badly needed in forestry and in the timber industry.

The reconstruction of agriculture will also require great advances in irrigation, soil conservation, the regulation of rivers, and the consolidation of peasant properties, which are often split up into small widely dispersed strips. All this will require systematic work based on foreign example, advice, and experience. The coöperation of foreign countries and the advice of their technical experts will be vitally important; Denmark, the United States, and Czechoslovakia could certainly be of great assistance.

This is not, of course, a program to be carried out overnight, but is a long-range plan.[17] In order to succeed in some regions it will require a change in the peasant's attitude and even in his inherited way of life. A high level of popular education is a prerequisite for modern farming, and, consequently, in order to bring the agriculture of the Southeast up to the level of that of Western and Central Europe, education and enlightenment along both technical and general lines will be necessary. Agriculture, here, must undergo a process of commercialization, not an easy step from the still rather patriarchal and precapitalistic system existing in some parts.

A well-organized system of coöperatives of all kinds could be a great help, especially in furnishing a very badly needed credit organization. But only among an enlightened peasantry can there be much hope of the kind of coöperative organization that has become almost essential for prosperous agriculture in Europe. Furthermore, in order

---

[16] See, for instance, for Yugoslavia: O. Frangeš, "Die treibenden Kräfte der wirtschaftlichen Strukturwandlungen in Jugoslavien," *Weltwirtschaftliches Archiv*, XLVIII (1938), 309–33. This was written before its author became convinced of the advantages of a big complementary economic empire led by Germany.

[17] N. F. Hall, *op. cit.*, p. 56.

to achieve real progress in agriculture within a reasonable length of time a great deal of capital will be required.

The development envisaged here will step by step abolish the appalling poverty now prevalent in some areas. It will expand the domestic market in general and improve the export situation, as a result of greater diversification, standardization of goods, and better commercial and financial organization. Undoubtedly it will provide greater employment opportunities throughout the whole economy. But, in spite of these advantages, the modernization of agriculture alone will not be sufficient to relieve the pressure of the population on the land. In spite of the losses in human lives that most of these countries have suffered during the war there is reason to expect that the population pressure will continue.[18] It was estimated that prewar agricultural production could have been reduced by one third fewer people. Therefore there was a surplus agricultural population in this whole area—of several million—comparable to the industrial unemployed. This explains sufficiently why even a rapid introduction of a modern agricultural economy cannot be expected to provide full employment for the whole agricultural population.

There is not much prospect that collectivization along Russian lines would be a real remedy for the rural poverty that is due to over-population. In Russia, collectivization was part of a comprehensive program providing great opportunities for employment in the construction of huge industries. Increase in food production, there, has been brought about not so much by reforming peasant life as by colonization, that is, by opening up new areas for cultivation. But this possibility does not exist in Southeastern Europe. Furthermore, because of the low total income, more equal distribution of income could not greatly alleviate peasant poverty. There was, in fact, much greater income equality than in Western and Central Europe. An exception in this respect was Hungary, where 37 per cent of the land was owned by 0.2 per cent of the total number of landowners and where 50 per cent of the farming population owned no land.[19] A system of big estates also existed in some parts of Poland. A land reform in Hungary—which is to be expected after the war—could improve the position of the great masses of the farm population, which, due

18 A. Reithinger, *op. cit.*, p. 19. See also Nicholas Mirkovich, "Die Bevölkerungsentwicklung Yugoslaviens," *Weltwirtschaftliches Archiv*, L (1939).
19 D. Warriner, *Economics of Peasant Farming*, Chapter IX, and *Eastern Europe After Hitler*, pp. 4, 13.

to the general conditions of development and the less intense population pressure, should be in a position to attain a higher standard of living than the peasants in some other parts of this region. But, in general, other population outlets must be found.[20] With no large-scale emigration possibilities in sight, such as existed in the decades before 1914, the only alternative is *industrialization*.

INDUSTRY

Practically, the solution is to continue the industrialization which was begun in some countries even before 1914 and in others after the First World War but which progressed more rapidly after 1931. However, if the results of these efforts are scrutinized it will be found that the total number of people employed in industry in 1937 in all five agricultural countries was not much greater than that in Czechoslovakia alone, and the number of workers in factories and the value of industrial production was even smaller than in Czechoslovakia.[21] It would appear, therefore, that the results achieved were not commensurate with the degree of industrial protection and support in these countries, and in particular with the excessively high prices of all kinds of industrial goods which were common in the agricultural countries of this region.

The natural resources required for building up new industries and expanding old ones are present. The whole field of processing agricultural commodities that employ new methods is open for development, and the timber and various mineral resources of the area will not be difficult to exploit. There will also be ample opportunities in many consumer-goods industries. Progress in the production of investment goods will be slower because of the requirements of greater skill, capital, and industrial experience, and the need of a large market. Further, in the interest of the economic progress of this region in general and its coöperation with the rest of the world in particular,

[20] "For the solution of the difficult problem of the pressure of populations on the land only a carefully worked out long-term policy can be expected to be successful." N. F. Hall, *Memorandum*, p. 56.

[21] In Yugoslavia the increase in the number of industrial workers between 1929 and 1937, about half a million, was not enough to absorb the increase in the agricultural population. (Total population increased yearly by 200,000 or by 1.8 million over this period). See O. Frangeš, Die treibenden Kräfte der wirtschaftlichen Strukturwandlung in Yugoslavien, p. 327. Except in Hungary, the results were no better in other countries.

its new industries should avoid those fields for which the area is not well suited and they should not be coupled with direct or indirect protection of such a nature as to disrupt again the desired price relationships.

It is not meant to imply that new industries should be created without the benefit of any protection. The argument that a demand for protection indicates the artificial nature of a new industry does not apply here. Even the argument that production costs will be higher at first should not be accepted as a final barrier to industrial development, for if the output per worker is lower than in more advanced countries, the productivity of labor for the economy as a whole will be raised above its present level because of the limited productivity in agriculture. Without reference then to the fact that even advanced industrial countries recognized as reasonable the demand for protection of new industries—at least in the form of protective duties for infant industries—this should itself justify a certain degree of tariff protection for the necessary industrialization of the region.[22]

The creation of new industries will in many cases require foreign technical assistance and certainly foreign financial help. Foreign capital will also be greatly needed for investments which, although not directly connected with production, are indispensable for real development and for creating the conditions necessary for greater domestic market and economic progress in general. Because of the extremely limited railway and highway facilities, the lack of utilities and of electrification, and the exploitation of water power as compared even with Central European standards, any extensive economic progress will call for huge investment in public works. There will be a great opportunity for international investment and development

---

[22] See Mihail Manoilescu, "Zusammenarbeit zwischen Ost und Westeuropa auf neuer Grundlage," *Weltwirtschaftliches Archiv*, XLI (1935), 155–73, and also by the same author, "Arbeitsproduktivität und Aussenhandel," *ibid.*, XLII (1935), 13–43, and "Die theoretische Problematik des Aussenhandels," *ibid.*, LI (1940), 1–76. He points out that by expanding industrial production which absorbs idle agricultural labor the productivity of all labor in the economy will tend to rise. He argues from this that if an agricultural country like Rumania is able to produce goods formerly imported, it would be disadvantageous to continue to import them even if domestic production is more expensive, because the national income would rise as labor employed in agriculture shifts to more productive employment in industry. Although Manoilescu's thesis is too general in its application it is nevertheless a good illustration of the special nature of this problem in retarded areas like those of Southeastern Europe, which calls for a different kind of approach.

Similar arguments related to Yugoslavia regarding the much higher productivity of labor in industry rather than agriculture are found in N. Mirkovich, *op. cit.*, p. 117.

organizations which can bring together the surplus savings of the advanced industrial states and the capital needs of the backward countries.[23]

If it should be suggested that these countries could accumulate the capital needed to meet the great demand for investments of various kinds by indirect compulsory savings arising from a forced reduction in national consumption, as was done in Russia, then this is another fallacy. It must be remembered that Russia was able to obtain most of the necessary raw materials at home in ample quantities; this does not apply to this region even if regarded as a unit,[24] and much less to the separate small states. Further, Russia's vast resources made it possible for her to take the chance of great waste in carrying out her program of industrialization. Finally, there is the general question of whether the people, freed after the war and expecting improved living conditions will be willing to bear sacrifices similar to those borne by the Russians in carrying out their industrial program.

There remains the problem of the economic and social system most appropriate to these countries. Some of the basic economic problems will not be solved by the setting up of any system regardless of its nature: poverty, the lack of capital, relative overpopulation in agriculture can be overcome only by a constructive program based upon increased production, importation or formation of capital, and general economic progress.

The whole policy of economic development for retarded countries is a long-range program requiring comprehensive and really constructive planning. It must aim at a general gradual rebuilding of the national economies and must be accompanied by a changed attitude on the part of the people toward economic problems. It should aim primarily to increase the standards of living, to expand the domestic market. Improved export possibilities should result from and go hand in hand with the first two. The program must embrace general education, the improvement of public utilities, transportation, and the technique of production in all its details. It should be an ambitious program with far-reaching goals, which can be attained only through hard, systematic work over a considerable period of time.

[23] See L. L. Lorwin, *International Economic Development, Public Works and Other Problems,* Washington, D.C., 1942; it contains various projects for public works in this region as they existed before the war.
[24] G. D. H. Cole, *op. cit.,* p. 62.

The need of comprehensive international as well as domestic planning is evident. Yet it should not be forgotten that in this part of Europe during the last decade planning was understood to mean government control involving supervision and often direction of every ordinary business transaction. The experience with this kind of planning in the last few years before the war was anything but encouraging. The prevalent attitude was one of unfriendliness toward private business, which nevertheless was needed more in these countries than in others. More attention was paid to changing the distribution of a small total national income than to devising methods to support the increase of the national income. There was in the agricultural countries a "full fledged state machinery far beyond the needs of the peasant economy" and certainly far beyond its ability to maintain it.[25]

There is little reason to expect that this situation will change after the war by itself. On the contrary one factor exists which may even increase the tendency toward bureaucratic management and regimentation of economic life. In some of these areas—Austria, Hungary, Rumania, Czechoslovakia (especially in her eastern part)—the Jews held important positions in industry, banking, and trade; this has been destroyed by the Nazi persecutions or by various measures taken by the national governments. And the Jews, like any minority, preferred to rely upon their own business ability rather than to depend upon the politically influenced bureaucracy.

Those who suggest a government-controlled and even regimented economy frequently use arguments that are common in the Western industrial states. Mention is very often made of the necessity of controlling big business and monopolies, of taking over key industries and of preventing the recurrence of fiscal policy supported by industry. Such arguments scarcely apply even to advanced Czechoslovakia. They certainly cannot supply a satisfactory basis for the desired policy in the agricultural countries, where no private monopolies and very few heavy industries or cartels exist, and where industry's influence on general political action has been far too weak to be blamed for appeasement or for the pacts with the Fascists. On the contrary, the power of the political rulers was undoubtedly decisive; in Hungary the big landowners backed the political regime.

25 D. Warriner, *Eastern Europe after Hitler,* p. 16: "Throughout the Balkans it is the bureaucrat not the capitalist or the landowner or the large peasant who exploits the worker."

Whatever the social and economic regime in the backward countries, it must be based on the assumption that the goal of planning and of government control is not merely to supervise big business and its expansion or to check the power of monopolies, but the much harder task of organizing productive forces, relieving poverty, supplying capital, and creating a dynamic trend to replace the present static one. A comparison with the pioneers in the overseas countries would be appropriate, but the difficulties in the present case are greater because of the population problem. A certain analogy with the Russian solution is apparent, but the Russian resources and opportunities are lacking. Therefore, the only policy which has a hope of success is one infused with a dynamic spirit and with a clear understanding that the goal is a general increase—not a redistribution—of national income. It must be a policy powerful and stable enough to ensure security and tolerance, and liberal enough to inspire real coöperation.

17

REGIONAL ORGANIZATION AND FOREIGN TRADE

IT IS OBVIOUS that such a far-reaching program will be possible only if world confidence is restored in general. The principles of the "Atlantic Charter" and the whole concept of the "United Nations" envisage provisions in the peace treaties and in the postwar international organization for the basically essential political security. It is to be hoped that the simultaneous establishment of an international economic authority with several agencies devoted to specific most important economic tasks will assure the pursuit of a policy of expanding world trade and intimate economic coöperation. An international authority should guarantee that the world economy will not again relapse into restrictive economic nationalism. It will be essential to prevent the recurrence of a situation in which economic conditions are blamed for political insecurity, while at the same time it is argued that economic consolidation is impossible because of the unstable political conditions—as was usually the case at international conferences in the interwar period.

The countries of Central and Southeastern Europe are so situated that their policy must be interrelated with the general policy of Europe and will, in turn, be influenced by it. They can achieve real success only through international political and economic coöperation. Nevertheless, it certainly cannot be expected that these countries will, after the experience of the last decade, have the old faith either in international collective security or in alliances between a large and a small power. They will rather attempt to secure greater safety by very close coöperation among themselves, assuming that the big powers will also promote this coöperation. The movement for union will be stimulated if these countries become convinced that they will receive large-scale coöperation and aid as they succeed in establishing intimate and mutually helpful relations among themselves. The concept of a European economic federation might be logically the best solution for them. But in view of the fact that such a European federation would not be possible for political as well as economic reasons—at least not for a long time—the demand for organization of regional groups must be envisaged. Indeed, all the proposals for a postwar settlement in this part of Europe recommend some sort of federation. The reasons given for this view are rather clear, and, at first, convincing.

Defense against renewed aggression by a big power is the basic political argument. On the economic side there is certainly a good case for the argument that the organization of the region into a single large bloc or into several relatively large blocs would undoubtedly accelerate the badly needed economic development of the whole area, and would make possible—with its greater market—a more efficient division of production, would increase the national income and build up the economic strength of the nations, providing the means of an adequate defense against any aggressor. The history of the last decades has taught us that any step which could promote a real economic rapprochement in this region and work, at the same time, in the direction of greater international coöperation, should be supported, and should be met by a flexible commercial policy. It would not be wise to dwell on orthodox patterns of federations or similar formations—assuming, always, that the purpose of the whole arrangement is, in fact, economic rapprochement and coöperation. Good faith must be proved by the willingness of these countries to maintain trade with the rest of the world on reasonable terms beginning with a lowering of their prewar customs tariffs, if their trade partners will do likewise.

Although we consider political and economic organizations of a regional character as very important for this part of Europe, we cannot omit certain qualifications in order to clear up some misconceptions.

First, it should be pointed out that the formation of a large unit will not be a panacea which by its mere existence will settle all the difficult economic and social problems that we have discussed. Secondly, as our analysis has shown, no customs union consisting of the small countries of Central and Southeastern Europe could or should be self-sufficient. Its prosperity will still depend on achieving real progress in general economic development and on the integration of this part of Europe with the economies of the advanced industrial states.[1]

It is evident that any such union will be possible only if it satisfies the political as well as the economic requirements of the nations con-

[1] D. Warriner, *Eastern Europe After Hitler,* p. 36.

cerned and it must have a definite economic and political program based upon common aims. Any coöperation between the nations of this region requires a real peace backed by international solidarity of purpose, and must start from the conviction that no nation in this area can profit by trying to acquire a piece of another country or by dominating another nation. It must be realized that far greater gains can be achieved through economic progress resulting from the mutual coöperation of all. The "beggar your neighbor" policy must be discarded in the relations between states as well as between the various groups within each state. No federation could endure in which the level of living of one member state is reduced to the advantage of the other members. The safety of this whole region and the stability of the entire Continent demand the separation from Germany of Austria and of the natural historic borders of Czechoslovakia. And in general, it is to be expected that the national boundaries established in this region by the peace treaties after the last war will not be substantially changed [2]—it would be difficult to find others more suitable to the principle of self-determination.

The creation of a consolidated unit demands not only real political peace but also similarity of political and social structure within the nations themselves. It is to be expected that the war will speed up the necessary social and political reforms and introduce the principles of democracy.

It is generally admitted that the economic sovereignty of states must be limited in order to establish a broader framework for close economic coöperation.[3] However, there is as yet no common agreement either as to what the regional extent of such blocs should be or as to the nature of their internal organization.

It is not our intention to deal here with the question of how far the political relations between the nations concerned will support the idea of federation. Political difficulties—many of them of historic origin, some of which may, of course, have been revived by developments before and during the present war—may continue to hamper economic progress. But it may also be that these nations, when

[2] Paul Birdsdall, *Versailles, Twenty Years After*, p. 7. Because of the mixture of populations in Central Europe, complete self-determination is impossible. Recent history has justified the commissioners in taking account of strategic factors in the award of boundaries to the new states.

[3] See Edvard Beneš, "The Organization of Postwar Europe," *Foreign Affairs*, XX (1942), No. 2, p. 239.

they are liberated from Nazi occupation or domination, will overcome many of their old feuds and prejudices and draw nearer together.

We must, however, examine certain economic prerequisites of action, particularly since most of the proposals for regional groups are not very explicit as to the economic organization of the federations put forth. Some of them go so far as to suggest the unification into one bloc of the countries between Germany, Italy, and Russia—the whole area from the Baltic to the Black and Aegean Seas. This means bringing together Poland, Czechoslovakia, Austria, Hungary, Rumania, Yugoslavia, Bulgaria, Albania, and Greece. Among other more modest schemes, the agreement between the Czechoslovak and Polish governments and a similar one between the Greek and Yugoslav governments propose to establish an economic federation with a customs union and coördinated monetary, fiscal, and social policy; in both cases it was suggested that neighboring countries might join the bloc later on.

A really efficient form of federation would undoubtedly call for a full customs union, but the function of a customs union is different in a planned economy than in a liberal one. In a liberal economy the creation of a customs union with the removal of customs duties between the members might prove adequate in itself substantially to increase trade between them and to work towards an adjustment and unification of their economies. On the other hand, the growth of economic planning and intervention, ranging all the way from the issuance of certain general directions to the supervision of regular daily business transactions, complicates the whole nature of the problem. It is clear that a customs union could not be expected to fulfill its purpose if it were concluded between one country with private foreign trade and another with a government foreign-trade monopoly or with its trade centrally planned and controlled. Serious difficulties might also arise if very important branches of production were owned by the government in one country while private enterprise prevailed in the other, or if the general objectives of planned economy greatly differed between the member states. In either situation the mere existence of a customs union would not of itself bring about the expected mutual adjustment of the member economies, nor would it be powerful enough to create the desired price equilibrium between them. Therefore, in an interventionist economy the need for uniform policy could not be limited to customs tariffs and monetary and financial policy, but should embrace all important aspects of economic policy if the real benefits customarily associated with a customs union are to be obtained. Hence, under these conditions the concept must be enlarged from that of a customs union to that of an economic union.

With an interventionist regime this type of economic coöperation consequently requires a higher degree of homogeneity between the economies of the member states than does a customs union in a liberal economy.

If this area of Central and Eastern Europe were inhabited by a single nation, previously divided into several independent states, it would doubtless be much easier to attain the objectives of such a far-reaching program, even if great cultural, social, and economic differences existed. But, in fact, the area is far from homogeneous. Substantial differences exist in the standard of living and in the economic and social structure. Czechoslovakia and Austria, especially, have highly developed and diversified industries, whereas in the agricultural countries many of the industrial enterprises have grown up only because of the protectionism of the last decades. In Czechoslovakia and in parts of Austria (both these countries are highly protected) and of Hungary, agricultural production is intensive, but in many sections of Southeastern Europe and in Poland it is extensive, and, with the lack of modern equipment, the yield per acre is often less than half that of Czechoslovakia.

Assuming that at the end of the war a definite economic program will be framed for this area, the period of rehabilitation and relief, during which there will be no great problem of finding export markets, should be used to initiate and support a policy of economic unification here. Some of the obstacles to real economic rapprochement will have disappeared, and in many respects it will be possible to start with a clean slate. It is desirable therefore to avoid both the creation of new vested interests during this period and the revival of the influence of various old pressure groups. Certainly the international economic authorities helping in the reconstruction and development work should support any possibility leading to political and economic rapprochement, at the same time preventing any policy which could work in the opposite direction.

Nevertheless, it remains to be seen whether the process of adjustment will advance far enough and whether the general political situation will be favorable enough to make it advisable or feasible to form a very large full-fledged economic union. While the advantages of a greater market constitute an argument in support of such a unit, it would be wrong to assume, for instance, that a completely complementary economy would result. Even though the industrial countries included could sell a large part of their surplus manufactured products within the regional area they could absorb only a minor fraction of the total surplus of the agricultural sections. Moreover, for obvious reasons the population problem could not be solved by introducing free migration within this region. And, in spite of having greater potential resources than Germany, this bloc would not be self-sufficient; its very size might encourage further protection of the domestic market, for there is a greater danger of such policy in large than in small units.

Finally, assuming the permanent existence if not the growth of government intervention—this would depend upon whether the Western or Russian influence is stronger, and as yet there is no possibility of guessing which will be—the task of any sort of governing body for the area from the Baltic to the Black Sea would be enormous. Only a government with extensive over-all powers of planning and control —and with a high degree of decentralization of administration— could master a situation of such complexity. That this would not make the economy flexible is clear.

But it is very doubtful whether the various schemes which have so far been proposed for an economic union of all Central and Eastern Europe do, indeed, have in mind a genuine customs or economic union providing free trade within the unit and thus building up a single big market. One scheme of federation [4] which proposes a real constitution for a Central European Commonwealth includes a customs union admitting internal tariffs for manufactured articles for a period of not more than five years. But agricultural produce is to be subject to marketing regulations, requiring special agreements between the national governments. Thus although there would be a free internal market for industrial products there would be a planned market for agricultural goods. This proposition is hardly likely to be very durable.

Another author is also in favor of a customs union for the whole big bloc, but he assumes that there will be planned management

[4] See M. Hodža, *Federation in Central Europe*, p. 173.

within a large customs union which will make possible a symmetrical development of agriculture and industry in all parts of the confederation.[5] This planned management can hardly be understood as advancing the idea of free intertrade, even though subject for a certain time to internal customs duties; it looks more like a planned management of the trade between the members of a confederation. This is not an isolated example but the reflection of an attitude frequently found in various circles.

This is, of course, a new concept of what might be described as a planned customs union. Although it calls for a common tariff for trade with the rest of the world, it does not automatically imply a real economic adjustment within the union. The plan could even be interpreted as admitting not only intermember customs duties but also a system of import permits, of import monopolies, or of a totally managed trade between the member states of a customs union. Knowing the good intention of the author, we understand that he prefers to work out a mutual adjustment of the economies of the members by comprehensive planning within the whole federation instead of through the free operation of the economic forces arising from the removal of the internal trade barriers.

Nevertheless, the real danger of a new protectionist policy within the bloc would have to be checked. Intertrade customs duties would certainly be demanded, but they should be strictly limited as to the period of their duration. It would be no help in the reconstruction of this area if measures apparently leading to economic readjustment in reality meant only a new shift in the source of imports, as was the case under the Rome Protocols and the Little Entente.

We should not be misled by the term "customs union" when it is used not to imply a large internal market but to represent a planned intertrade with all kinds of preferential treatment. It would be better to avoid the phrase for international coöperation of this type and to use instead a managed preferential regime.[6] Such a solution is desirable only where there is reasonable hope that it will lead ultimately to real economic rapprochement and adjustment.

But should the difficulties connected with such ambitious schemes as a Central and Eastern European Commonwealth be very complex,

[5] L. Feierabend, "Czechoslovakia and Central Europe," *Journal of Central European Affairs*, II (1943), 367.
[6] Probably greater emphasis would be placed upon control of intertrade than upon the common customs tariff.

instead of creating complicated and artificial mechanisms it would be wiser to begin on a more modest scale with regard to both the size and the nature of the federation and to progress gradually towards greater economic unification of the whole region, starting with a genuine customs union where conditions allow it.

In all probability some groups of countries would agree upon the creation of a full customs union; this would be true of countries having a somewhat similar economic and social structure and basic political attitudes. However, economic considerations will be recognized only if they conform to the political orientation of the partners. Failure to realize the reluctance of all these nations to enter any bloc menacing their freedom, perhaps in the future, would be highly unrealistic.

The question of which countries will unite will ultimately be decided by the people themselves, and a considerable period may be required before real progress can be achieved in this field. From the *economic* point of view we could suggest either countries with most similar structure or, alternatively, a group in which agriculture and industry are somewhat balanced. But we must realize that the combined agricultural import requirements of Czechoslovakia and Austria could be met almost entirely by the export surplus of any one of these agricultural countries—Hungary, Rumania, and Yugoslavia.

Theoretically there appear to be several possibilities. As to similarity of structure one group is composed of the predominantly agricultural countries in the Southeast, a second group of Czechoslovakia and Austria (the more advanced parts of Poland and Hungary are somewhat similar in structure). Poland's commercial ties with the rest of the region between the Baltic and Black Seas were not very strong, being particularly weak with the agricultural states. In the last years before the war only about 10 per cent of her total import came from all these countries (8 per cent from Austria and Czechoslovakia alone) and only a little more than 11 per cent of her exports went to them (more than 9 per cent to Czechoslovakia and Austria alone). However, even the reëstablishment of pre-1930 trade relations between Poland and the two industrial countries could double their mutual trade. A full-fledged Czechoslovak–Polish customs union could definitely increase their mutual exchange of commodities and provide a really huge market.

A broader basis could be supplied by forming a customs union between Czechoslovakia, Austria, Hungary, and Yugoslavia (and, possibly, Rumania), with close economic coöperation with Poland. Such a customs union could substantially increase the market available to its members, and greatly help the agriculture of two of the partners. The Rumanian export trade has always tended toward the West, and she has ample resources for building up a strong national economy. Close economic ties could perhaps be established also between the Balkan States, with Yugoslavia acting as a bridge between them and the possible economic union mentioned above. It should be emphasized once more that under no circumstances should greater blocs be instrumental in raising the level of customs tariffs.

Should the immediate formation of a customs union of wide scope be faced with too great difficulties it would be advisable to organize close regional coöperation, possibly in the form of a clearly defined preferential regime of limited duration, for even if prodded by international authorities the process of genuine rapprochement might take time. It is evident that such a regime should be permitted only if it is organized to foster freer trade and the mutual adjustment of the economies of the members, and in no case if it is designed to increase the trade barriers with nonmember states. Although there might be objections on principle to such action as contrary to the letter of the most-favored-nation clause, the lessons of the past should indicate that such regional solutions should not be excluded from postwar trade organization. Had the major powers, including the United States, been less strongly opposed to such a regime in the Danubian countries, had they been less desirous of pursuing their special interests, and had they advised and encouraged the introduction of such a scheme, a regional arrangement might have led, in the course of time, to closer economic rapprochement. It would be very helpful to include a provision for this type of organization in the peace treaties as a limited alternative to economic union. There should also be clear provision for the liquidation of the preferential system either by transforming it into an economic union or by abandoning it completely.[7] All possible steps toward establishing closer economic coöperation and the weaving of strong ties between these

---

[7] Percy W. Bidwell points to the usefulness of regional agreement between industrially backward countries to promote desirable diversification (such as the recent agreement between Brazil and Argentina) and remarks that industrially advanced nations should not prevent such arrangements by insisting on the most-favored-nation clause. Each case should be decided on its merits.—"Controlling Trade after the War," *Foreign Affairs,* XXI (1943), 309.

countries should be taken. Just as economic interventionism and planning have forced a change in the concept of customs unions, so will it be desirable to devise new flexible forms of close economic coöperation, always designed to promote a freer flow of goods, not depending too much upon the orthodox methods which were appropriate in different economic circumstances.

The formation of such regional groups, although certainly important and in the interest of all participating nations, will be no panacea applicable to all these complicated problems. Such an organization can be successful only if it faces the fundamental issues. In our case these are: a program for the development of the backward regions, a policy leading to greater integration of the European economy, and a policy fostering the expansion of world trade and the abandonment of the ideas of autarky, of big protected economic units, and of exaggerated economic nationalism. Politically, regional pacts should be negotiated within an established framework of international order, ensuring peace by some effective universal force.[8] The small countries of Europe would benefit greatly from a period of freer trade and it would be in their political as well as economic advantage to do their utmost to support liberal trade. In a world of protectionism the smaller nations are bound to get a worse deal than the bigger countries can obtain with their greater bargaining power.

This whole problem of regional coöperation would, of course, change completely if there should be centrally controlled national economies with no great emphasis upon the international division of production. In such a system, obviously, the most-favored-nation clause and the whole idea of foreign trade change in meaning and nature; trade becomes regimented and planned by the governments, which also take care of economic adjustment. A system of indirect barter would dominate. In this case, the only regional unity possible might be close coöperation between the national economic authorities or reciprocal preferential treatment between neighbors.

The expected economic development of the retarded agricultural areas will, obviously, work important changes in their foreign trade. On the whole, this will tend to increase in volume, but because of the large-scale expansion of domestic production it will come to represent a smaller proportion of all economic activity. In this connection, one of the most important parts of the whole program should be to devote maximum attention to the development of the domestic

[8] J. B. Condliffe, *Agenda for a Postwar World*, pp. 78–79.

markets in these countries in order to realize the great possibilities for expansion available there. This is something that was greatly neglected after the First World War.

As to the expected changes in foreign trade, the progressive industrialization will tend to be accompanied by increased imports of overseas raw material and reduced imports of consumer goods, especially those which can be produced from domestic raw materials. Similarly there will be an increase in the imports of various investment goods, and, as the standard of living rises, the demand for colonial products will increase as will that for certain high-quality industrial products such as tractors, electro-technical equipment, automobiles, railway equipment, heavy machinery, many chemicals and pharmaceutical products, precision instruments, business machines, and so forth.

There will, of course, be corresponding changes in the nature of exports. As diversification of agriculture progresses, the emphasis upon the export of the old staple agricultural products will be reduced, but there will be larger exports of specialized crops: protective foods, fodder, raw materials, semifinished goods, and also processed agricultural goods, forestry products, and others.

The structure of this trade clearly indicates, once more, that it can function only within the framework of multilateral trade, because chiefly through exports to other European states will Southeastern Europe be able to acquire the foreign exchange needed for purchases of overseas raw materials and colonial goods.

It is evident that the economic progress in the agricultural countries will react very favorably upon the economies of Austria and Czechoslovakia, who, following the trade policy which is to be expected and desired, should be able to regain their former position in foreign trade. However, they will need to adjust the composition of their trade to suit the changes in the other economies; Czechoslovakia will have to continue her policy of shifting the structure of her export from mass goods to high-quality products. As an important step toward the economic integration of Europe, the whole development of the backward countries should interlock closely with the new, that is, with the expected agricultural policies of the industrial countries. The whole set-up should work toward a large-scale increase in the mutual trade, with favorable effects upon the economic progress of all.[9]

9 See N. F. Hall, *op. cit.* pp. 64 ff.

The foreign trade of Central and Southeastern Europe could also be favorably affected by the expected increase in economic coöperation between the U.S.S.R. and the rest of the world. Soviet Russia could certainly become a great buyer of many industrial products and could also furnish various raw materials. The extent of this trade is hardly to be forecast; the potentialities are great. There is still another new possibility in foreign trade. Just as we can assume that there will be economic progress in this part of Europe so is it safe to expect a similar development in the Near East. Before the war both the agricultural and industrial countries of the group in question extended their trade with Egypt, Palestine, Iran, Syria, and Turkey and there is reason to believe that the war will accelerate progress in this part of the world and lead to increased trade especially with the neighboring parts of Europe.

The policy of economically integrating the backward areas of Europe with the advanced industrial countries could introduce a new phase in the economic history of that continent. For a second time within a relatively short period there will be a chance to organize and carry out such a program, to extend progress, to strengthen and consolidate Europe economically, socially, and also, of course, politically. Clearly this would favorably influence the whole world economy. It will be a hard task, requiring the help and coöperation of other nations, particularly of the advanced Western countries. But extending this aid will bring a good return, not only in an expansion of economic and trade opportunities but also in supporting their own world position. Finally, only a powerful and balanced economy can provide the region with a basis for a defense against future aggression.

As for Germany, because of her economic structure and geographical position, she will remain an important partner in the trade of this whole region, but the new postwar policy must build up a strong economic system free of German domination or control.

The world which saw Germany as the foremost factor in the development and organization of Central and Southeastern Europe will have to revise its view. The Western Powers must realize that it is at least as important to entertain close economic relations with these countries as with Germany. An ultimate change in the economic and social status of this neglected region will provide a new and safer balance for Europe as a whole. The retarded regions will themselves be energized and transformed.

BIBLIOGRAPHY

LEAGUE OF NATIONS PUBLICATIONS

Chiffres essentiels du commerce exterieur des pays danubiens. 1932. II.B.3.
Commercial Policy in the Inter-War Period. 1942. II.A.6.
Considerations in the Present Evolution of Agricultural Protectionism. 1935. II.B.7.
Enquiry into Clearing Agreements. 1935. II.B.6.
Europe's Trade. 1941. II.A.1.
International Trade Statistics.
Network of World Trade. 1942. II.A.3.
Population and Agriculture with Special Reference to Agricultural Over-population. 1939. Conference on Rural Life 3.
Preliminary Investigation into Measures of a National or International Character for Raising the Standard of Living. 1938. II.B.4.
Report on Exchange Control. 1938. II.A.10.
Review of World Trade.
Statistical Year-Book.
World Economic Conference. Geneva, 1927.
World Economic Survey.
World Production and Prices, 1937–38. 1938. II.A.11.

INTERNATIONAL INSTITUTE OF INTELLECTUAL COÖPERATION, PARIS

Bobtcheff, Constantin N. Reglementation du commerce et politique commerciale en Bulgarie. Sofia, 1939.
Buday, K. Exchange Control in Hungary.
Commerce entre la Roumanie et les etats Danubiens, Le. 1937.
Commerce exterieur de la Roumanie pendant la periode 1920–1938, Le. 1939.
Development of Hungary's Foreign Trade between 1920 and 1936, The. 1939.
Dumitresco, Stefan. Les Matières premières en Roumanie. 1939.
Hantos, Elemer. Le Régionalisme économique en Europe. 1939.
Hungarian External Economic Policy. Memorandum made by a Hungarian study group under the chairmanship of W. Heller. 1939.
Kerschagl, Richard. Foreign Exchange Restrictions in Central Europe. 1939.
Kuyucak, Hazin Atif. Exchange Control in Turkey. 1939.

Madgearu, V. Le Contrôle des changes en Roumanie. 1939.

Obradovič, S. D. La Politique commerciale de la Jugoslavie. Beograd, 1939.

Piatier, A. Exchange Control: a General Survey. 1940.

Pintos, J. D. Le Contrôle des changes en Grêce. 1939.

Tasca, H. J. World Trading Systems. 1939.

Tchakaloff, A., and S. Zagoroff. Le Contrôle des changes en Bulgarie. 1939.

Wright, Carl Major. Provisional Report on the Study of Danubian Problems. 1939.

Yovanovitch, A. Le Contrôle des changes en Jugoslavie. 1939.

OTHER REFERENCES

Annual Reports and other regular publications of the National Bank of the following countries: Austria, Bulgaria, Czechoslovakia, Hungary, Rumania, Yugoslavia and of the Bank of Greece.

Armstrong, Hamilton Fish. "Danubia: Relief or Ruin." Foreign Affairs, X (1932).

—— Europe between Wars. New York, 1934.

Basch, Antonín. Czechoslovak Economy during the Crisis. Prague, 1937. (In Czech.)

—— The Economic Crisis of the Danubian Countries and the Reagrariasation of Europe. Prague, 1935. (In Czech.)

—— "Probleme der Devisenkontrolle." Mitteilungen des Verbandes oester. Banken und Bankiers, Vienna, XIV, No. 9–10.

Basch, Antonín, and J. Dvořáček. Austria and Its Economic Existence. Prague, 1925.

Beneš, Eduard. "The Organization of Postwar Europe." Foreign Affairs, XX (1942).

Bidwell, Percy W. "Controlling Trade after the War." Foreign Affairs, XXI (1943).

Birdsall, Paul. Versailles, Twenty Years After. New York, 1941.

Bonnell, Allen Thomas. German Control over International Economic Relations. Urbana, Ill., 1940.

Brandt, Carl. "The Crisis in German Agriculture." Foreign Affairs, X (1932).

—— "German Agricultural Policy." Journal of Farm Economics, XIX, No. 1 (1937).

Buell, Raymond Leslie. Poland, Key to Europe. New York, 1939.

Clark, Colin. The Conditions of Economic Progress. London, 1940.

Cole, G. D. H. Europe, Russia, and the Future. New York, 1942.

Condliffe, J. B. Agenda for a Postwar World. New York, 1942.

—— Reconstruction of World Trade. New York, 1941.

Decken, Hans von der. "Die Intensivierung der Europäischen Landwirtschaft." Vierteljahreshefte des deutschen Institutes für Konjunkturforschung, 1940–41, No. 2–3.

Deyanowa, Milka. "Die Staatlichen Massnahmen zur Förderung der Ausfuhr der Agrarprodukte Bulgariens." *Weltwirtschaft. Arch.*, LI (1940).

Dietz, C. V. "Measures for Combating the Agricultural Crisis in Germany." *Proceedings of the Third International Conference of Agricultural Economists*, Oxford, 1935.

Einzig, Paul. The Exchange Clearing System. London, 1935.

—— Hitler's New Order in Europe. London, 1941.

Ellis, Howard S. Exchange Control in Central Europe. Cambridge, Mass., 1941.

Evelpidi, E. "Die landwirtschaftliche Krise in Griechenland." *Weltwirtschaft. Arch.*, LI (1940).

Fabian Society, London, International Research Section. Hitler's Route to Bagdad. London, 1939.

Feierabend, L. "Czechoslovak Agriculture." *The Banker*, June, 1938, Annex.

—— "Czechoslovakia and Central Europe." *Journal of Central European Affairs*, II (1943).

Feis, Herbert. Europe, the World Banker, 1870–1914. New Haven, Conn., 1930.

Fischer, Werner A. Devisenclearing. Berlin, 1937.

Fisher, Allan G. B. "The German Trade Drive in Southeastern Europe." *International Affairs*, XVIII, No. 2 (1939).

Frangeš, O. von. "Die Donaustaaten Südosteuropas und der deutsche Grosswirtschaftsraum." *Weltwirtschaft. Arch.*, XXXVIII (1934).

—— "Die treibenden Kräfte der wirtschaftlichen Strukturwandlungen in Yugoslavien." *Weltwirtschaft. Arch.*, XLVIII (1938).

Funk, Walter. *Wirtschaftsordnung im neuen Europa.* Vienna, 1941.

German Institute for Business Research, Berlin. Weekly Reports.

Geshkoff, Theodor I. Balkan Union in Southeastern Europe. New York, 1940.

Gordon, Margaret. Barriers to World Trade. New York, 1941.

Gratz, Gustav, and R. Schüller. Die äussere Wirtschaftspolitik Oesterreich-Ungarns. Vienna, 1925.

Gross, Hermann. Südosteuropa: Bau und Entwicklung der Wirtschaft. Leipzig, 1937.

Guillebaud, C. W. "Hitler's New Economic Order in Europe." *Economic Journal*, London, 1940.

Häfner, Kurt. "Zur Theorie der mengemässigen Einfuhrregulierung." *Weltwirtschaft. Arch.*, XLI (1935).

Hanč, J. Tornado across Eastern Europe: the Path of Nazi Destruction from Poland to Greece. New York, 1942.

Hertz, Friedrich. Die Produktionsgrundlagen der oester Industrie vor und nach dem Kriege imbesondere im Vergleich mit Deutschland. Vienna, 1917.

Heuser, Heinrich. Control of International Trade. London, 1939.

Hodža, M. Federation in Central Europe. London, 1942.

Holt, John B. German Agricultural Policy, 1918–1934. Chapel Hill, N.C., 1936.

Horna, M. J. Mayer, and A. Šourek. Neue Wege der Handelspolitik, Prague, 1936.

Hubbard, G. E. Eastern Industrialization and Its Effect on the West. 2d ed., Oxford, 1938.

Institut für Konjunkturforschung, Berlin. Vierteljahreshefte zur Konjunkturforschung.

Jaszi, Oscar. "The Economic Crisis in the Danubian States." *Social Research*, II, No. 1 (1935).

—— "Feudal Agrarianism in Hungary." *Foreign Affairs*, XVIII (1938).

Joint Committee of the Carnegie Endowment for International Peace and the International Chamber of Commerce. International Economic Reconstruction. Improvement of Commercial Relations between Nations: the Problem of Monetary Stabilization. 2d ed., Paris, 1936.

Jones, J. Elwyn. Hitler's Drive to the East. New York, 1937.

Kerner, R. J., and H. N. Howard. The Balkan Conferences and the Balkan Entente, 1930–1935. Berkeley, Calif., 1936.

Kroymann, Kurt. Clearing und Kompensation in Aussenhandel. Hamburg, 1935.

Krugmann, Robert W. Südosteuropa und Grossdeutschland. Breslau, 1939.

Lamer, Mirko. "Die Wandlungen der ausländischen Kapitalanlagen auf dem Balkan." *Weltwirtschaft. Arch.*, XLVII (1938).

Layton, W., and C. Rist. The Economic Situation of Austria. Geneva, 1925.

Liepmann, H. Tariff Levels and the Economic Unity of Europe. New York, 1938.

Lorwin, L. L. International Economic Development, Public Works, and Other Problems. National Resources Planning Board, Washington, D.C., 1942.

Lossos, Harold. Bilanz der deutschen Devisenbewirtschaftung. Jena, 1940.

Luckas, Hans. Theorie der Devisenzwangswirtschaft auf Grund der deutschen und ausländischen Erfahrungen in der Zeit 1914–40. Jena, 1940.

Macartney, C. A. Problems of the Danube Basin, Cambridge, 1942.

Machray, Robert. The Struggle for the Danube and the Little Entente, 1929–1938. London, 1938.

Madden, John T., M. Nadler, and H. C. Sauvain. America's Experience as a Creditor Nation. New York, 1937.

Manoilescu, Mihail. "Arbeitsproduktivität und Aussenhandel." *Weltwirtschaft. Arch.*, XLII (1935).

—— "Die theoretische Problematik des Aussenhandels." *Weltwirtschaft. Arch.*, LI (1940).

—— "Zusammenarbeit zwischen Ost und Westeuropa auf neuer Grundlage." *Weltwirtschaft. Arch.*, XLI (1935).

Matolcsy, M. S., and S. Varga. The National Income of Hungary, 1924–25 to 1936–37. London, 1938.

Meyer, Fritz. "Die Sicherung der autonomen Wirtschaftsentwicklung im Bereich der Aussenwirtschaft." *Weltwirtschaft. Arch.*, LIII (1941).

Mirkovich, Nicholas. "Die Bevölkerungsentwicklung Yugoslaviens." *Weltwirtschaft. Arch.*, L (1939).

Mitnizky, Mark. "Germany's Trade Monopoly in Eastern Europe." *Social Research*, VI (1939).

Morgan, O. S., ed. Agricultural Systems of Middle Europe. New York, 1933.

Müller, Carl Hermann. Grundriss der Devisenbewirtschaftung. Berlin, 1939.

Pasvolsky, Leo. Economic Nationalism of the Danubian States. New York, 1928.

Pertot, Vladimir. "Einige Entwicklungstendenzen im Aussenhandel der Balkanländer." *Weltwirtschaft. Arch.*, L (1939).

—— "Die Weizenregulierung in Jugoslavien." *Weltwirtschaft. Arch.*, XLV (1937).

Predöhl, Andreas. "Die sogenannten Handelshemnisse und der Preisaufbau der Weltwirtschaft." *Weltwirtschaft. Arch.*, LII (1940).

Reithinger, A. Das wirtschaftliche Gesicht Europas. Stuttgart-Berlin, 1936.

Ritter, Karl. "Germany's Experience with Clearing Agreements." *Foreign Affairs*, XIV (April, 1936).

Rouček, Joseph. The Politics of the Balkans. New York, 1939.

Royal Institute of International Affairs, London. The Balkan States. 1936.

—— Europe under Hitler. 1941.

—— The Problem of International Investments. 1937.

—— Raw Materials. 1939.

—— South-Eastern Europe: a Brief Survey. 1940.

—— South-Eastern Europe: a Political and Economic Survey. 1939.

—— Survey of International Affairs, 1930–38.

Schacher, Gerhard. Mitteleuropa und die westliche Welt. Prague, 1936.

Staley, Eugene. World Economy in Transition. New York, 1939.

Stisser, Reinhold. "Die deutsche Getreidemarktordnung." *Weltwirtschaft. Arch.*, XLVII (1938).

Ten Years of the National Bank of Czechoslovakia. Prague, 1936.

U.S. Department of Agriculture. Foreign Agriculture. Bulletin No. 12, 1940.

—— World Trade Barriers in Relation to American Agriculture. Washington, D.C., 1933.

Wagemann, Ernst. Der neue Balkan. Hamburg, 1939.

Warriner, Doreen. Eastern Europe after Hitler. London, 1940.

—— Economics of Peasant Farming. London, 1939.

INDEX

Agrarian Bloc, 60

Agricultural countries, 60; German economic policy detrimental to, 3-4, 41 ff., 46, 196 ff.; freedom must be regained after war, 4, 250; industrialization, 25; industrial production, 79 f., (table), 152n; industrial employment, 80n; impact of the crisis (1930–31), 35-50; compared to South America, 36 f.; products and exports before the crisis (1930–31), 37 ff.; exports, value, 40; need of foreign capital, 51; long-term indebtedness, 53; preferential problem pressed by, 62; import-licensing system, 78 ff.; monetary adjustments, 132-52; wholesale price level, 136; the period of recovery (1936–37), 197; chief economic problems, 198; population pressure, 234, 242; food consumption (table), 237n; see also Bulgaria; Greece; Hungary; Rumania; Yugoslavia

—— balance of payments: (1932), 58; foreign debt and, 75 f., 198

—— trade: with industrial countries, under clearing agreements, 87-88; with Austria, 126; with Germany, 184, 199, 204; (tables), 181, 194, 195; foreign, 41, 90 ff.; vs. competition in world markets, 41, 50, 196 f., 199 f., 204

Agricultural products, of the agricultural countries, 37 ff.; (table), 38; prices and price adjustments, 43, 94, 238; in world trade (table), 45; in percentage of world production (table), 230; yield per hectare and ratio of farm population to farm land, 232 f.

—— exports: Balkan, 16; duties on, 27; efforts to foster, 59; preferential customs treatment asked of League of Nations, 60; valorization of domestic prices and, 144; under the Rome Protocols, 159-65

Agricultural protectionism, see under Protectionism

Agricultural surpluses, Germany as market for, 3

Agriculture, chief occupation of Austria-Hungary, 5; Hungary, 6; Balkan countries, 6, 11; necessity for development of, 235 ff., 239 f.; diversification, 241

Argentina, refused consent to preferential system for cereals, 63

Armament production, 80, 223

Austria, annexation by Germany, 1, 203-15; national income before World War I, 5; standard of living before World War I, 6; tourist trade, 9; postwar economic development, 19-20; as creditor nation, 20; monetary and financial reform, 22; tariffs, 26; protection of agricultural products, 28; foreign trade, 28; balance of trade, 30, 31, 121-31; financial and economic situation examined by League of Nations, 32; attitude toward a Danubian economic union, 33; as market for the agricultural countries, 37, 39, 203; agricultural production and trade, 47, 126n; short-term credits arranged for, 52; moratorium, 54; League of Nation loans to, 55, 128; Germany's attempt to establish customs union with, 62, 65; Tardieu Plan proposal, 63; marketing difficulties, 66n; import-licensing system, 79 f.; and clearing agreements, 83; decline in exports, 90; devaluation of currency, 95n, 124; preferential duty granted to Yugoslavia, 97n; wholesale price index, 113n, 130; industrial production, 117-18, 130; sources of income, 121; effect of 1931 crisis, 123; introduction of foreign-exchange control, 123 ff.; reduction of import surplus, 125, 127; bilateralism and clearing agreements, 125 ff.; and the clearing countries, 127 f.; foreign debts, 128; Rome Protocols, 159-65; credit balance and investments in Danubian area, 205; trade with Danubian area (table), 206; protectionism, 238

Austro-Hungarian Monarchy, dissolution, 1; sometimes regarded as ideal economic unit, 5; agriculture chief occupation, 5; domestic market insufficiently developed, 6; foreign trade, 6 ff.; imports, 7; foreign investments in, 9-10; economic development retarded, 10; as source of Rumanian imports, 11; trade with Serbia and Bulgaria, 12; with Greece, 13; economic development, 15; customs unit, 17

Autarky, 46, 218n, 221, 238

Balance of payments, Czechoslovakia, 24; agricultural countries, 51; Danubian